Pathways To The Past

Each volume stands alone as an Individual Book
Each volume stands together with others
to enhance the value of your collection

Build your Personal, Pastoral or Church Library
Pathways To The Past contains an ever-expanding list of
Christendom's most influencial authors

Augustine of Hippo
Athanasius
E. M. Bounds
John Bunyan
Brother Lawrence
Jessie Penn-Lewis
Bernard of Clairvaux
Andrew Murray
Watchman Nee
Arthur W. Pink
Hannah Whitall Smith
R. A. Torrey
A. W. Tozer
Jean-Pierre de Caussade
Thomas Watson
And many, many more.

The Fundamental Doctrines of the Christian Faith

R. A. Torrey

The Fundamental Doctrines of the Christian Faith

Published By Parables
June, 2018

All Rights Reserved. No part of this book may be reproduced or utilized in any form or by any means, electronic or mechanical, including photocopying, recording, or by any information storage and retrieval system, without permission in writing from the author.

ISBN 978-1-945698-62-0
Printed in the United States of America

Readers should be aware that Internet Web sites offered as citations and/or sources for further information may have been changed or disappeared between the time this was written.

The Fundamental Doctrines of the Christian Faith

R. A. Torrey

R. A. TORREY

I
Inspiration, or to What Extent Is the Bible Inspired of God?

"For no prophecy ever came by the will of man, but men spake from God, being moved by the Holy Spirit."—2 Pet. 1:21.

"All Scripture is given by inspiration of God, and is profitable for doctrine, for reproof, for correction, for instruction in righteousness; that the man of God may be perfect, thoroughly furnished unto all good works."—2 Tim. 3:16, 17.

Our subject this morning is "The Inspiration of the Bible, or to What Extent Is the Bible Inspired of God?" The subject is of vital and fundamental importance. If we can make it clear that the writers of the various books of the Bible were inspired of God in a sense that no other men were ever inspired of God, that they were so gifted and taught and led and governed by the Holy Spirit in their utterances as recorded in the Bible, that they taught the truth and nothing but the truth, that their teachings were absolutely without error,—then we have in the Bible a court of final appeal and of infallible wisdom to which we can go to settle every question of doctrine or duty. But if the writers of the Bible were "inspired" only in the vague and uncertain sense that Shakespeare, Browning and many other men of genius were inspired, only inspired to the extent that their minds were made more keen to see the truth than ordinary men, but still only in such a way that they made mistakes, or chose the wrong word to express their thought, so that we must recast their thought by discovering, if we may, what the inspired thought back of the uninspired words was, then we are all at sea, in hopeless confusion, so that each generation must settle for itself what the Holy Spirit meant to say through the blundering reporters; and it is absolutely certain that no generation can determine with anything approximating accuracy what the Spirit meant, and so no generation can arrive at the truth, but simply promulgate blunders for the next and wiser generation to correct, to be corrected in turn by the next generation that follows it. Thank God that this latter subtle but popular doctrine can be proven to be utterly untrue!

There is great need of crystal clear teaching on this subject, because our colleges and seminaries and pulpits and Sunday schools and religious papers are full of teaching that is vague, inaccurate, misleading, un-Scriptural, and oftentimes grossly false. There are many in these days who say "I believe that the Bible is inspired" when by "inspired" they do not mean at all what you understand or what the mighty men of faith in the past meant by "inspired." They often say that they "believe the Bible is the Word of God," when at the same time they believe it is full of errors.

Now the Bible is as clear as crystal in its teachings and claims regarding itself, and either those claims are true, or else the Bible is the biggest fraud in all the literature of the human race. The position held by so many to-day, that the Bible is a good book, perhaps the best book in the world, but at the same time it is full of errors that must be corrected by the higher wisdom of our day, is utterly illogical and absolutely ridiculous. If the Bible is not what it claims to be, it is a fraud—an outrageous fraud.

What does the Bible teach and claim concerning itself? What does it teach and claim regarding the fact and extent of its own inspiration?

I. THE WORK OF THE HOLY SPIRIT IN APOSTLES AND PROPHETS DIFFERENT IN CHARACTER FROM HIS WORK IN ALL OTHER PERSONS

The first thing that the Bible teaches on this point and claims for itself is, that the work of the Holy Spirit in apostles and prophets, in the various human authors of the different books of the Bible, differs from His work in other men, even in other believers in Christ. It teaches that the Holy Spirit imparts to apostles and prophets an especial gift for an especial purpose. We find this clearly taught in

1 Cor. 12:4, 8-11, 28, 29, where we read, "Now there are diversities of gifts, but the same Spirit. . . . (8) for to one is given through the Spirit the word of wisdom; and to another the word of knowledge, according to the same Spirit; (9) to another faith, in the same Spirit; and to another gifts of healing, in the same Spirit; (10) and to another workings of miracles (powers); and to another prophecy; and to another discerning of spirits; to another divers kinds of tongues, and to another the interpretation of tongues; (11) but all these worketh the one and the same Spirit, dividing to each one severally even as He will. . . . (28) And God hath set some in the church, first apostles, secondly prophets, thirdly teachers, then miracles, then gifts of healings, helps, governments, divers kinds of tongues. (29) Are all apostles? are all prophets? are all teachers? are all workers of miracles?" This chapter is the fullest and clearest chapter in the Bible on the subject of the various gifts of the Holy Spirit. It is the classical chapter on the whole subject, and the teaching of these verses is as plain as language can make it, and it states in terms, the meaning of which is unmistakable, that the gift bestowed on apostles and prophets differed in kind from the gifts bestowed on other believers, even though those believers were filled with the Holy Spirit. Not only did the work of the Holy Spirit in the apostles and prophets differ from His work in men of genius, but even from His work in other believers. These verses make it as plain as day that the doctrine which has become so common and so popular in our day, that the work of the Holy Spirit in preachers and teachers and in ordinary believers, illuminating them and guiding them into the truth and into the understanding of the Word of God, is the same in kind and differs only in degree from the work of the Holy Spirit in Apostles and Prophets is thoroughly unscriptural and untrue. This doctrine overlooks what is here so clearly stated and so carefully elucidated, that while there is "the same Spirit" "there are diversities of gifts" "diversities of ministrations," "diversities of workings" (1 Cor. 12:406 R. V.) and that not all are Prophets or Apostles. (1 Cor. 12:29.)

Those who desire to minimise the difference between the work of the Holy Spirit in Apostles and Prophets, and His work in other men, often refer to the fact that the Bible itself says that Bezaleel, the architect of the tabernacle, was to be "filled with the Spirit of God, in wisdom, and in understanding, and in knowledge, and in all manner of workmanship," "to devise the work of the tabernacle" (Ex. 31:1-11), as a proof that the inspiration of the Prophet does not differ in kind from the inspiration of the artist or the architect. This argument at first glance seems plausible, but when we bear in mind the facts about the tabernacle, especially the fact that the tabernacle was to be built after the pattern shown to Moses in the mount (Ex. 25:8, 9, 40) and that therefore it was itself a revelation from God, a prophecy, a setting forth of the truth of God, the argument loses all its force. The tabernacle was the Word of God done into wood, gold, silver, brass, cloth, skin, etc., just as truly the Word of God and the revealing of God's truth as if the truth were printed on a page. So, of course, Bezaleel needed to be inspired, he was a prophet, a prophet who uttered his prophecies in the details of the tabernacle. There is much reasoning about inspiration to-day that appear at first sight very learned, but that will not bear much scrutiny or candid comparison with the teachings of the Word of God. There is nothing in the Bible more inspired than the tabernacle, and if the destructive critics would study the tabernacle more carefully and thoroughly they would be led to give up their ingenious but untenable theories, not only about the construction of the tabernacle, but about many other things as well. I have never heard or known of a single destructive critic who had ever given a thorough study to the real meaning of the tabernacle in all its parts, or who had any considerable understanding of the types of Scripture. I have challenged the critics in the University centres of England, Ireland and Scotland to name one single destructive critic who had ever made any thorough study of the types, and no one has ever attempted to even suggest one.

II. TRUTH HIDDEN FROM MEN FOR AGES, AND WHICH THEY HAD NOT DISCOVERED AND COULD NOT DISCOVER, BY THE UNAIDED PROCESSES OF HUMAN REASONING, HAS BEEN REVEALED TO APOSTLES AND PROPHETS IN THE SPIRIT

The second thing taught in the Bible regarding the inspiration of the Apostles and Prophets, the inspiration of the various authors of the books of the Bible, is that truth hidden from men for ages, and which they had not discovered, and could not discover, by the unaided processes of human reasoning, even human reasoning at its very best and highest, has been revealed to Apostles and Prophets in the Holy Spirit. We find this very clearly taught in Eph. 3:2-5: "If so be that ye have heard of the dispensation of that grace of God which was given me to you-ward; (3) how that by revelation was made known unto me the mystery, as I wrote before in few words, (4) whereby when ye read, ye can perceive my understanding in the mystery of Christ; (5) which in other generations was not made known unto the sons of men, as it hath now been revealed unto his holy apostles and prophets in the Spirit." The meaning of these words is unmistakable. Paul here declares in words the meaning of which is perfectly plain, that God "in the Spirit" had revealed "unto His holy apostles and prophets" "the mystery of Christ" which in former generations had not been made known unto the sons of men, which they had not discovered and could not discover except by revelation from God; Paul and the other apostles and prophets knew it by direct revelation from God himself through the Holy Ghost. The teaching is inescapable that the Bible contains truth that men never had discovered and never could have discovered if left to themselves, but truth which the Father in great grace has revealed to His children through His servants the prophets and apostles. We see in this the folly, a folly so common in our day, of seeking to test the statements of Scripture by the conclusions of human reasoning, or by the intuitions of the "Christian consciousness." The revelation of God transcends human reasoning, and therefore human reasoning cannot be its test. Furthermore, a consciousness that is truly and fully Christian is the product of the study and absorption of Bible truth. It is not the test of the truth of the Bible,—it is the product of meditation on the Bible. If our "consciousness" differs from the statements of the Bible, it is not as yet a fully "Christian consciousness," and the thing for us to do is not to try to pull God's revelation down to the level of our consciousness but to tone our consciousness up to the level of God's Word.

III. THE REVELATION MADE TO THE PROPHETS BY THE HOLY SPIRIT WAS INDEPENDENT OF THEIR OWN THINKING

The third thing that the Bible makes perfectly clear as to the inspiration of the Prophets and Apostles is, that the revelation made by God through His Holy Spirit to the Prophets was independent of the Prophets' own thinking, that it was made to them by the Spirit of Christ which was in them, and that they themselves oftentimes did not thoroughly understand the full meaning of what the Spirit was saying through them, and that what they said was a subject of diligent search and inquiry to their own mind as to its meaning. This comes out very plainly in 1 Pet. 1:10-12, "Concerning which salvation the prophets sought and searched diligently, who prophesied of the grace that should come to you; searching what time, or what manner of time the Spirit of Christ which was in them did point unto, when it testified beforehand the sufferings of Christ and the glories that should follow them. Unto whom it was revealed, that not unto themselves, but unto you, did they minister these things which now have been announced unto you through them that preached the Gospel unto you by the Holy Spirit sent forth from Heaven; which things angels desire to look into." Here again the meaning is as clear as day and inescapable. We are told that the prophets had a revelation made to them by the Holy Spirit, the meaning of which they did not thoroughly comprehend, and that they themselves "sought and searched diligently" as to the meaning of this revelation which was made to them and which they recorded. The Spirit, through them testified beforehand the sufferings of Christ (e.g. in Isa. 53:3, Ps. 22) and the glories that should follow them. They recorded what the Spirit testified, but what it meant they did not thoroughly understand. It was not merely that their minds were made keen to see things which they would not otherwise see, and which they therefore more or less accurately recorded. No, there was a very definite revelation, arising not from their own minds at all, but from the Spirit of God Who made the revelation to them and this they recorded, but it was not of themselves to that extent that they themselves wondered as to what its meaning might be. What they recorded was not at all their own thought, it was the thought of the Holy Spirit who spoke through them. How utterly different this conception is from that which is so persistently taught in many of our colleges and theological seminaries and pulpits,—how utterly different it is from the conception that was taught a week ago to-day in one of the pulpits of our own city.

IV. NO PROPHETIC UTTERANCE WAS OF THE PROPHET'S OWN WILL, BUT THE PROPHET SPOKE FROM GOD AND THE PROPHET WAS CARRIED ALONG BY THE HOLY SPIRIT AND NOT BY HIS OWN IMPULSE OR REASONING IN WHAT HE SAID

The fourth thing that the Bible makes perfectly clear is, that not one single prophetic utterance was of the prophet's own will (i.e., it was not in any sense merely what he wished to say), but in every instance the Prophet spoke from God, and the Prophet was carried along in the prophetic utterance by the Holy Spirit, regardless of his own will or thought. We find this stated practically in so many words in 2 Pet. 1:21 where we read: "For no prophecy (literally, not a prophecy) ever came (literally, was brought) by the will of man; but men spake from God being moved (literally, carried along, or borne) by the Holy Spirit." There can be no honest mistaking of the meaning of this language. The Prophet never thought that there was something that needed to be said and therefore said it, but God took possession of the prophet, carried him along in his utterance, by the power of the Holy Spirit, and he spake, not from his own consciousness, and not from his own reasoning, nor from his own intuition, but "from God." As God's messenger he spoke what God told him to say.

V. THE HOLY SPIRIT WAS THE REAL SPEAKER WHO SPOKE IN THE PROPHETIC UTTERANCES

The fifth thing that the Bible teaches regarding the Inspiration of the Prophets and the Apostles and their utterances, is that the Holy Spirit was the real speaker in the prophetic utterances, that what was said or written was the Holy Spirit's Word that was upon the Apostle's tongue, and not the word of the Prophet or Apostle. This is said in the Bible in so many words, over and over again. For example, in Heb. 3:7 we read: "Wherefore, even as the Holy Spirit saith, To-day if ye shall hear His voice, harden not your hearts, etc." The author of the epistle to the Hebrews is quoting Ps. 95:7, 8 and says that what the Psalmist is recorded as saying "the Holy Spirit saith." Again in Heb. 10:15, 16, we read: "And the Holy Spirit also beareth witness to us; for after He had said, This is the covenant that I will make with them after those days, saith the Lord: I will put my laws on their heart, and upon their mind also will I write them." Now the author of the Epistle to the Hebrews is quoting Jer. 31:33, and he does not hesitate to say that the testimony that Jeremiah there bore is the testimony of the Holy Ghost, that the Holy Ghost was the real speaker.

Again we read in Acts 28:25, 26 that Paul said, "Well spake the Holy Spirit through Isaiah the prophet, unto your fathers, (26) saying, Go thou unto this people and say, By hearing ye shall hear and shall in no wise understand; and seeing ye shall see, and shall in no wise perceive, etc." Here Paul is quoting Isaiah's words as recorded in the 6th chapter of Isaiah, the 9th and 10th verses, and he distinctly says that the real speaker was not Isaiah, but "the Holy Spirit" who spoke "through Isaiah the prophet."

Turning now to the old Testament we read in 2 Sam. 23:2 this assertion by David regarding the things that he said and wrote: "The Spirit of Jehovah spake by me, and his word was upon my tongue." There can be no mistaking the meaning of these words on the part of any one who goes to the Bible to find out what it really claims and teaches. The Holy Spirit was the real speaker in the prophetic utterance. It was the Holy Spirit's utterance that was upon the prophet's tongue. The prophet was simply the mouth by which the Holy Spirit spoke. Merely as a man, except as the Holy Spirit taught him and used him, the prophet was fallible as other men are fallible, but when the Spirit was upon him, when he was taken up and borne along by the Holy Spirit, then he became infallible in his teachings; for his teachings were not his, but the teachings of the Holy Spirit. It was God who was then speaking, not the Prophet. For example, Paul merely as a man, even as a Christian man, doubtless had many mistaken notions on many things, and was more or less subject to the ideas and opinions of his time, but when he taught as an Apostle, under the power of the Holy Spirit he was infallible, or rather the Spirit who taught through him was infallible, and the teachings that resulted from the Spirit's teaching through him, were infallible, as infallible as God. Common sense demands of us that we carefully distinguish between what Paul may have thought as a man, and what he actually taught as an apostle. In the Bible we have the record of what he taught as an Apostle. Some one may cite as a possible exception to this statement 1 Cor. 7:6, 25, where he says: "But this I say by way of concession, not of commandment. . . . Now concerning virgins, I have no commandment of the Lord, but I give my judgment, as one that hath obtained mercy of the Lord to be trustworthy." There are those who think that Paul does not seem to have been sure here that he had the word of the Lord in this particular matter, but that is not the meaning of the passage. The meaning of v. 6 is that his teaching which he had just given was by way of concession to their weakness, and not a commandment as to what they must do. And the teaching of v. 25 is that the Lord, during His earthly life, had given no commandment on this subject, but that Paul was giving his judgment; but he says distinctly that he was giving it as one who had obtained mercy of the Lord to be trustworthy and furthermore, in the 40th verse of the chapter he distinctly says that in his judgment he had the Spirit of God. But even allowing that the other interpretation of this passage is the correct one, and that Paul was not absolutely sure in this case that he had the Word of the Lord and the mind of the Lord, that would only show that where Paul was not absolutely sure that he was teaching in the Holy Ghost he was careful to note the fact, and this would only give additional certainty to all other passages that he wrote.

It is sometimes said that Paul taught in his earlier epistles that the Lord would return during his lifetime, and that in this matter he certainly was mistaken. But Paul never taught in his earlier epistles, or any other epistles, he never taught anywhere, that the Lord would return during his lifetime. This assertion is contrary to fact. He does say in 1 Thess. which was his first epistle, the 4th chapter and 17th verse: "Then we that are alive, that are left, shall together with them (i.e., the believers who had already fallen asleep) be caught up in the clouds, to meet the Lord in the air; and so shall we ever be with the Lord." He does here put himself in the same class with those who were still alive when he wrote the words. He naturally and necessarily did not include himself with those who had already fallen asleep. In speaking of the Lord's return he does not say nor hint that he will be still alive when the Lord returns. It is quite probable that Paul did believe at this time that he might be alive when the Lord returned but he never taught that he would be alive. The attitude of expectancy is the true attitude in all ages for every believer. This was the attitude that Paul took until it was distinctly revealed to him that he would depart before the Lord came. I think it very probable that Paul in the earlier part of his ministry was inclined to believe that he would live until the coming of the Lord, but the Holy Ghost kept him from so teaching, and also kept him from all other errors in his teachings.

VI. THE HOLY SPIRIT IN THE APOSTLES GAVE NOT ONLY THE THOUGHT, BUT THE WORDS IN WHICH THE THOUGHT WAS TO BE EXPRESSED

The 6th thing that the Bible makes clear as to the inspiration of the apostle and prophets is that, the Holy Spirit in the Prophets and Apostles gave not only the thought but also gave the words in which the thought was to be expressed. We find this very clearly stated in 1 Cor. 2:13: "Which things also we speak, not in words which man's wisdom teacheth, but which the Holy Spirit teacheth; combining spiritual things with spiritual words." One of the most popular of the false theories of Inspiration in our day is that the Holy Spirit was the author of the thought, but that the Apostles were left to their own choice of words in the expression of the thought, and that therefore in studying the Bible we cannot emphasise the exact meaning of the words, but must try to find the thought of God that was back of the words, and which the writer has more or less inaccurately expressed. There are many teachers in our theological seminaries to-day, and in our pulpits, who speak very sneeringly and superciliously of those who believe in Verbal Inspiration,—i.e., those who believe that the Holy Spirit chose the very words in which the thought he was teaching was to be expressed, but however sneeringly they may speak of those who believe in Verbal Inspiration, certainly the Bible claims that it was verbally inspired. The passage which I have just read makes it as plain as language can possibly make it that the "words" in which the Apostle spoke were not "words which man's wisdom teacheth, but which the Spirit teacheth." Now if this is not the fact, if only the thought that was given to Paul was the thought of God, and he clothed the thought in his own words, then Paul was a thoroughly deceived man on a fundamental point, in which case no dependence at all can be placed in his teachings on any point, or else he was a deliberate fraud, in which case the quicker we burn up his books the better for us and all concerned. There is no possibility of finding any middle ground, and the attempts to find a middle ground have landed those who have tried it in all kinds of absurdities. If you have an exact and logical mind, you must take your choice between Verbal Inspiration and bald infidelity. Paul distinctly states that the words in which he conveyed to others the truth that was revealed to him were the words which the Holy Spirit taught him. The Holy Spirit himself has anticipated all these modern ingenious, but wholly unbiblical and utterly illogical and entirely false theories regarding his own work in the Apostles. The theory that "the concept" was inspired but the words in which the concept was expressed were not, was anticipated by the Holy Spirit Himself and exploded 1800 years before our supposedly wise 19th century theological teachers conceived it, and attempted to foist it upon an unsuspecting public. It was exploded eighteen centuries before it was exploited. Furthermore, the theory is absurd in itself. As the only way in which thought can be conveyed from one mind to another, from one man's mind to another man's mind, or from the mind of God to the mind of man is by words, therefore if the words are imperfect the thought expressed in those words is necessarily imperfect. The theory is an absurdity on its very face, and it is difficult to see how intelligent men could have ever deceived themselves into believing such a thoroughly illogical theory. If the words are not inspired the Bible is not inspired. Let us not deceive ourselves; let us face facts.

Furthermore, the more carefully and minutely one studies the wording of the statements of this wonderful book—the Bible—the more he will become convinced of the marvellous accuracy of the very words used to express the thought. To a superficial thinker the doctrine of Verbal Inspiration may appear questionable or even absurd, but any regenerate and Spirit-taught man who ponders the words of the Scripture day by day, and year after year, will become thoroughly and immovably convinced that the wisdom of God is in the very words used as well as in the thought which is expressed in the words. It is a significant and deeply impressive fact that our difficulties with the Bible rapidly disappear as we note the precise language used. The changing of a word or letter, or of a tense, case or number, would oftentimes land us in contradiction or untruth, but taking the words exactly as written, difficulties disappear and truth shines forth. Countless times people have come to me with apparent difficulties and supposed contradictions in the Bible and asked a solution, and I have pointed them to the exact words used and the solution was found in taking the words exactly as written. It was because they changed in a slight degree the very words that God spoke that a difficulty had seemed to arise. The Divine origin of nature shines forth more and more clearly the more closely we examine it under the microscope. As by the use of a powerful microscope we see the perfection of form and the adaptation of means to end in the minutest particles of matter, we are overwhelmingly convinced that God, a God of infinite wisdom and power, a wisdom extending down to the minutest parts of matter, is the author of the material universe: so likewise the divine origin of the Bible shines forth more and more clearly under the microscope. The more minutely we study the Bible the more we note the perfection with which the turn of a word reveals the absolute thought of God.

An important question, and a question that has puzzled many writers at this point, is: If the Holy Spirit is the author of the very words of Scripture how do we account for the variations in style and diction? How is it, for example, that Paul always used Pauline language, and John used Johannean language, and Peter used language that was characteristic of himself? The answer to this question is very simple and is two-fold: First, even though we could not account at all for this fact, it would have little weight against the explicit statement of God's Word with any one who is humble enough and wise enough to recognise that there are a great many things which he cannot account for at all which could be easily accounted for if he knew a little more. It is only the man who has such amazing and stupendous conceit that he thinks he knows as much as God, in other words, that he is infinite in wisdom, who will give up an explicit statement of God's Word simply because he sees a difficulty in the way of the acceptance of that statement, which he in his limited knowledge cannot solve. But there is a second answer, and an all-sufficient one, and that is this: these variations in style and diction are easily accounted for. The Holy Spirit is infinitely wise. He Himself is the Creator of Man, and of man's power of speech, and therefore he is quite wise enough and has quite enough facility in the use of language in revealing truth to and through any individual to use words, phrases and forms of expression that are in that person's ordinary vocabulary and forms of thought, and He is also quite wise enough to make use of that person's peculiar individuality in revealing the truth through him. It is one of the marks of the Divine wisdom of this book that the same Divine truth is expressed with absolute accuracy in such widely variant forms of expression.

VII. ALL SCRIPTURE IS INSPIRED OF GOD

The seventh thing that the Bible makes plain regarding the work of the Holy Spirit in the various writers of Scripture, is that all Scripture, that is everything contained in all the books of the Old and New Testament, is inspired of God. We are distinctly taught this in 2 Tim. 3:16, 17. Here we read, "All Scripture (more exactly, every Scripture) is given by inspiration of God (more literally, God-breathed), and is profitable for doctrine, (or teaching), for reproof, for correction, for instruction in righteousness (rather, instruction which is in righteousness), that the man of God may be perfect (rather, complete) thoroughly furnished (better, furnished completely) unto all good works (rather, every good work)." An attempt has been made to obscure the full force of these words by a revised translation given in both the English Revision and American Standard Version. In this revised translation, the words are rendered as follows: "Every Scripture inspired of God is also profitable for teaching, for reproof, for correction, for instruction which is in righteousness; that the man of God may be complete, furnished completely unto every good work." There is absolutely no warrant in the Greek text for changing

"Every Scripture is given by inspiration of God and is profitable for doctrine, etc.," into "Every Scripture inspired of God is also profitable for teaching, etc." "Every" is in the Greek. There is no "is" in the Greek. It must be supplied, as is often the case in translating from Greek into English. "Is" must be supplied somewhere, either before "given by inspiration" (or God-breathed), or else supplied after it, in the latter case necessitating the change of "and" into "also" (a change which is possible, but very uncommon); and there is not a single instance in the New Testament outside of this in which two adjectives coupled by the simplest copulative "and (kai)" are ripped apart and the "is" placed between them and an "and" changed into "also." The other construction, that of the Authorised Version, is not at all uncommon. The translation of the Revisers does violence to all customary usage of the Greek language. But we do not need to dwell upon that, for, even accepting the changes given in the Revision, the thought is not essentially changed; for if Paul had said what the revisers make him say that "Every Scripture inspired of God is also profitable for teaching, etc.," there can be no question but by "every scripture inspired of God" he referred to every Scripture contained in the Old Testament. Here, then, taking whichever translation you will, we have the plain teaching that every Scripture of the Old Testament is "God-breathed" or "inspired of God." Certainly if we can believe this about the Old Testament there is no difficulty in believing it about the New, and there can be no question that Paul claimed for his own teaching an equal authority with the O. T. teaching. This we shall see clearly under the next head. And not only did Paul so claim, but the Apostle Peter also classes the teaching of Paul with the O. T. teaching as being "Scripture." Peter says in 2 Pet. 3:15, 16, "Even as our beloved brother Paul also, according to the wisdom given unto him, wrote unto you; (as also in all his epistles, speaking in them of these things, wherein are some things hard to be understood, which the ignorant and unstedfast wrest, as they do also the other Scriptures, unto their own destruction." Here Peter clearly speaks of Paul's epistles as being "Scripture."

VIII. THE BIBLE IS THE WORD OF GOD

The eighth thing that the Bible teaches concerning the extent of the inspiration of its writings is that because of this inspiration of Prophets and Apostles, the writers of the Bible, the whole Bible as originally given becomes the absolutely inerrant Word of God. In the O. T. David says of his own writings, in 2 Sam. 23:2, a passage already referred to, "The Spirit of Jehovah spake by me, and His Word was upon my tongue." In Mark 7:13 Our Lord Jesus Himself calls the law of Moses "the Word of God." He says "making void the Word of God by your tradition, which ye have delivered." In the verses immediately preceding, He has been drawing a contrast between the teachings of the Mosaic law (not merely the teachings of the Ten Commandments, but other parts of the Mosaic law as well) and the traditions of the Scribes and Pharisees, and has shown how the traditions of the Scribes and Pharisees flatly contradicted the requirements of the law as given through Moses, and in summing up the matter he says in the verse just quoted, that the Scribes and Pharisees made void "the Word of God" by their traditions, thus calling the law of Moses "the Word of God." When I was in England a high dignitary and scholar in the Church of England in a private correspondence tried to call me down by saying that the Bible nowhere claimed to be "the Word of God," but I replied to him by showing him that not only did the Bible claim it, but that the Lord Jesus Himself said in so many words that the law given through Moses was "the Word of God." In 1 Thess. 2:13 the Apostle Paul claims that his own epistles and teachings are "the Word of God." He says: "And for this cause we also thank God without ceasing, that when ye received from us the word of the message, even the word of God, ye accepted it not as the word of men, but as it is in truth, the word of God, which also worketh in you that believe." Here the Apostle Paul claims for his own teaching in the most absolute way that the message that he gave was "the Word of God." When we read the words that Jeremiah wrote and Isaiah wrote and Paul wrote and John wrote and James wrote and Jude wrote and the other Bible writers wrote, we are reading what God says. We are not listening to the voice of man, but we are listening to the voice of God. "The

Word of God" which we have in the Old and New Testaments, as originally given, is absolutely inerrant down to the smallest word and smallest letter or part of a letter. Our Lord Jesus Himself says of the Pentateuch in Matt. 5:18: "For verily I say unto you, till heaven and earth pass away, one jot or one tittle shall in no wise pass away from the law till all things be accomplished." Now a "jot" is the Hebrew character "yodh," the smallest character in the Hebrew alphabet, less than half the size of any other letter in the Hebrew alphabet, and a "tittle" is a part of a letter, the little horn put on some of the Hebrew consonants, less than the cross we put on a "t," and here our Lord says that the law given through Moses was absolutely inerrant, down to its smallest letter or part of a letter. That certainly is verbal inspiration with a vengeance. Again he said, as recorded in John 10:35, after having quoted from the 82nd Psalm and the 6th verse, as conclusive proof of a point, "The Scripture CANNOT BE BROKEN," thus asserting the absolute irrefragability or inerrancy and finality of the Scriptures. If the Scriptures as originally given were not the inerrant Word of God, then not only is the Bible a fraud, but Jesus Christ Himself was utterly misled and is therefore utterly unreliable as a teacher. I have said that the Scriptures of the Old and New Testaments as originally given were absolutely inerrant, and the question of course arises to what extent is the Authorized Version, or the Revised Version, the inerrant Word of God. The answer is simple; they are the inerrant Word of God just to that extent that they are an accurate rendering of the Scriptures of the Old and New Testaments as originally given, and to all practical intents and purposes they are a thoroughly accurate rendering of the Scriptures of the Old and New Testaments as originally given. There are, it is true, many variations in the many manuscripts we possess, thousands of variations, but by a careful study of these very variations, we are able to find with marvellous accuracy what the original manuscripts said. A very large share of the variations are of no value whatever, as it is evident from a comparison of different manuscripts that they are mistakes of a transcriber. Many other variations simply concern the order of the words used, and in translating into English, in which the order of words is often different from what it is in the Greek, the variation is not translatable. Many other variations are of small Greek particles, many of which are not translatable into English any way. When all the variations of any significance have been reduced to the minimum to which it is possible to reduce them by a careful study of manuscripts, there is not one single variation left that affects any doctrine held by the evangelical churches, and the Scriptures as we have them to-day translated into our English language, either in the A. V. or R. V., are to all practical intents and purposes the inerrant Word of God.

II

The Christian Conception of God, or the God of the Bible as Distinguished from the God of Christian Science and the God of Modern Philosophy

"God is Spirit."—John 4:24.

"God is Light."—1 John 1:5.

"God is Love."—1 John 4:8, 16.

Our subject this morning is "The Christian Conception of God, or The God of the Bible as Distinguished from the God of Christian Science and the God of Modern Philosophy." I have three texts: John 4:24: "God is Spirit." 1 John 1:5: "God is Light." 1 John 4:8, 16: "God is Love." These three texts give three of the most remarkable statements that were ever uttered and set before us in the clearest possible way the Christian conception of God as distinguished from every other conception of God. The Christian Scientists constantly quote one of our texts: "God is Love." In fact they quote it more than almost any other passage in the Bible, but they do not mean at all by "God is Love" what 1 John 4:8 or 1 John 4:16 evidently mean when taken in their connection. By "love" the Christian Scientists do not mean a personal attribute of God, but an impersonal abstraction which is itself God. Mrs. Eddy frankly and flatly denies the personality of God. The Christian Scientists not only say, "God is love," but they also say, "Love is God." They not only say, "God is good," but they also say, "Good is God." To say "Love is God" is an utterly different statement from saying, "God is love." You might just as well say "Spirit is God," because God says, "God is spirit," but all spirit is not God. Or you might as well say, "Light is God," because "God is light," but light is not God and love is not God, though God is love and God is light and God is spirit. What is meant by "love" in the inspired statement, "God is Love"? What is meant by the statement, "God is Love," is shown by the definition or description of love given in the context and in the immediately preceding chapter—1 John 3:13-18. These verses clearly show that by the statement in 1 John 4:8 and 1 John 4:16, "God is Love" is not meant that God is an abstract quality, "love," and that the abstract quality of love is God, but what is meant is that God is a person whose whole being and conduct are dominated by the quality of love, that is, by a desire for and delight in the highest welfare of others. This will be evident to you if I read from the immediately preceding chapter (1 John 3:13-17): "Marvel not, brethren, if the world hateth you. (14) We know that we have passed out of death into life, because we love the brethren. He that loveth not abideth in death. (15) Whosoever hateth his brother is a murderer: and ye know that no murderer hath eternal life abiding in him. (16) Hereby know we love, because he laid down his life for us: and we ought to lay down our lives for the brethren. (17) But whoso hath the world's goods, and beholdeth his brother in need, and shutteth up his compassion from him, how doth the love of God abide in him? (18) My little children, let us not love in word, neither with the tongue; but in deed and truth." And from this chapter (1 John 4:7-17): "Beloved, let us love one another: for love is of God; and every one that loveth is begotten of God, and knoweth God. (8) He that loveth not knoweth not God; for God is love. (9) Herein was the love of God manifested in us, that God hath sent his only begotten Son into the world that we might live through him. (10) Herein is love, not that we loved God, but that he loved us, and sent his son to be the propitiation for our sins. (11) Beloved, if God so loved us, we also ought to love one another. (12) No man hath beheld God at any time: If we love one another, God abideth in us, and his love is perfected in us: (13) Hereby we know that we abide in him and he in us, because he hath given us of his spirit. (14) And we have beheld and bear witness that the father hath sent the Son to be the Saviour of the world. (15) Whosoever shall confess that Jesus is the son of God, God abideth in him, and he in God. (16) And we know and have believed the love which God hath in us. God is Love; and he that hath abideth in love abideth in God, and God abideth in him. (17) Herein is love made perfect with us, that we may have boldness in the day of judgment; because as he is, even so are we in this world."

The God of what is called "Modern Philosophy" is "The Absolute," and by "The Absolute" is generally meant a cold abstraction and not a clear, definite and warm personality Who loves, grieves, suffers, and Who works intelligently for others. And oftentimes the God of modern philosophy is not only "in all things" but is all things and all things are God. Such a God is no God at all. Whereas the God of the Bible, as we shall see as we proceed, is a Divine Person who exists apart from the world which He has created and Who existed before the world He created, Who bears definite relations to the world He has made and Who works along definite and clearly revealed lines. So we come face to face with the question, What sort of a Being is the God of the Bible, the real God, the one true God, the God of Christianity, the only God Whom we should worship and love and obey? The Kaiser also talks much about God and his followers are fond of saying, "Gott mit uns," but if any one will carefully study the Kaiser's utterances it becomes plain that he does not mean by God the God of the Bible, the Christian God, the God and Father of our Lord Jesus Christ.

I. GOD IS SPIRIT

First of all "God is Spirit." This we read in our first text: John 4:24, "God is Spirit." You will note that in your Bible, both the Authorised and Revised Versions, you read, "God is a Spirit." But there is no indefinite article in the Greek language, and wherever it is necessary in the English translation to fit the English idiom, it has to be supplied, and it is supplied, in this case. But there is really no reason for supplying it here any more than there is for supplying it in 1 John 4:8 and translating, "God is a Love," or in 1 John 1:5 and translating "God is a Light." The preferable translation is as I have given it: "God is Spirit." This is a definition of the essential nature of God. What does it mean? Our Lord Jesus Himself has defined what is meant by "spirit" in Luke 24:39, where He is recorded as saying after His resurrection: "See My hands and My feet, that it is I Myself; handle Me, and see, for a spirit not flesh and blood, as ye behold Me having." It is evident from these words of our Lord that spirit is that which is contrasted to body. That is to say, spirit is incorporeal, invisible reality. To say, "God is Spirit" is to say that God is essentially incorporeal and invisible (cf. 1 Tim. 6:16), that God in His essential nature is not material but immaterial and invisible, but none the less real. This thought is also found in the very heart of that revelation of Himself which God made to Moses in the first division of the Old Testament. For example, we read in Deut. 4:15-18: "Take ye therefore good heed unto yourselves; for ye saw no manner of form on the day that Jehovah spake unto you in Horeb out of the midst of the fire; (16) lest ye corrupt yourselves, and make you a graven image in the form of any figure, the likeness of male or female, (17) the likeness of any beast that is on the earth, the likeness of any winged bird that flieth in the Heavens. (18) The likeness of anything that creepeth on the ground, the likeness of any fish that is in the water under the earth." This is a plain declaration way back fifteen centuries before Christ, of the spirituality of God in His essential nature. God is essentially invisible spirit.

But it is also clearly revealed in the Word of God that "spirit" may be manifested in visible, bodily form. We read in John 1:32 these words of John the Baptist speaking about what his own eyes had seen: "And John bore witness, saying, I have beheld the Spirit descending as a dove out of heaven; and it abode upon him." Here, then, we see Him who was essentially spirit manifesting Himself in a bodily, visible form.

Furthermore in the Bible we are told that God has manifested Himself in visible form. We read in Ex. 24:9, 10: "Then went up Moses, and Aaron, Nadab, and Abihu, and seventy of the elders of Israel: (10) and they saw the God of Israel; and there was under his feet as it were a paved work of sapphire stone, and as it were the very heaven for clearness."

What they saw was not God in His essential nature as Spiritual Being. Indeed, what we see when we see one another is not our essential self, but the house we live in, and so John could say, as he does say in John 1:18: "No man hath seen God at any time." And so I could say to you now that you do not see me. Nevertheless, it was a real manifestation of God Himself that they saw, and so it could also be said, and said truthfully, that they had seen God, as it could be truthfully said, "you see me."

Furthermore still, though God is essentially spirit, God has a visible form. This is taught in the most unmistakable terms in Phil. 2:6, where we are told of our Lord Jesus that He existed originally "in the form of God." The Greek word which is translated "form" in this passage means "visible form," "the form by which a person or thing strikes the vision," "the external appearance." It cannot mean anything else. This is the definition given in the best Greek-English lexicon of the New Testament, of the word here translated "form." Now as Jesus existed originally "in the form of God," it is evident that God Himself must have a form, this form in which our Lord Jesus is said to have existed originally.

That God in His external form, though not in His invisible essence, is seeable, is also clear from Acts 7:55, 56, where we read: "But he (i.e., Stephen), being full of the Holy Ghost, looked up steadfastly into heaven, and saw the glory of God, and Jesus standing on the right hand of God, and said, Behold, I see the heavens open, and the Son of man standing on the right hand of God." Now if God has not a form that can be seen, then, of course, the Lord Jesus could not be seen standing upon the right hand of God. God is, as we shall see later, everywhere; but God is not everywhere in the same sense. There is a locality where God is visibly and manifestly present in a way in which He is not present anywhere else. There is a place where He is present visibly and manifests Himself as He does not elsewhere. The place of God's visible presence and full manifestation of Himself is Heaven, though in His spiritual presence He pervades the universe. This is evident from many passages in the Scriptures. For example, it is clear from the prayer that our Lord taught us—a portion of Scripture that many accept who reject most of the Bible. Our Lord began the prayer that He taught His disciples with these words "Our Father Which Art in Heaven." If these words mean anything, they certainly mean that God, our Father, is in heaven in a way in which He is not elsewhere. That was where God was when Jesus was addressing Him. We read again in Matt. 3:17: "Lo, a voice out of the heavens, saying, this is my beloved Son, in whom I am well pleased." If these words mean anything, they mean that God was in heaven and that His voice came out of the heavens to the Lord Jesus who was here on earth. Again in John 14:28 Jesus is recorded as saying:

"Ye heard how I said to you, I go away and I come again unto you. If ye loved me, ye would have rejoiced, because I go unto the Father: for the Father is greater than I." If these words mean anything, taken in the light of the events that were to follow on the next day and the days following, they mean that Jesus was going away from the place where He then was—earth—to another place where He was not when He spoke, i.e., heaven—and that in going to heaven he was going to where God was, from earth where God was not in the sense in which He was in heaven. Again we read in Acts 11:9: "A voice answered the second time out of heaven, What God hath cleansed make not thou common." Here again God is represented as speaking from heaven where He was. Again our Lord Jesus Christ is recorded in John 20:17 as saying to Mary Magdalene after His resurrection: "Touch me not; for I am not yet ascended unto the Father: but go unto my brethren and say to them, I ascend unto my father and to your father and my God and your God," from which it is unmistakably evident that in the conception of our Lord Jesus after His resurrection there was a place where God was and to which He was going, and that place was up in heaven. There is no possibility of explaining this away by saying it is a figure of speech, the whole passage loses its meaning by any such interpretation, and to attempt to so explain it is a trick and a subterfuge that will not bear close examination. Again the Apostle Paul tells us regarding our Lord Jesus Christ that God the Father "raised Him from the dead, and made Him to sit at His right hand in the heavenly places" (Eph. 1:20) which makes it as clear as language can make anything that there is a place, heaven, where God is in a sense that He is nowhere else, and where one can be placed at His right hand. The same thing is evident from the verses that we have already quoted in another connection, Acts 7:55, 56, where we are told that Stephen "being full of the Holy Ghost, looked up steadfastly into heaven and saw the glory of God, and Jesus standing at the right hand of God, and said, Behold, I see the heavens open, and the Son of man standing on the right hand of God." The meaning of these words to anybody who wishes to know what words are intended to convey and not merely to distort them to fit his own conception, is that God is in heaven locally present. There is no escaping this by any fair, honest interpretation. Men who are skilful in the art of discrediting truth by giving it bad names, and names that sound very scholarly, may call this "anthropomorphism," and that sounds very learned. Nevertheless, be it "anthropomorphism" or what not, this is the clear teaching of the Word of God in spite of this or any other frightful terms used to scare immature college boys and immature college girls. There is no mistaking that this is the teaching of the Bible, and we have already proven that the Bible is God's Word, and is to be taken at its face value in spite of all the attempts that men, who "counting themselves wise, have become fools," make to explain it away.

II. GOD IS A PERSON

The next thing that the Bible teaches about God is that God is a person. That is to say He is a being who knows, feels, loves, hears prayer, speaks, acts, a being who acts intelligently upon us and upon whom we can act.

While God is in all things, He is a personality distinct from the persons and things in which He is, which He has created. The Bible, both in the Old and New Testaments is full of this vital conception of "a living God" as distinguished from the mere cold abstraction of "The Absolute," or "The Infinite," or "The Supreme Being," or "The Great First Cause" of which "Modern Philosophy" loves to prate. For example, we read in Jer. 10:10-16: "But Jehovah is the true God; he is the living God, and an everlasting king: at his wrath the earth trembleth, and the nations are not able to abide his indignation. (11) Thus shall ye say unto them, the gods that have not made the heaven and the earth, these shall perish from the earth, and from under the heavens. (12) He hath made the earth by his power, he hath established the world by his wisdom, and by his understanding hath he stretched out the heavens. (13) When he uttereth his voice, there is a tumult of waters in the heavens, and he causeth the vapours to ascend from the ends of the earth; he maketh lightnings for the rain, and bringeth forth the wind out of his treasuries. (14) Every man is become brutish and is without knowledge; every goldsmith is put to shame by his graven image; for his molten image is falsehood, and there is no breath in them. (15) They are vanity, a work of delusion; in the time of their visitation they shall perish. (16) The portion of Jacob is not like these; for he is the former of all things; and Israel is the tribe of his inheritance: Jehovah of hosts is his name." In this passage God is distinguished from idols which are things and not persons, things which "speak not" "cannot act," "cannot do good neither is it in them to do evil"; and we are told that Jehovah is wiser than "all the wise men." Is "the living God," "an everlasting King," a being who hath "wrath and indignation," separate from His creatures—"at His wrath the earth trembleth and the nations are not able to abide His indignation."

In Acts 14:15 we read: "Sirs, why do ye these things? We also are men of like passions with you, and bring you good tidings, that ye should turn from these things unto the living God, who made heaven and earth and sea, and all that in them is." Here also we have the representation of God as a personal being distinct from His created work, and also to be clearly distinguished from the idols which are not living gods. In 1 Thess. 1:9, the converts at Thessalonica are represented as turning from dead gods, "idols, to serve the living and true God."

In 2 Chron. 16:9 we are told that "The eyes of Jehovah run to and fro throughout the whole earth, to show himself strong in the behalf of them whose heart is perfect toward him," and in Ps. 94:9, 10 we read: "He that planteth the ear, shall he not hear? He that formed the eye, shall he not see? He that punisheth nations, shall not he correct? Even he that teacheth men knowledge?" This is clearly the representation of a personal God and not a mere abstraction like "The Absolute," or "The Infinite," or "The Supreme Being." The clear distinction between God, who is immanent in all things, and dwells in believers, and the beings and persons in whom He dwells, is brought out very clearly by our Lord Himself in John 14:10: "Believest thou not that I am in the Father and the Father in me? The words that I say unto you I speak not from myself: But the Father abiding in me doeth his work." And again in the 24th verse of the same chapter where our Lord Jesus distinguishes between His own personality and that of the Father, who dwelt in Him, in these words:

"He that loveth me not keepeth not my words: and the word which ye hear is not mine, but the Father's who sent me." This conception of God pervades the entire Bible. The view of God presented in the Bible is utterly different from the conception of Pantheism and Buddhism and Theosophy and Christian Science. This conception is found in the opening words of the Bible, Gen. 1:1: "In the beginning God created the heaven and the earth." Here the God of the Bible is clearly differentiated from the so-called God of Pantheism, and the God of Christian Science. And this same conception of God is found in the last chapter of the Bible, and it is found in every chapter of the Bible between the first and the last. The God of the Bible is a Personal Being Who, while He created all things and is in all things, is a distinct personality separate from the persons and things He has created.

III. GOD'S PRESENT RELATION TO THE WORLD AND TO MEN

We turn now to a consideration of the present relation of this Personal God presented to us in the Bible, to the world He has created and to the men whom He has created.

1. In the first place we find that God sustains, governs and cares for the world He has created. He shapes the whole present history of the world. This comes out again and again. A few illustrations must suffice. We read in Ps. 104:27-30: "These wait all for thee, that thou mayest give them their food in due season. (28) Thou givest unto them, they gather; thou openest thy hand, they are satisfied with good. (29) Thou hidest thy face, they are troubled; thou takest away their breath, they die, and return to their dust. (30) Thou sendest forth thy spirit, they are created; and thou renewest the face of the ground." And again in Ps. 75:6, 7: "For neither from the east, nor from the west, nor yet from the south, cometh lifting up. (7) But God is the judge: he putteth down one, and lifteth up another." All these passages and others that could be cited, set forth the same conception of God's present relation to the world which He has created. They show, as we have said, that God sustains, governs and cares for the work He has created; that He shapes the whole present history of the world.

2. Now let us look at His relation to the affairs of men. We will find that God has a present, personal interest and an active hand in the affairs of men; that He makes a path for His people and leads them; that He delivers, saves and punishes. Here four illustrations from the Bible must suffice. First of all Joshua 3:10: "And Joshua said, Hereby ye shall know that the living God is among you, and that he will without fail drive out from before you the Canaanite, and the Hittite, and the Hivite, and the Perizzite, and the Girgashite, and the Amorite, and the Jebusite." Now turn to Dan. 6:20-22, 26, 27. "And when he came near unto the den to Daniel, he cried with a lamentable voice: the king spake and said to Daniel, O Daniel, servant of the living God, is thy God, whom thou servest continually, able to deliver thee from the lions? (21) Then said Daniel unto the king, O king, live for ever. (22) My God hath sent his angel, and hath shut the lions' mouths, and they have not hurt me: forasmuch as before him innocency was found in me; and also before thee, O king, have I done no hurt." . . . "(26) I make a decree, that in all the dominion of my kingdom men tremble and fear before the God of Daniel; for he is the living God, and stedfast for ever, and his kingdom that which shall not be destroyed and his dominion shall be even unto the end. (27) He delivereth and rescueth, and he worketh signs and wonders in heaven and in earth, who hath delivered Daniel from the power of the lions." Now turn to 1 Tim. 4:10: "For to this end we labour and strive, because we have our hope set on the living God, who is the Saviour of all men, specially of them that believe," and now turn to Heb. 10:28-31: "A man that hath set at nought Moses' law dieth without compassion on the word of two or three witnesses: (29) Of how much sorer punishment, think ye, shall he be judged worthy, who hath trodden under foot the Son of God? and hath counted the blood of the covenant wherewith he was sanctified an unholy thing, and hath done despite unto the Spirit of grace? (30) For we know him that said, Vengeance belongeth unto me, I will recompense. And again, The Lord shall judge his people. (31) It is a fearful thing to fall into the hands of the living God." In all of these passages we have this same conception of God in His relation to man, viz., that God has a personal interest and an active hand in the affairs of men; that He makes a path for His people and leads them; that He

delivers, saves and punishes them.

The God of the Bible is to be clearly distinguished not merely from the God of the Pantheists who has no existence separate from His creation, but also from the God of the Deists who has created the world and put into it all the necessary powers of self-government and development and set it going and left it to go of itself. The God of the Bible is a God who is personally and actively present in the affairs of the universe to-day. He sustains, governs, cares for the world He has created, He shapes the whole present history of the world. He has a present personal interest and an active hand in the affairs of men and He it is that is back of all the events that are occurring to-day. He reigns and makes even the wrath of men to praise Him, and the remainder of wrath doth He restrain. The Kaiser may rage, armies may clash, force and violence and outrage may seem triumphant for the passing hour, but God stands back of all; and through all the confusion and the discord and the turmoil and the agony and the ruin, through all the outrageous atrocities that are making men's hearts stand still with horror, He is carrying out His own purposes of love and making all things work together for good to those who love Him.

III

The Christian Conception of God—The Infinite Perfection and Unity of God

"God is Light."—1 John 1:5.

"God is Love."—1 John 4:8, 16.

"With God All Things are Possible."—Matt. 19:26.

"His Understanding is Infinite."—Ps. 147:5.

We are to consider again to-day the Christian conception of God. We saw a week ago to-day that God is Spirit, that God is a person and that God has a personal interest and an active hand in the affairs of men to-day, that He sustains, governs and cares for the world He has created and that He shapes the whole present history of the world.

I. THE INFINITE PERFECTION OF GOD

The next thing to be noted about the Christian conception of God is, that God is perfect and infinite in all His intellectual and moral attributes and in power.

1. First of all, fix your attention upon our first text: "God is Light" (1 John 1:5). These three words form a marvellously beautiful and overwhelmingly impressive statement of the truth. They set forth the Absolute Holiness and Perfect Wisdom of God. The words need rather to be meditated upon than to be expounded. "In Him is no darkness at all." That is to say, in Him is no darkness of error, no darkness of ignorance, no darkness of sin, no darkness of moral imperfection or intellectual imperfection of any kind. The three words, "God is Light," form one of the most beautiful, one of the most striking and one of the most stupendous statements of truth that was ever penned.

2. To come to things more specific, the God of the Bible is omnipotent. This great truth comes out again and again in the Word of God. One direct statement of this great truth especially striking because of the connection in which it is found, occurs in Jer. 32:17, 27: "Ah Lord Jehovah! Behold, thou hast made the heavens and the earth by thy great power and by thine outstretched arm: there is nothing too hard for thee." Here it is Jeremiah who makes the statement, but in the 27th verse it is Jehovah Himself who says: "Behold, I am Jehovah, the God of all flesh: is there anything too hard for me?"

In Job 42:2 we read these words of Job, when at last he has been brought to see and to recognise the true nature of Jehovah: "I know that thou canst do all things and that no purpose of thine can be restrained." In Matt. 19:26 our Lord Jesus says: "With God all things are possible." Taking these passages together, we are plainly taught by our Lord Himself and by others that God can do all things, that nothing is too hard for Him, that all things are possible with Him. In a word, that God is omnipotent. A very impressive passage in the book of Psalms setting forth this same great truth is Ps. 33:6-9: "By the word of Jehovah were the heavens made, and all the host of them by the breath of his mouth. (7) He gathereth the waters of the sea together as a heap: he layeth up the deeps in storehouses. (8) Let all the earth fear Jehovah: let all the inhabitants of the world stand in awe of him. (9) For he spake, and it was done; he commanded, and it stood fast." Here we see God by the mere utterance of His voice bringing to pass anything that He desires to be brought to pass. We find this same lofty conception of God in the very first chapter of the Bible, that chapter that so many people who imagine themselves scholarly are telling us is outgrown and not up to date, and yet which contains some of the sublimest utterances that were ever written, unmatched by anything that any philosopher or scientist or platform orator is saying to-day. The very first words of that chapter read: "In the beginning God created the heaven and the earth" (Gen. 1:1), a description of the origin of things that has never been matched for simplicity, sublimity and profundity; and two verses further down, in the third verse, we read: "And God said, Let there be light: and light was." These words need no comment. There is here a sublimity of thought in the setting forth of the omnipotence of God's mere word before which any truly intelligent and alert soul will stand in wonder and awe. There is nothing in poetry or in philosophical dissertation, ancient or modern, that can for one moment be put in comparison with these sublime words. Over and over again the thought is brought out in the Word of God that all nature is absolutely subject to God's will and word. We see this, for example, in Ps. 107:25-29: "For he commandeth, and raiseth the stormy wind, which lifteth up the waves thereof. (26) They mount up to the heavens, they go down again to the depths: their soul melteth away because of trouble. (27) They reel to and fro, and stagger like a drunken man, and are at their wits' end. (28) Then they cry unto Jehovah in their trouble, and he bringeth them out of their distresses. (29) He maketh the storm a calm, so that the waves thereof are still." Another description of a similar character is found in Nahum 1:3-6: "Jehovah is slow to anger, and great in power, and will by no means clear the guilty: Jehovah hath his way in the whirlwind and in the storm, and the clouds are the dust of his feet. (4) He rebuketh the sea, and maketh it dry, and drieth up all the rivers: Bashan languisheth, and Carmel and the flower of Lebanon languisheth. (5) The mountains quake at him, and the hills melt; and the earth is upheaved at his presence, yea, the world, and all that dwell therein. (6) Who can stand before his indignation? and who can abide in the fierceness of his anger? His wrath is poured out like fire, and the rocks are broken asunder by him." What a picture we have here of the omnipotence and awful majesty of God!

Not only is nature represented as being absolutely subject to God's will and word, but men also are represented as being absolutely subject to His will and word. For example, we read in Jas. 4:12-15: "One only is the lawgiver and judge, even he who is able to save and to destroy: But who art thou that judgest thy neighbour? (13) Come now, ye that say, to-day or to-morrow we will go into this city, and spend a year there, and trade, and get gain: (14) Whereas ye know not what shall be on the morrow. What is your life? For ye are a vapour that appeareth for a little time, and then vanisheth away. (15) For that ye ought to say, if the Lord will, we shall both live, and do this or that."

Happy is the man who voluntarily subjects himself to God's will and word, but whether we voluntarily subject ourselves to God's will and word or not, we are subject to His will and word whether or no. The angels also are subject to His will and word (Heb. 1:13, 14) and even Satan himself is, although entirely against his own will, absolutely subject to the will and word of God, as is evident from Job 1:12 and Job 2:6.

The exercise of God's omnipotence is limited by His own wise and holy and loving will. God can [61]do anything, but will do only that which infinite wisdom and holiness and love dictate. This comes out, for example, in Isa. 59:1, 2: "Behold, Jehovah's hand is not shortened, that it cannot save; neither his ear heavy, that it cannot hear: (2) But your iniquities have separated between you and your God, and your sins have hid his face from you, that he will not hear."

3. The God of the Bible is also omniscient. In 1 John 3:20 we read: "God knoweth all things." Turning to the Old Testament, in Ps. 147:5, we read: "Great is our Lord, and mighty in power; his understanding is infinite." The literal translation of the last clause of this passage is "Of his understanding there is no number." In these passages it is plainly declared that "God knoweth all things" and that "His understanding is infinite." In Job 37:16 Elihu the messenger of God is represented as saying that Jehovah is "perfect in knowledge." Along the same line, in Acts 15:18 we read: "Known unto God are all his works from the beginning of the world." The Revised Version makes a change in the translation of this verse but this change does not alter the sense of the truth here set forth that God knows all His works and all things from the beginning of the world. Known to Him is everything from the most vast to the most minute detail. In Ps. 147:4 we are told that, "He telleth the number of the stars; he knoweth them all by name." While in Matt. 10:29 we are told that not a sparrow falleth to the ground without Him. The stars in all their stupendous magnitude and the sparrows in all their insignificance are all equally in His mind.

We are further told that everything has a part in His purpose and plan. In Acts 3:17, 18, the Apostle Peter says of the crucifixion of our Lord, the wickedest act in all the history of the human race:

"And now, brethren, I wot that in ignorance ye did it, as did also your rulers. But the things which God foreshowed by the mouth of all the prophets, that his Christ should suffer, he thus fulfilled." In Acts 2:23 Peter declared on the day of Pentecost (although the crucifixion of the Lord Jesus was the wickedest act in all history) that nevertheless the Lord Jesus was "Delivered up by the determinate council and foreknowledge of God." According to the Psalmist (Ps. 76:10) God takes the acts of the wickedest men into His plans and makes the wrath of men to praise Him, and the remainder of wrath doth He restrain. Even the present war with all its horrors, with all its atrocities, with all its abominations and all its nameless wickednesses, was foreknown of God and taken into His own gracious plan of the ages; and He will make every event in this present war, even the most shocking things, designed by the vilest conspiracy of unprincipled men, utterly unhuman and beastly men and Devil inspired men, work together for good to those who love God, for those who are the called according to His purpose (Rom. 8:28).

The whole plan of the ages, not merely of the centuries, but of the immeasurable ages of God, and every man's part in it, has been known to God from all eternity. This is made very clear in Eph. 1:9-12, where we read: "Having made known unto us the mystery of his will, according to his good pleasure which he purposed in him unto a dispensation of the fullness of the times, to sum up all things in Christ, the things in the heavens, and the things upon the earth; in him, I say, in whom also we were made a heritage, having been foreordained according to the purpose of him who worketh all things after the counsel of his will; to the end that we should be to the praise of his glory, we who before hoped in Christ." And in Eph. 3:4-9, we read: "Wherefore when ye read, ye can perceive my understanding in the mystery of Christ; which in other generations was not made known unto the sons of men, as it is now revealed unto his holy prophets and apostles in the Spirit; to wit, that the Gentiles are fellow-heirs, and fellow-members of the body, and fellow-partakers of the promise in Christ Jesus through the gospel, whereof I was made a minister, according to the gift of that grace of God which was given me according to the working of his power.

Unto me, who am less than the least of all saints, was this grace given, to preach unto the Gentiles the unsearchable riches of Christ; and to make all men see what is the dispensation of the mystery which from all ages has been hid in God who created all things." There are no after-thoughts with God. Everything is seen, known, purposed and planned for from the outset. Well may we exclaim: "Oh, the depth of the riches both of the wisdom and knowledge of God: how unsearchable are his judgments and his ways past finding out." (Rom. 11:33.) God knows from all eternity what He will do to all eternity.

    4. God is also absolutely and infinitely holy. This is a point of central and fundamental importance in the Bible conception of God. It comes out in our first text: "God is light, and in him is no darkness at all." John when he wrote these words gave them as the summary of "The message which we have heard from God." (1 John 1:5.) In Isa. 6:3 in the vision of Jehovah which was given to Isaiah in the year that King Uzziah died, the "seraphim," or "burning ones," burning in their own intense holiness, are represented as standing before Jehovah with covered faces and covered feet and constantly crying, "Holy, holy, holy, is Jehovah of Hosts." And in 1 Pet. 1:16 God cries to us, "Be ye holy, for I am holy."

    This thought of the infinite and awe-inspiring holiness of God pervades the entire Bible. It underlies everything in it. The entire Mosaic system is built upon and about this fundamental and central truth. Its system of washings; the divisions of the tabernacle; the divisions of the people into ordinary Israelites, Levites, Priests and High Priests, who were permitted different degrees of approach to God under strictly defined conditions, insistence upon sacrifices of blood as the necessary medium of approach to God; God's directions to Moses in Ex. 3:5, to Joshua in Josh. 5:15, the punishment of Uzziah in 2 Chron. 26:16-26, the strict orders to Israel in regard to approaching Sinai when Jehovah came down upon it; the doom of Korah, Dathan and Abiram in Num. 16:1-33; and the destruction of Nadab and Abihu in Lev. 10:1-3: all these were intended to teach, emphasise and burn into the minds and hearts of the Israelites the fundamental truth that God is holy, unapproachably holy. The truth that God is holy is the fundamental truth of the Bible, of the

Old Testament and the New Testament, of the Jewish religion and the Christian religion. It is the preëminent factor in the Christian conception of God. There is no fact in the Christian Conception of God that needs more to be emphasised in our day than the fact of the absolute, unqualified and uncompromising holiness of God. That is the chief note that is lacking in Christian Science, Theosophy, Occultism, Buddhism, New Thought, the New Theology and all the base but boasted cults of the day. That great truth underlies those fundamental doctrines of the Bible,—the Atonement by Shed Blood and Justification by Faith. The doctrine of the holiness of God is the keystone in the arch of Christian truth.

5. God is also love. This truth is declared in one of our texts. The words "God is love" are found twice in the same chapter (1 John 4:8, 16). This truth is essentially the same truth as that "God is light" and "God is holy," for the very essence of true holiness is love, and "light" is "love" and "love" is "light."

6. Furthermore, God is not only perfect in His intellectual and moral attributes and in power, He is also omnipresent. This thought of God comes out in both the Old Testament and the New. In Ps. 139:7-10 we read: "Whither shall I go from thy Spirit? Or whither shall I flee from thy presence? (8) If I ascend up into heaven, thou art there: If I make my bed in Sheol, behold thou art there. (9) If I take the wings of the morning, and dwell in the uttermost part of the sea; (10) Even there shall thy hand lead me, and thy right hand shall hold me." There is no place where one can flee from God's presence, for God is everywhere. This great truth is set forth in a remarkable way in Jer. 23:23, 24: "Am I a God at hand, saith Jehovah, and not a God afar off? (24) Can any hide himself in secret places that I shall not see him? saith Jehovah. Do not I fill heaven and earth? saith Jehovah."

Last week we saw that God has a local habitation, that there is a place where He exists and manifests Himself in a way in which He does not manifest Himself everywhere; but while we insist upon that clearly revealed truth, we must also never lose sight of the fact that God is everywhere. We find this same truth set forth by Paul in his sermon to the Epicurean and Stoic philosophers on Mars Hill, Acts 17:24-28: "The God that made the world, and all things therein, he, being Lord of heaven and earth, dwelleth not in temples made with hands: (25) Neither is served by men's hands as though he needed anything, seeing he himself giveth to all life and breath and all things. (26) And he made of one every nation of men who dwell on all the face of the earth, having determined their appointed seasons, and the bounds of their habitations. (27) For in him we live, and move, and have our being; as certain even of your own poets have said, for we are also his offspring."

From these passages we see that God is everywhere. He is in all parts of the universe and near each individual. In Him each individual lives and moves and has his being. He is in every rose and lily and blade of grass.

7. There is one other thought in the Christian conception of God that needs to be placed alongside of His omnipresence and that is His eternity. God is eternal. His existence had no beginning and will have no ending, He always was, always is and always shall be. God is not only everywhere present in space, He is everywhere present in time. This conception of God appears constantly in the Bible. We are told way back in Gen. 21:33 that Abraham called "On the name of Jehovah, the everlasting God." In Isa. 40:28 we read this description of Jehovah: "Hast thou not known? Hast thou not heard? The everlasting God, Jehovah, the creator of the ends of the earth, fainteth not, neither is weary; there is no searching of his understanding." Here again He is called "The Everlasting God." Habakkuk in Hab. 1:12 sets forth the same conception of God. He says, "Art not thou from everlasting, O Jehovah my God, mine holy one?" The Psalmist gives us the same representation of God in Ps. 90:2, 4: "Before the mountains were brought forth, or ever thou hast formed the earth and the world, even from everlasting to everlasting thou art God. (4) For a thousand years in thy sight are but as yesterday when it is passed, and as a watch in the night." We have the same representation of God in the 102nd Ps., verses 24-27: "I said, O my God, take me not away in the midst of my days: Thy years are throughout all generations. (25) Of old didst thou lay the foundation of the earth; and the heavens are the work of thy hands. (26) They shall perish, but thou shalt endure; yea, all of them shall wax old like a garment; as a vesture shalt thou change them, and

they shall be changed; (27) But thou art the same, and thy years shall have no end."

The very name of God, His covenant name, Jehovah, sets forth His eternity. He is the eternal "I am," the One who is, was and ever shall be. (Cf. Ex. 3:14, 15.)

II. THERE IS ONE GOD

One more fact about the Christian conception of God remains to be mentioned and that is: There is but one God. The Unity of God comes out again and again in both the Old Testament and the New. For example, we read in Deut. 4:35: "Jehovah he is God. There is none else beside him." And in Deut. 6:4 we read: "Hear O Israel: Jehovah our God is one Jehovah." Turning to the New Testament in 1 Tim. 2:5 we read: "There is one God, one mediator also between God and man, himself man, Christ Jesus." And in Mark 12:29 our Lord Jesus Himself says: "Hear O Israel, the Lord our God, the Lord is one."

But we must bear in mind the character of the Divine Unity. It is clearly revealed in the Bible that in this Divine Unity, in this one Godhead, there is a multiplicity of persons. This comes out in a variety of ways.

1. First of all, the Hebrew word translated "One" in these various passages given denotes a compound unity, not a simple unity. (Cf. 1 Cor. 3:6-8; 1 Cor. 12:13; John 17:22, 23; Gal. 3:28.)

2. In the second place, the Old Testament word most frequently used for God is a plural noun. The Hebrew grammarians and lexicographers tried to explain this by saying that it was the "pluralis majestatis," but the very simple explanation is that the Hebrews, in spite of their intense monotheism, used a plural name for God because there is a plurality of persons in the one Godhead.

3. More striking yet, as a proof of the plurality of persons in the one Godhead, is the fact that God Himself uses plural pronouns in speaking of Himself. For example, in the first chapter of the Bible, Gen. 1:26, we read that God said: "Let us make man in our image, after our likeness." And in Gen. 11:7, He is further recorded as saying: "Go to, let us go down, and there confound their language, that they cannot understand one another's speech." In Gen. 3:22 we

read: "And Jehovah God said, Behold, man is become as one of us to know good and evil." And in that wonderful vision to which reference has already been made, in which Isaiah saw Jehovah, we read this statement of Isaiah's in Isa. 6:8: "And I heard the voice of the Lord, saying, Whom shall I send, and who will go for us? Then said I, Here am I; send me."

4. Another illustration of the plurality of persons in the one Godhead in the Old Testament conception of God is found in Zech. 2:10, 11; where Jehovah speaks of Himself as sent by Jehovah in these words: "Sing and rejoice, O daughter of Zion; for, lo, I come, and I will dwell in the midst of thee, saith Jehovah. (11) And many nations shall join themselves to Jehovah in that day, and shall be my people and I will dwell in the midst of thee, and thou shalt know that Jehovah of hosts hath sent me unto thee." Here Jehovah clearly speaks of himself as sent by Jehovah, thus clearly indicating two persons in the Deity.

5. Another indication of the plurality of persons in the Godhead in the Old Testament conception of God is found in the fact that "The Angel of Jehovah" in the Old Testament is at the same time distinguished from and identified with Jehovah.

6. This same thought of the plurality of persons in the one Godhead is brought out in John 1:1, where we reach the very climax of this thought. Here we are told in so many words: "In the beginning was the word and the word was with God and the word was God." We shall see later, when we come to study the Deity of Christ and the Personality and Deity of the Holy Spirit, that the Lord Jesus and the Holy Spirit are clearly designated as divine beings and at the same time distinguished from one another, and from God the Father. So it is clear that in the Christian conception of God while there is but one God there is a multiplicity of persons in the one Godhead.

In these two sermons on "The Christian Conception of God" we have very inadequately stated that conception. This conception of God runs through the whole Bible from the first chapter of the book of Genesis to the last chapter of Revelation, and this is one of the many marvellous illustrations of the divine unity of the Book. How [72]wonderful is that Book, in that there is this unity of thought on this very profound doctrine pervading the whole book!

It is a clear indication that the Bible is the Word of God. There is in the Bible a profounder philosophy than is found in any human philosophy, ancient or modern, and the only way to account for it is that God Himself is the author of this incomparable philosophy. What a wondrous God we have! How we ought to meditate upon His person! With what awe and at the same time with what delight we should come into His presence and bow before Him in adoring contemplation of the wonder and beauty and majesty and glory of His being!

IV
The Deity of Jesus Christ

"Now while the Pharisees were gathered together, Jesus asked them a question, saying, What think ye of the Christ? whose son is He?"—Matt. 22:41, 42.

The question that our Lord Jesus here puts to the Pharisees is the most fundamental question concerning Christian thought and faith that can be put to anybody in any age. Jesus Christ Himself is the centre of Christianity, so the most fundamental questions of faith are those that concern the person of Christ. If a man really holds right views concerning the person of Jesus Christ he will sooner or later get right views on every other question. If he holds a wrong view concerning the person of our Lord Jesus Christ, he is pretty sure to go wrong on everything else sooner or later. What think ye of Christ? That is the great central question, that is the vital question.

And the most fundamental question concerning the person of Christ is, is Jesus Christ really God? Not merely is He Divine, but is He actually God? When I was a boy, to say you believed in the Divinity of Christ, meant that you believed in the real Deity of Christ, that you believed that Jesus was actually a Divine person, that He was God. It no longer means that. The Devil is wise, shrewd, subtle, and he knows that the most effectual way to instil error into the minds of the inexpert and unwary is to use old and precious words and put a new meaning into them. So when his messengers masquerading as "ministers of righteousness" seek to lead, if possible, the elect astray, they use the old precious words but with an entirely new and entirely different and entirely false meaning. They talk about "the Divinity of Christ," but they do not mean at all by it what intelligent Christians in former days meant by it. Just so they talk of "the atonement," but they do not mean at all by the atonement the substitutionary death of Jesus Christ in our place, by which eternal life is secured for us. And oftentimes when they talk about Christ they do not mean at all our Lord and Saviour Jesus Christ, the actual historic Jesus of the four gospels, they mean an ideal Christ, or a Christ principle. So our subject this morning is not the Divinity of Christ, but the Deity of Christ, and our question is not is Jesus Christ Divine, but is Jesus Christ God? Was that person who was born at Bethlehem nineteen hundred and twenty-one years ago, and who lived thirty-three or thirty-four years here upon earth as recorded in the four gospels of Matthew, Mark, Luke and John, who was crucified on Calvary's cross, who rose from the dead the third day, and was exalted from earth to heaven, to the right hand of the Father, was He God manifested in the flesh, was He God embodied in a human being? Was He and is He a being worthy of our absolute faith, and supreme love, and our unhesitating obedience, and our whole-hearted worship, just as God the Father is worthy of our absolute faith and supreme love and unhesitating obedience and our whole-hearted worship? Should all men honour Jesus Christ even as they honour God the Father (John 5:23)? Not merely is He an example that we can wisely follow, or a Master whom we can wisely serve, but is He a God Whom we can rightly worship?

I presume that most of us do believe that He was God manifested in the flesh, and that He is God to-day at the right hand of the Father, but why do you believe so? Are you so intelligent in your faith, and therefore so well grounded in your faith, that no glib talker or reasoner, no Unitarian or Russellite or Christian Scientist or Theosophist, or other errorist can confuse you and upset you and lead you astray? It is important that we be thoroughly sound in our faith at this point, and thoroughly well-informed, wherever else we may be in ignorance or error, for we are distinctly told in John 20:31 that "These are written, that ye may believe that Jesus is the Christ, the Son of God; and that believing, ye may have life in His name." It is evident from these words of the inspired Apostle John that this question is not merely a matter of theoretical opinion, that it is a matter that concerns our salvation. It is to confirm and instruct you in your blessed faith, your saving faith in Jesus Christ as a Divine person, that I speak this morning. When I studied the subject of the Divinity of Christ in the theological seminary I got the impression that there were a few proof-texts in the Bible that conclusively proved that He was Divine. Years later I found that there were not merely a few proof-texts that proved this, but that the Bible in many ways and in countless passages clearly taught that Jesus Christ was God manifest in the flesh. Indeed I found that the Doctrine of the Deity of Jesus Christ formed the very warp and woof of the Bible.

I. DIVINE NAMES

The first line of proof of the absolute Deity of our Lord Jesus is that many names and titles clearly implying Deity are used of Jesus Christ in the Bible, some of them over and over again, the total number of passages reaching far into the hundreds. Of course, I can give you only a few illustrations. Turn with me first of all to Rev. 1:17, "And when I saw him, I fell at his feet as one dead. And he laid his right hand upon me saying, Fear not; I am the first and the last." The context shows clearly that our Lord Jesus was the speaker, and here our Lord Jesus distinctly calls Himself "the First and the Last." Now this beyond a question is a Divine name, for in Isa. 44:6 we read, "Thus sayeth Jehovah, the king of Israel, and his redeemer, Jehovah of hosts: I am the first, and I am the last; and besides me there is no God." In Rev. 22:12, 13, our Lord Jesus says that He is the Alpha and Omega. His words are, "Behold, I come quickly; and my reward is with me, to render to each man according as his work is. I am Alpha and Omega, the first and the last, the beginning and the end." Now in this same book in the first chapter and the eighth verse the Lord God declares that He is the Alpha and the Omega. His words are, "I am the Alpha, and the Omega, saith the Lord God, which is and which was and which is to come, the Almighty." In 1 Cor. 2:8, the Apostle Paul speaks of our crucified Lord Jesus as "the Lord of glory." His exact words are, "Which none of the princes of this world knew: for had they known it, they would not have crucified the Lord of glory." There can be no question that "the Lord of glory" is Jehovah God, for we read in Ps. 24:8-10, "Who is this king of glory? Jehovah strong and mighty, Jehovah mighty in battle. Lift up your heads, O ye gates; yea lift them up, ye everlasting doors, and the king of glory will come in. Who is the king of glory? Jehovah of hosts. He is the king of glory." And we are told in the passage already referred to that our crucified Lord Jesus was the King of Glory, therefore He must be Jehovah. In John 20:28 Thomas addressed the Lord Jesus as his Lord and his God, "And Thomas answered and said unto him, My Lord and my God." Unitarians have endeavoured to get around the force of this utterance of Thomas by saying that Thomas was excited and that he was not addressing the Lord Jesus, but was saying "my Lord and my God" as an ejaculation of astonishment, just in the way that profane people sometimes use these exclamations to-day, but this interpretation is impossible, and shows to what desperate straits the Unitarians are driven; for Jesus Himself commended Thomas for seeing it and saying it. Our Lord Jesus' words immediately following those of Thomas are, "Because thou hast seen me, thou hast believed: blessed are they that have not seen, and yet have believed" (John 20:29). In the correct translation of Titus 2:13, the translation given in the English revision, not in the American Standard Revision, our Lord Jesus is spoken of as, "our great God and Saviour Jesus Christ." In Rom. 9:5, Paul tells us that "Christ is over all, God blessed forever." The Unitarians have made desperate efforts to overcome the force of these words, but the only fair translation and interpretation of the words that Paul wrote in Greek are the translation and interpretation found in both our Authorised and Revised Versions. There can be no honest doubt to one who goes to the Bible to find out what it actually teaches, and not to read his own thought into it, that Jesus is spoken of by various names and titles that beyond a question imply Deity, and that He in so many words is called God. In Heb. 1:8 it is said in so many words, of the Son, "But unto the Son he saith, thy throne, O God, is for ever and ever; a sceptre of righteousness is the sceptre of thy kingdom." If we should go no further it is evidently the clear and often repeated teaching of the Bible that Jesus Christ was really God.

II. DIVINE ATTRIBUTES

But there is a second line of proof that Jesus Christ was God, a proof equally convincing, and that is, all the five distinctively Divine attributes are ascribed to Jesus Christ, and "all the fulness of the Godhead" is said to dwell in Him. There are five distinctively Divine attributes, that is five attributes that God alone possesses. These are Omnipotence, Omniscience, Omnipresence, Eternity, and Immutability. Each one of these distinctively Divine attributes are ascribed to Jesus Christ. First of all, omnipotence is ascribed to Jesus Christ. Not only are we taught that Jesus had power over disease and death and winds and sea and demons, that they were all subject to His word, and that He is far above all principality, and power, and might, and dominion, and every name that is named, not only in this world but also in the world to come (Eph. 1:20-23), but in Heb. 1:3 it is said in so many words that He "Upholds all things by the word of his power." Omniscience is also ascribed to Him. We are taught in the Bible that Jesus knew men's lives, even their secret history (John 4:16, 19), that He knew the secret thoughts of men, knew all men, knew what was in man (Mark 2:8; Luke 5:22; John 2:24, 25) which knowledge we are distinctly told in 2 Chron. 6:30 and Jer. 17:9, 10, God only possesses, but we are told in so many words in John 16:30 that Jesus knew "all things," and in Col. 2:3 we are told that in Him "are hid all the treasures of wisdom and knowledge." Omnipresence is also ascribed to Him. We are told in Matt. 18:20 that where two or three are gathered together in His name, that He is in the midst of them, and in Matt. 28:20 that wherever His obedient disciples should go He would be with them, even unto the end of the age, and in John 14:20 and 2 Cor. 13:5 we are told that He dwells in each believer, in all the millions of believers scattered over the earth. In Eph. 1:23 we are told in so many words that He "filleth all in all." Eternity is also ascribed to Him. We are told in John 1:1 that "in the beginning was the Word, and the Word was with God, and the Word was God." In John 8:57 Jesus Himself said, "Verily, verily, I say unto you, before Abraham was, I am." Note that the Lord Jesus did not merely say that "before Abraham was I was," but that "before Abraham was, I am," thus declaring Himself to be the eternal "I am." Even in the Old Testament we have a declaration of the eternity of the Christ who was to be born in Bethlehem. In Micah 5:2 we read, "But thou, Bethlehem Ephratah, though thou be little among the thousands of Judah, yet out of thee shall he come forth unto me that is to be ruler in Israel; whose goings forth have been from of old, from everlasting." And in Isa. 9:6 we are told of the child that is to be born, "For unto us a child is born, unto us a Son is given; and the government shall be upon his shoulder; and his name shall be called Wonderful, Counsellor, the Mighty God, the Everlasting Father, the Prince of Peace." And in Heb. 13:8 we are told that "Jesus Christ is the same yesterday, and to-day, and for ever." His immutability is also taught in the passage just quoted from Hebrews, and in the first chapter of the same book, the twelfth verse we are told that while even the heavens change, the Lord Jesus does not change. The exact words are, "They shall perish, but thou remainest: They all shall wax old as doth a garment; and as a mantle shalt thou roll them up, as a garment, and they shall be changed: but thou art the same. And thy years shall not fail." So we see that each one of the five distinctly Divine attributes were ascribed to our Lord Jesus Christ. And in Col. 2:9 we are told in so many words, "In him dwelleth all the fulness of the Godhead bodily" (i.e., in a bodily form). Here again we might rest our case, for what has been said under this head, even if taken alone, clearly proves the absolute Deity of our Lord Jesus Christ. It shows that He possessed every perfection of nature and character that God the Father possesses.

III. DIVINE OFFICES

But we do not need to rest the case here. There is a third unanswerable line of proof that Jesus Christ is God, namely, all the distinctively Divine offices are predicated of Jesus Christ. There are seven distinctively Divine offices. That is to say, there are seven things that God alone can do, and each one of these seven distinctively Divine offices are ascribed to Jesus Christ. The seven distinctively Divine offices are: Creation, Preservation, Forgiveness of Sin, the Raising of the Dead, the Transformation of Bodies, Judgment, and the Bestowal of Eternal Life, and each of these is ascribed to Jesus

Christ. Creation is ascribed to Him. In Heb. 1:10 these words are spoken to our Lord: "And thou, Lord, in the beginning hast laid the foundation of the earth; and the heavens are the works of thy hands." The context clearly shows that the Lord addressed is the Lord Jesus. In John 1:3 we are told that "All things were made through him; and without him was not anything made that was made." Preservation of the universe and of everything is also ascribed to Him in Heb. 1:3 where it is said of the Lord Jesus, "Who being the brightness of his glory, and the express image of his (i.e., God's) substance and upholding all things by the word of his power, when he had by himself purged our sins, sat down on the right hand of the majesty on high." The forgiveness of sin is ascribed to Him. He Himself says in Mark 2:5-10 when His power to forgive sins was questioned, because that was recognised as a Divine power, "That ye may know that the Son of man hath power on earth to forgive sins." The future raising of the dead is distinctly ascribed to Him in John 6:39, 44, "And this is the Father's will which hath sent me, that of all which He hath given me I should lose nothing, but should raise it up at the last day. No man can come to me, except the Father which hath sent me draw him: and I will raise him up at the last day." The transformation of our bodies is ascribed to Him in Phil. 3:21, R. V. In 2 Tim. 4:1 judgment is ascribed to Him: we are told that He shall "judge the quick and the dead." Jesus Himself declared that He would be the judge of all mankind, and emphasised the fact of the Divine character of that office. In John 5:22, 23 He said, "For neither doth the Father judge any man, but He hath given all judgment unto the Son, that all men may honour the Son, even as they honour the Father." The bestowal of eternal life is ascribed to Him time and time again. In John 10:28 He Himself says, "And I give unto them eternal life, and they shall never perish, neither shall any man pluck them out of my hand." And in John 17:1, 2, He says, "Father, the hour is come; glorify thy Son, that the Son may glorify thee: even as thou gavest Him authority over all flesh, that to all whom thou hast given him, He should give eternal life." Here then we have the seven distinctively Divine offices all predicated of Jesus Christ. This alone would prove that He is God, and we might rest the case here, but there are still other proofs of His absolute Deity.

IV. STATEMENTS WHICH IN THE OLD TESTAMENT ARE MADE DISTINCTLY OF JEHOVAH, GOD, TAKEN IN THE NEW TESTAMENT TO REFER TO JESUS CHRIST

The fourth line of proof of the absolute Deity of Jesus Christ is found in the fact that over and over again statements which in the Old Testament are made distinctly of Jehovah, God, are taken in the New Testament to refer to Jesus Christ. We have not time to illustrate this at length, but will give but one illustration where many might be given. In Jer. 11:20 the prophet says, "But, O Lord of hosts, that judgest righteously, that triest the reins and the heart, let me see thy vengeance on them: for unto thee have I revealed my cause." Here the prophet distinctly says that it is Jehovah of Hosts who judgest and triest the reins and the heart. And in the 17th chapter and the tenth verse Jeremiah represents Jehovah Himself as saying the same thing in these words, "I, Jehovah, search the heart, I try the reins, even to give every man according to his ways, according to the fruit of his doings." But in the New Testament in Rev. 2:23 the Lord Jesus says, "I am he which searcheththe reins and the hearts: and I will give unto every one of you according to your works." We are distinctly told in the context that it is "The Son of God" who is speaking here. So Jesus claims for Himself in the N. T. what Jehovah in the O. T. says is true of Himself and of Himself alone, and in very many other instances statements which in the Old Testament are made distinctly of Jehovah, God, are taken in the N. T. to refer to Jesus Christ. This is to say, in New Testament thought and doctrine Jesus Christ occupies the place that Jehovah occupies in Old Testament thought and doctrine.

V. THE WAY IN WHICH THE NAME OF GOD THE FATHER AND JESUS CHRIST THE SON ARE COUPLED TOGETHER

The fifth line of proof of the absolute Deity of our Lord is found in the way in which the name of Jesus Christ is coupled with that of God the Father. In numerous passages His name is coupled with the name of God the Father in a way in which it would be impossible to couple the name of any finite being with that of the Deity. We have time for but a few of the many illustrations that might be given. A striking instance is in the words of our Lord Himself in John 14:23 where we read, "Jesus answered and said unto him, If a man love me, he will keep my words: and my Father will love him, and he will come unto him, and make [86]our abode with him." Here our Lord Jesus does not hesitate to couple Himself with the Father in such a way as to say "we," i.e., God the Father and I will come and make our abode with him. In John 14:1 He says, "Let not your heart be troubled: Believe in God, believe also in me." If Jesus Christ was not God this is shocking blasphemy. There is absolutely no middle ground between admitting the Deity of Jesus Christ and charging Christ with the most daring and appalling blasphemy of which any man in all history was ever guilty.

VI. DIVINE WORSHIP TO BE GIVEN TO JESUS CHRIST

There is a sixth line of proof of the absolute Deity of our Lord Jesus. Those already given have been decisive, each one of the five has been decisive, but this, if possible, is the most decisive of them all, and that is, that we are taught in so many words that Jesus Christ should be worshipped as God, both by angels and men. In numerous places in the gospels we see Jesus Christ accepting without hesitation a worship which good men and angels declined with fear, and which He Himself taught should be rendered only to God (Matt. 28:9; Luke 24:52; Mark 14:33; cf. Acts 10:25, 26; Rev. 22:8, 9, R. V.; Matt. 4:9, 10). A curious and very misleading comment is made in the margin of the American Standard Revision upon the meaning of the word translated "worship" in these passages, and that is that "the Greek word translated worship denotes an act of reverence, whether paid to a creature or to the Creator." Now this is true, but it is utterly misleading; for while this word is used to denote "an act of reverence paid to a creature" by idolators, our Lord Jesus Himself distinctly says, using exactly the same Greek word, "Thou shalt worship the Lord thy God, and Him only shalt thou serve," and on the other hand He says in John 5:23 that "All men should honour the Son even as they honour the Father." And in Rev. 5:8, 9, 12, 13 the four living creatures and the four and twenty elders are represented as falling down before the Lamb and offering worship to Him just as worship is offered to Him that sitteth upon the throne, i.e., God the Father. In Heb. 1:6 we are told in so many words, "And again, when he bringeth in the first begotten into the world, he saith, and let all the angels of God worship him." One night in the inquiry room in Chicago I stepped up to an intelligent looking man at the back of the room and said to him, "Are you a Christian?" He replied, "I do not suppose you would consider me a Christian." I said, "Why not?" He said, "I am a Unitarian." I said, "What you mean then is that you do not think that Jesus Christ is a person who should be worshipped." He replied, "That is exactly what I think," and added, "the Bible nowhere says we ought to worship Him." I said, "Who told you that?" He replied, "My pastor," mentioning a prominent Unitarian minister in the City of Boston. I said, "Let me show you something," and I opened my Bible to Heb. 1:6 and read, "And again, when he bringeth in the first begotten into the world, he saith, and let all the angels of God worship him," and he said, "Does it say that?" I handed him the Bible and said, "Read it for yourself," and he read it and said, "I did not know that was in the Bible." I said, "Well it is there, isn't it?" "Yes it is there." Language could not make it plainer. The Bible clearly teaches that Jesus, the Son of God, is to be worshipped as God by angels and men, even as God the Father is worshipped.

VII. INCIDENTAL PROOFS OF THE DEITY OF JESUS CHRIST

The six lines of proof of the Deity of Jesus Christ which I have given you leave no possibility of doubting that Jesus Christ is God, that Jesus of Nazareth is God manifest in a human person, that He is a being to be worshipped, even as God the Father is worshipped; but there are also incidental proofs of His absolute Deity which, if possible, are in some ways even more convincing than the direct assertions of His Deity.

1. Our Lord Jesus says in Matt. 11:28, "Come unto me, all ye that labour and are heavy laden, and I will give you rest." Now any one that makes a promise like that must either be God, or a lunatic,

or an impostor. No one can give rest to all who labour and are heavy laden who come to him unless he is God, and yet Jesus Christ offers to do it. If He offers to do it and fails to do it when men come to Him, then He is either a lunatic or an impostor. If He actually does it, then beyond a question He is God. And thousands can testify that He really does it. Thousands and tens of thousands who have laboured and were heavy laden and crushed, and for whom there was no help in man, have come to Jesus Christ and He actually has given them rest. Surely then He is not merely a great man, He is God.

2. Again in John 14:1 Jesus Christ demands that we put the same faith in Him that we put in God the Father, and promises that in such faith we will find a cure for all trouble and anxiety of heart. His words are, "Let not your heart be troubled; believe in God, believe also in me." It is clear that He demands that the same absolute faith be put in Himself that is to be put in God Almighty. Now in Jer. 17:5, scripture with which our Lord Jesus was perfectly familiar, we read "Thus saith Jehovah: Cursed is the man that trusteth in man," and yet with this clear curse pronounced upon all who trust in man, Jesus Christ demands that we put trust in Him just as we put trust in God. It is the strongest possible assertion of Deity on His part. No one but God has a right to make such a demand, and Jesus Christ, when He makes this demand, must either be God or an impostor, but thousands and tens of thousands have found that when they did believe in Him just as they believe in God, their hearts were delivered from trouble no matter what their bereavement or circumstances might be.

3. Again, the Lord Jesus demanded supreme and absolute love for Himself. It is clear as day that no one but God has a right to demand such a love, but there can be no question that Jesus did demand it. In Matt. 10:37 He said to His disciples, "He that loveth father or mother more than me is not worthy of me; and he that loveth son or daughter more than me is not worthy of me." And in Luke 14:26, 33, He says, "If any man cometh unto me, and hateth not his own father, and mother, and wife, and children, and brethren, and sisters, yea, and his own life also, he cannot be my disciple. . . . So therefore whosoever he be of you that renounceth not all that he hath, he cannot be my disciple." There can be no question

that this is a demand on Jesus' part of supreme and absolute love to Himself, a love that puts even the dearest relations of life in an entirely secondary place. No one but God has a right to make any such demand, but our Lord Jesus made it, and, therefore, He must be God.

4. In John 10:30 the Lord Jesus claimed absolute equality with the Father. He said, "I and the Father are one."

5. In John 14:9 our Lord Jesus went so far as to say, "He that hath seen me, hath seen the Father." He claims here to be so absolutely God that to see Him is to see the Father Who dwelleth in Him.

6. In John 17:3 He says, "And this is eternal life, to know thee, the only true God, and him whom thou didst send, even Jesus Christ." In other words, he claims that the knowledge of Himself is as essential a part of eternal life as knowledge of God the Father.

Conclusion: There is no room left to doubt the absolute Deity of Jesus Christ. It is a glorious truth. The Saviour in whom we believe is God, a Saviour for whom nothing is too hard, a Saviour who can save from the uttermost and save to the uttermost. Oh, how we should rejoice that we have no merely human Saviour, but a Saviour that is absolutely God. On the other hand, how black is the guilt of rejecting such a Saviour as this! Whoever refuses to accept Jesus as his Divine Saviour and Lord is guilty of the enormous sin of rejecting a Saviour Who is God. Many a man thinks he is good because he never stole, or committed murder, or cheated. "Of what great sin am I guilty?" he complacently asks. Have you ever accepted Jesus Christ? "No." Well, then you are guilty of the awful and damning sin of rejecting a Saviour Who is God. "But," you answer, "I do not believe that He is God." That does not change the fact nor lessen your guilt. Questioning a fact or denying a fact never changes it, regardless of what Mary Baker Eddy may say to the contrary. Suppose a man had a wife who was one of the noblest, purest, truest women that ever lived, would her husband's questioning her purity and nobility change the fact? It would not. It would simply make that husband guilty of awful slander, it would simply prove that man to be an outrageous scoundrel. So denying the Deity of Jesus Christ, does not make his Deity any less a fact, but it does make the denier of His

Deity guilty of awful, incredible, blasphemous slander. It does prove you who deny His Deity to be———. I leave your own conscience to finish the sentence.

Jesus Christ a Real Man

"And the word became flesh, and dwelt among us (and we beheld his glory, glory as of the only begotten from the Father), full of grace and truth."—John 1:14.

"Who, existing in the form of God, counted not the being on an equality with God a thing to be grasped, but emptied himself, taking the form of a servant, being made in the likeness of man; and being found in fashion as man, he emptied himself, becoming obedient even unto death, yea the death of the cross."—Phil. 2:6-8.

"There is one God, one mediator also between God and men, himself man, Christ Jesus."—1 Tim. 2:5.

Our subject in this chapter is "Jesus Christ a Real Man." I have three texts, and the substance of all that I shall say is these three texts. The first text is John 1:14: "And the word became flesh, and dwelt among us (and we beheld his glory, glory as of the only begotten from the Father), full of grace and truth." The second text is Phil. 2:6-8: "Who, existing in the form of God, counted not the being on an equality with God a thing to be grasped, but emptied himself, taking the form of a servant, being made in the likeness of man; and being found in fashion as a man, he emptied himself, becoming obedient even unto death, yea the death of the cross." And the third text is 1 Tim. 2:5: "There is one God, one mediator also between God and man, himself man, Christ Jesus."

We saw in the preceding chapter that Jesus Christ was God, that in Him dwelt all the fullness of the Godhead bodily, that He possessed all the distinctively divine attributes, that He exercised all the distinctively divine functions, that He occupied the position in New Testament thought that Jehovah occupied in Old Testament thought, that He was a being worthy of our absolute faith, our supreme love, our unhesitating obedience, and our whole-hearted worship, that He was God and is God. But in the passages which we have taken for our texts to-day, we are told that this Divine One, who had existed from all eternity with God, the Father, and who was God, became a man. In becoming a man, He did not cease to be God; but the Word, the Eternal Word, which was with God and was God, took human nature upon Himself. While He was very God of very God, He was real man, as truly and completely a man as any man who ever walked on this earth. The doctrine of the real humanity of Christ is as essential a part of the Christian faith as the doctrine of His real Deity. There is one very large class of people who do not see the real Deity of Jesus Christ. They are in fundamental error. There is another large class of people who see only His Deity, and who do not see the reality of His manhood. They also are in error. A doctrine of a Saviour who is only man is false doctrine; and a doctrine of a Saviour who is only God is equally false doctrine. The doctrine of the Bible is that, One Who from all eternity was God in the person of Jesus of Nazareth became man. There are many passages in the Bible which set forth the Deity of our Lord Jesus in a way that is unmistakable and inescapable. There are many other passages in the Bible which set forth the complete humanity of our Lord Jesus in a way which is equally unmistakable and inescapable. It is with the doctrine of His real humanity, i.e., that He was a real man, that we are concerned this morning.

I. THE HUMAN PARENTAGE OF JESUS CHRIST

First of all, the Bible teaches us that Jesus Christ had a human parentage. We read in Luke 2:7, "And she (i.e., Mary) brought forth her first born Son; and she wrapped him in swaddling clothes, and laid him in a manger, because there was no room for them in the inn." Here we are told that our Lord Jesus Christ, though supernaturally conceived, was Mary's Son. Mary was as truly His mother as God was His Father. He had a human parentage as truly as He had a divine parentage. In the first chapter of this same Gospel of Luke, in the 35th verse, we read, "And the angel answered and said unto her (i.e., Mary), the Holy Spirit shall come upon thee, and the power of the Most High shall overshadow thee: wherefore also the holy thing, which is begotten shall be called the Son of God." He was called the Son of God because He was begotten directly by the power of the Holy Spirit; but the Holy Spirit came upon Mary and she became the mother of this One who was to be called the "Son of God." Not only was He descended from Mary and in that way of human parentage, we are clearly told also in Rom. 1:3 that God's Son "Was born of the seed of David according to the flesh." And in Acts 2:30 we are told that He was "The fruit of his (i.e., David's) loins, according to the flesh." And in Hebrews 7:14, we are told that "Our Lord sprang out of Judah." While we are told in Gal. 4:4 that "When the fulness of the time came, God sent forth His Son," we are also told with equal plainness in the same verse that this Son of God was "Born of a woman." The human parentage of our Lord and Saviour Jesus Christ was just as real and just as essential a part of His personality as His divine parentage.

II. THE HUMAN PHYSICAL NATURE OF JESUS CHRIST

But not only did Jesus Christ have a human parentage, He had a human physical nature, a human body. This comes out in the first of our texts, "The Word Became Flesh," and in Hebrews 2:14 we are taught "Since then the children are sharers in flesh and blood, he also (i.e., our Lord Jesus also) himself in like manner partook of the same; that through death he might bring to naught him that had the power of death, that is, the devil." Words could not make it plainer that our Lord Jesus had a real human body, a real human physical nature. Indeed, the Apostle John teaches us in 1 John 4:2, 3, that not to believe in the actuality of His human body, is a mark of the Anti-Christ. He says, "Hereby know ye the Spirit of God: every spirit that confesseth that Jesus Christ is come in the flesh is of God: and every spirit that confesseth not Jesus is not of God: and this is the spirit of the anti-Christ, whereof ye have heard that it cometh; and now it is in the world already." There were those in John's day who denied the reality of Jesus' human nature, who asserted that His body was only a seeming or apparent body, that it was an illusion, or as the Christian Scientists now put it, "mortal thought," and John, speaking in the wisdom and power of the Holy Ghost, asserts that this doctrine is a mark of the Anti-Christ. It is the one supreme mark to-day, that "Christian Science" is of the Anti-Christ.

Jesus Christ not only had a human body during His life here upon earth, but after His resurrection He still had a human body. The Millennial Dawnists (Pastor-Russellites) teach us that this is not so; that, whereas before His incarnation He was wholly a spiritual being, that at His incarnation He became wholly a human being, and that since His death and resurrection He is wholly a divine being: all of which is not Scriptural, and therefore is not true. He himself said after His resurrection, "See my hands and my feet, that it is I myself: handle me, and see; for a spirit hath not flesh and bones, as ye behold me have. And when he said this, he showed them his hands and his feet" (Luke 24:39, 40). And to Thomas in John 20:27, after Thomas had doubted the reality of His resurrection, He said, "Reach hither thy finger, and see my hands; and reach hither thy hand, and put it into my side: and be not faithless but believing." Not only after His resurrection while still here on earth did He have a real human body, but He still has a human body in the glory. In that wonderful view into heaven that was given to Stephen at the time he was stoned and killed we read in Acts 7:55, 56, "But he, being full of the Holy Spirit, looked up steadfastly into heaven, and saw the glory of God, and Jesus standing on the right hand of God, and said, Behold I see the heavens opened, and the Son of man standing on the right hand of God." And when He comes again to take His rightful authority on this earth, He shall come with a human body, coming as "the Son of Man." He Himself said to the High Priest when He stood before him on trial, in Matt. 26:64, "Nevertheless I say unto you, henceforth ye shall see the son of man standing at the right hand of power and coming in the clouds of heaven." In this utterance of our Lord we have a declaration of His Deity, but an equally clear declaration that He was a real man, and that He will come again as a man with a human, though glorified body. Indeed, we are told in Phil. 1:20, 21 that when He does thus come, He is going to transform these our present human bodies, the bodies of our present humiliation, into the likeness of His own glorious body, His glorified human body.

III. SUBJECT TO HUMAN LIMITATIONS

But the reality and completeness of our Lord's human nature comes out not only in the fact that He had a human parentage and a human body: we are also clearly taught that, while as God he possessed all the attributes and exercised all the offices of Deity, as a man He was subject to human limitations.

1. He was subject to the physical limitations which are essential to humanity. In John 4:6 we read that Jesus Christ was weary. The words are "Jesus, therefore, being wearied with his journey, sat thus on the well: and it was about the sixth hour." But God is never weary. We read explicitly in Isa. 40:28 "Hast thou not known? Hast thou not heard? The everlasting God, Jehovah, the creator of the ends of the earth, fainteth not, neither is weary."

We are told in Matt. 8:24 that Jesus Christ slept. But God never sleeps. We read in Ps. 121:4, 5, "Behold he that keepeth Israel shall neither slumber nor sleep. Jehovah is thy keeper: Jehovah is thy shade upon thy right hand." By comparison of these two verses, we see distinctly that Jehovah never sleeps. Yet Jesus did sleep, so while He was Jehovah, He was not Jehovah only. He was man as truly as He was God.

In Matt. 21:18 we read that Jesus Christ hungered; in John 19:28 we read that Jesus Christ thirsted; in Luke 22:44 we read that Jesus Christ suffered physical agony, His agony was so great that He was on the point of dying with agony; and in 1 Cor. 15:3 we read that "Christ died," that His death is an essential part of the Gospel. Paul says in this passage, "For I delivered unto you first of all that which I received, how that Christ died for our sins according to the scriptures." It was no merely apparent death, it was a real death. It was no "illusion." Our salvation depends on the reality of His death. "Christian Science" cuts the very heart out of the Gospel. We are oftentimes asked was it the human nature of Jesus Christ that died or was it the divine nature that died. It was neither the one nor the other, natures do not die, a person dies. It was Jesus who died, the

Person who was at once God and man. We are told in so many words in 1 Cor. 2:8, that they "Crucified the Lord of glory," and we saw in the last chapter that the "Lord of Glory" is unquestionably a divine title. It was the one Person Jesus who was at once human and divine, who died upon the cross of Calvary.

2. He was also, as a man subject to intellectual and moral limitations.

We read in Luke 2:52, "Jesus advanced in wisdom and stature and in favour with God and man." As we are told here that He grew in wisdom, He must have been more perfect in wisdom after He grew than He was before He grew, and as He grew in favour with God and man, He must have attained to a higher type of moral perfection when He grew than He had attained to before He grew. While in the Babe of Bethlehem God was incarnate, nevertheless He was a real babe and grew not only in stature, but in wisdom and in favour with God and man. As a man He was limited in knowledge, He Himself says in Mark 13:32, "But of that day and that hour (i.e., the day and the hour of His own return) knoweth no man; no, not the angels which are in heaven, neither the Son but the Father." Of course, His knowledge was self-limited: to set an example for you and me to follow in His steps, He voluntarily as man put away His knowledge of the time of His own return.

Furthermore still, we are definitely and explicitly taught in Heb. 4:15 that Jesus Christ was "In all points tempted like as we are." But in bearing this in mind as being clear and complete proof of the reality of His humanity, not only physical but mental and moral, we should also bear in mind what is stated in the same verse, that He was tempted "Apart from Sin," i.e., that [102]there was not the slightest taint or tinge of sin in His temptation, not one moment's yielding to it in thought or desire or act. Nevertheless, He was tempted and overcame temptation in the same way that we may overcome it, by the Word of God and prayer. He Himself voluntarily placed Himself under the essential moral limitations that man is under in order to redeem man.

3. He was also, as a man, subject to limitations in the way in which He obtained power and in which He exercised power. Jesus Christ obtained the power for the Divine work that He did while

here upon earth, not by His incarnate Deity, but by prayer. We read in Mark 1:35, "And in the morning, a great while before day, he rose up and went out, and departed unto a desert place, and there prayed." And we read also that before He raised Lazarus from the dead, called him forth from the tomb by His Word, that He lifted up His eyes to God and said, "Father, I thank thee that thou heardest me," showing conclusively that the power by which He raised Lazarus from the dead was not His inherent, inborn, Divine power, but was power obtained by prayer. It is mentioned not less than twenty-five times that He prayed. He obtained power for work and for moral victory as other men do, by prayer. He was subject to human conditions for obtaining what He desired. He obtained power for the divine works and miracles which he wrought by the anointing of the Holy Spirit. We read in Acts 10:38, that "God anointed Jesus of Nazareth with the Holy Ghost and with power: who went about doing good, and healing all that were oppressed of the devil; for God was with him." And we are taught, furthermore, that He was subject during the days of His humiliation to limitations in the exercise of power. He himself said just before His crucifixion and subsequent glorification, in John 14:12, "Verily, verily, I say unto you, he that believeth on me, the works that I do shall he do also; and greater works than these shall he do; for I go unto my Father," the evident meaning of which is, that during the days of His flesh there was a limitation to His exercise of power, but after His glorification, when He was glorified with the Father with the glory which He had with Him since the world was, there would be no limitations to the exercise of His power, and therefore, that we, being united, not to our Lord Jesus in His humiliation, but in His exaltation and restoration to His divine glory, will do greater works than he did during the days of His humiliation.

IV. THE HUMAN RELATION OF JESUS CHRIST TO GOD

The completeness of the humanity of Jesus Christ comes out in still another matter, and that is, the relation that He bore to God as a man was the relation of a man, so that God was His God. He himself says to Mary in John 20:17, "Touch me not; for I am not yet ascended unto the father: but go unto my brethren, and say to them, I ascend unto my Father and your Father, and my God and your God." The evident meaning of this is that Jesus Christ's relation to God, the Father, was the relation of man. He speaks of God the Father as "My God." Though possessed of all the attributes and exercising all the functions of Deity, Jesus Christ the Son was subordinate to the Father. This explains utterances of our Lord which have puzzled many who believe in His Deity, such utterances, for example, as that in John 14:28, where Jesus says, "Ye have heard how I said unto you, I go away, and come again unto you. If ye loved me ye would rejoice, because I said, I go unto the Father: For my Father is greater than I." The question is often asked, "If Jesus Christ is God, how could the Father be greater than He?" The very simple answer to which is; that He, as the Son, was subordinate to the Father, equal to the Father in the possession of all the distinctively Divine attributes and exercising all the Divine offices, and as an object of our wholehearted worship, but subordinate to the Father in His office. Jesus Christ's relation to the Father is like the relation of the wife to the husband in this respect, that the wife may be fully the equal of the husband, but nevertheless, the "Head of the Woman is the Man," she is subordinate to the man, just as we are told in the same verse (1 Cor. 11:12) "The head of Christ is God," i.e., Jesus Christ the Son is subordinate to the Father.

It is evident from what we have read from God's Word, that Jesus Christ in every respect was a true man, a real man, a complete man. He was made "In all things" "like unto his brethren" (cf. Heb. 2:17). He was subject to all the physical, mental and moral conditions of existence essential to human nature. He was in every respect a real man. He became so voluntarily in order to redeem men. From all eternity He had existed "in the form of God" and could have remained "in the form of God," but if He had so remained, we would have been lost. Therefore, out of love to us, the fallen race, as we are taught in one of our texts (Phil. 2:5-8), He "Counted not the being on an equality with God a thing to be grasped, but emptied himself, taking the form of a servant, being made in the likeness of man; and being found in fashion as a man, he humbled himself, becoming obedient even unto death, yea, the death of the cross."

Oh, wondrous love! that out of love to us He should take our nature upon Him, turning His back upon the glory that had been His from all eternity and taking upon Himself all the shame and suffering that was involved in our redemption, and becoming one of us that He might die for us and redeem us! Oh, how wondrous the "Grace of our Lord Jesus Christ, that though He was rich yet for our sakes He became poor, that we through his poverty might become rich." (2 Cor. 8:9.) He partook of human nature that we might become partakers of the Divine nature. The philosophy of the divine and human natures of Christ, the philosophy of the New Testament, is a most wonderful philosophy, the most wonderful philosophy the world ever heard, and thank God it is a true philosophy.

But some one may ask, "How shall we reconcile the Bible doctrine of the true Deity of Jesus Christ with the Bible doctrine of the real human nature of Jesus Christ, the doctrine that He was real God with the doctrine that He was equally truly man?" The answer to this is very simple. Reconciling doctrines is not our main business. Our first business is to find out what the various passages in the Bible mean, taken in their natural, grammatical interpretation. Then, if we can reconcile them, well and good; if not, we should still believe them both and leave the reconciliation of the two apparently conflicting doctrines to our increasing knowledge as we go on communing with God and studying His Word. It is an utterly foolish and vicious principle of Biblical interpretation that we must interpret every passage of the Bible so that we can readily reconcile it with every other passage. It is this principle of interpretation that gives rise to a one-sided, and therefore untrue, theology. One man, for example, takes the Calvinistic passages in the Bible and believes them and twists and distorts the other passages; that teach the freedom of man, to make them fit with those that teach the sovereignty of God, and he becomes a one-sided Calvinist. Another man sees only those passages that clearly teach man's power of self-determination and seeks to twist all that teach the sovereignty of God and the foreordaining wisdom and will of God to fit into his ideas, and he becomes a one-sided Arminian, and so on through the whole gamut of doctrine. It is utter foolishness, to say nothing of presumption, to thus handle the Word of God deceitfully. Our business is to find out the plainly intended sense of a passage that we are studying, as determined by the usage of words, grammatical construction and context; and when we have found out the plainly intended meaning, believe it whether we can reconcile it with something else that we have found out and believe, or not. We should always remember that in many cases two truths, both clearly true, that at one time seemed utterly irreconcilable or flatly contradictory to one another, are now, with our increased knowledge seen to beautifully harmonise. So we should have no difficulty in recognising the fact that truths that still seem to us to be contradictory, do now perfectly harmonise in the infinite wisdom of God, and will some day perfectly harmonise to our minds when we approach more nearly to God's omniscience. The Bible, in the most fearless way, puts the absolute Deity of Jesus Christ in closest juxtaposition with the real manhood of Jesus Christ. For example, we read in Matt. 8:24, "And behold, there arose a great tempest in the sea, insomuch that the boat was covered with the waves; but He (Jesus) was asleep." Here we have a plain statement of the real manhood of our Lord, but two verses later, in the 26th verse, we read, "And He saith unto them, why are ye fearful, O ye of little faith? Then He arose, and rebuked the winds and the sea, and there was a great calm." Here we have a clear shining forth of His Deity, even the winds and the waves subject to His word. No wonder the disciples asked one another, "What manner of man is this that even the winds and the sea obey him?" (Matt. 8:27). The answer is plain: a Divine Man.

Again we read in Luke 3:21, "Now it came to pass, when all the people were baptised, that Jesus also having been baptised, and praying, . . ." Here we see Jesus in His humanity, baptised and praying. Surely this is a man. But in the remainder of the verse and in the next verse we read, "And the heaven was opened, and the Holy Spirit descended in a bodily form, as a dove, upon him, and a voice came out of heaven, Thou art my beloved Son; in thee I am well pleased." Here God with an audible voice declares Him to be Divine, to be His Son. Again in John 11:38 we read, "Jesus, therefore, again groaning in himself cometh to the tomb. Now it was a cave, and a stone laid against it." Here we see Jesus in His humanity, but four verses further down, the 43rd and 44th verses, we read, "And when He had thus spoken, He cried with a loud voice, Lazarus, come forth. And he that was dead came forth." Here again his Deity shines forth.

In Luke 9:28 we read, "And it came to pass about eight days after these sayings, that he took with him Peter and John and James, and went up into the mountain to pray." Here we very clearly see His humanity, His limitation, His dependence upon God; but in the very next verse, the 29th verse, we read, "And as He was praying the fashion of his countenance was altered and His raiment became white and glistering." Here we see His Divinity shining forth, and then again in the 35th verse, we read of the voice coming out of the cloud, saying, "This is my son, my chosen; hear ye him." Here His Deity unmistakably is seen again.

In Matt. 16:16, 17, we read, "And Simon Peter answered and said, thou art the Christ, the son of the living God. And Jesus answered and said unto him, Blessed art thou, Simon Bar-Jona: for flesh and blood hath not revealed it unto thee, but my father who is in heaven." Here is a clear declaration by Jesus Himself of His Deity. But four verses further down in the chapter, the 24th verse, we read, "From that time began Jesus to show unto his disciples that he must go up unto Jerusalem, and suffer many things of the elders and chief priests and scribes, and be killed, and the third day rise from the dead." Here we have the clearest declaration of the reality and completeness of His humanity.

In Heb. 1:6, we read of our Lord Jesus, "And when He (i.e., God the Father) again bringeth in the first-begotten into the world he saith, and let all the angels of God worship him." Here is a most unmistakable and inescapable declaration that Jesus Christ is a Divine Person, to be worshipped as God by angels as well as men, and two verses further down we read this further declaration of His absolute Deity, "But of the son he saith, Thy throne O God, is for ever and ever." Here again the Son is declared in so many words to be God, He is called God. But in the very next chapter, Heb. 2:18, we read, "For in that He himself hath suffered being tempted, He is able to succor them that are tempted." Here we have the clearest possible declaration of the reality of His human nature.

In Heb. 4:14 we read, "Having then a great high priest, who

hath passed through the heavens, Jesus the Son of God, let us hold fast our profession." Here we have a plain declaration of His Deity; but in the very next verse, we read, "For we have not an high priest that cannot be touched with the feeling of our infirmities; but one that hath been in all points tempted like as we are, yet without sin." One of the plainest declarations of the fullness and completeness of His humanity to be found in the Bible.

The doctrine of the Deity of Jesus Christ and the doctrine that Jesus Christ was a real man, go hand in hand in the Bible. What kind of a Saviour, what kind of a Lord Jesus, do you believe in? Do you believe in a Saviour that is a man and man only? Then you do not believe in the Saviour that is presented in the Bible. On the other hand, do you believe in a Saviour that is God and God only? Then you do not believe in the Saviour of the Bible. The Lord Jesus, our Lord and Saviour, presented to us in the Bible, is very God of very God and at the same time He is our brother, our fellowman, and is not ashamed to call us brethren. Oh, I thank God that I have a Saviour that is God, possessed of all the attributes and powers of Deity, all the perfections of Deity, a Saviour for whom nothing is too hard. I thank God that my Saviour is One who made the heavens and the earth, and who holds all the powers of nature and of history in His control; but I equally thank God that my Saviour is my brother man, One who was tempted in all points like as I am, One who is in a position to bear my sins, on the one hand because He is God, on the other hand because He is man. A merely divine Saviour could not be a Saviour for me. A merely human Saviour could not be a Saviour for me. But a Saviour in whom Deity and humanity meet; a Saviour who is at once God and man, is just the Saviour I need, and the Saviour that you need, a Saviour that is able to save to the uttermost all that come unto God through Him.

VI

The Personality of the Holy Spirit

"The Communion of the Holy Ghost."—2 Cor. 13:14.

Our subject this morning is "The Personality of the Holy Spirit." No series of sermons upon the Fundamentals of our Christian faith would be complete without a sermon on the Personality and Deity of the Holy Spirit. The doctrine of the Personality of the Holy Spirit is both fundamental and vital. Any one who does not know the Holy Spirit as a person has not attained to a complete and well-rounded Christian experience. Any one who knows God the Father and God the Son, but who does not know God the Holy Spirit has not attained unto the Christian conception of God, nor to a fully Christian experience. It may seem to you at first thought as if the doctrine of the Personality of the Holy Spirit were a purely technical and apparently impractical doctrine, but it is not so. As we shall see shortly, the doctrine of the Personality of the Holy Spirit is a doctrine of the very first practical importance.

I. THE IMPORTANCE OF THE DOCTRINE OF THE PERSONALITY OF THE HOLY SPIRIT

1. The Doctrine of the Personality of the Holy Spirit is of the highest importance from the standpoint of worship. If the Holy Spirit is a person and a Divine Person, and He is, and if we do not know Him as such, if we think of the Holy Spirit only as an impersonal influence or power, then we are robbing a Divine Person of the worship which is His due, and the love which is His due, and the confidence and surrender and obedience which are His due. And may I stop at this point to ask each one of you, "Do you worship the Holy Spirit?" Theoretically we all do, every time we sing the long metre Doxology,

"Praise God from whom all blessings flow,
Praise Him all creatures here below.
Praise Him above, ye heavenly hosts,
Praise Father, Son and Holy Ghost."

Theoretically we all do every time we sing the Gloria Patri: "Glory be to the Father and to the Son and to the Holy Ghost. As it was in the beginning, is now, and ever shall be, world without end. Amen." But it is one thing to do a thing theoretically and quite another thing to actually do it. It is one thing to sing words, quite another thing to realise the meaning and the force of the words that you sing. I had a striking illustration of this some years ago. I was going to a Bible Conference in New York State. I had to pass through a city four miles from the grounds where the Conference was held. I had a relative living in that city and on the way to the Conference stopped to call upon my relative, who went with me to the Conference. This relative was a Christian, she was much older than I, had been a Christian much longer than I, a member of the Presbyterian Church, brought up on the Shorter Catechism, and thoroughly orthodox. I spoke that morning at the Conference on the Personality of the Holy Spirit. When the address was over, we were waiting on the veranda of the hotel for the trolley to take us back to the city. My relative turned to me and said, "Archie, I never thought of it before as a person." Well, I had never thought of it as a person, but thank God I had come to know Him as a person.

2. In the second place, it is of the highest importance from a practical standpoint that we know the Holy Spirit as a person. If you think of the Holy Spirit, as so many even among Christian people do, as a mere influence or power, then your thought will be, "How can I get hold of the Holy Spirit and use it." But if you think of Him in the Biblical way as a Divine person, your thought will be, "How can the Holy Spirit get hold of me and use me?" Is there no difference between the thought of man, the worm, using God to thresh the mountain, or God using man, the worm, to thresh the mountain? The former conception is heathenish, it does not differ essentially from the conception of the African fetich worshipper who uses his god. The latter conception, of God the Holy Ghost

getting hold of and using us, is lofty and Christian. If you think of the Holy Spirit merely as an influence or power, your thought will be, "How can I get more of the Holy Spirit?" But if you think of Him in the Biblical way as a person, your thought will be, "How can the Holy Spirit get more of me?" The former conception, the conception of the Holy Spirit as a mere influence or power, inevitably leads to self-confidence, to self-exaltation, to the parade of self. If you think of the Holy Spirit as an influence or power and then fancy that you have received the Holy Spirit, the inevitable result will be that you will strut around as if you belonged to a superior order of Christians. I remember a woman who came to me one afternoon at the Northfield Bible Conference at the close of an address and said to me, "Brother Torrey, I want to ask you a question; but before I do, I want you to understand that I am a Holy Ghost woman." It made me shudder. It did not sound like it. But on the other hand, if you think of the Holy Spirit in the Biblical way as a Divine Person of infinite majesty, who comes to dwell in our hearts and take possession of us and use us, it leads to self-renunciation, self-abnegation, self-humiliation. I know of no thought that is more calculated to put one in the dust and keep one in the dust than this great Biblical truth of the Holy Ghost as a Divine Person coming to take up His dwelling in our hearts, and to take possession of our lives and to use us.

3. The doctrine of the personality of the Holy Spirit is of the highest importance from the standpoint of experience. Thousands and tens of thousands of Christian men and women can testify to an entire transformation of their experience through coming to know the Holy Spirit as a person. In fact, this address upon the Personality of the Holy Spirit which, for substance, I have given in almost every city in which I have ever held a series of meetings, is in some respects apparently the most abstruse and technical subject that I ever attempted to handle before a popular audience, and yet, notwithstanding that fact, more men and women have come to me at the close of the address and more have written to me, testifying of personal blessing received, than of any other address which God has permitted me to give.

II. FOUR LINES OF PROOF OF THE PERSONALITY OF THE HOLY SPIRIT

There are four separate and distinct lines of proof of the Personality of the Holy Spirit.

1. The first line of proof of the Personality of the Holy Spirit is that all the distinctive marks or characteristics of personality are ascribed to theHoly Spirit in the Bible. What are the distinctive characteristics of personality? Knowledge, feeling and will. Any being who knows and feels and wills is a person. Oftentimes when you say that the Holy Spirit is a person, people understand you to mean that the Holy Spirit has hands and feet and fingers and toes and eyes and ears and nose and mouth, and so on. But these are not the marks of personality, these are the marks of corporeity. Any being who knows, thinks and wills is a person whether he have a body or not. Now all these characteristics of personality are ascribed to the Holy Spirit in the Bible.

(1) Turn in your Bibles to 1 Cor. 2:11. "For what man knoweth the things of a man, save the spirit of man which is in him? Even so the things of God knoweth no man, but the Spirit of God." Here knowledge is ascribed to the Holy Spirit. The Holy Spirit in other words, is not a mere illumination that comes to your mind and mine whereby our minds are cleared and strengthened to see truth that they would not otherwise discover. The Holy Spirit is a Person who Himself knows the things of God and reveals to us what He Himself knows.

(2) Now turn to 1 Cor. 12:11: "But all these worketh that one and the selfsame Spirit, dividing to every man severally as He will." Here will is ascribed to the Holy Spirit. The thought clearly is that the Holy Spirit is not a divine power that we get hold of and use according to our will, but that the Holy Spirit is a person who gets hold of us and uses us according to His will. This is one of the most fundamental facts in regard to the Holy Spirit that we must bear in mind if we are to get into right relations to Him. More people are going astray at this point than almost any other. They are trying to get hold of some divine power which they can use according to their will. I do thank God that there is no divine power that I can get hold of and use according to my will. What could I, in my foolishness

and ignorance, do with a divine power, what evil I might work! But on the other hand, I am still more glad that while there is no divine power that I can get hold of and use according to my foolish will, there is a Divine Person who can get hold of me and use me according to His infinitely wise and loving will.

(3) Turn now to Rom. 8:27. "And he that searcheth the hearts knoweth what is the mind of the Spirit, because he maketh intercession for the saints according to the will of God." What I wish you to notice here is expression, "the mind of the Spirit." The Greek word here translated "mind" is a comprehensive word that has in it the ideas of both thought and purpose. It is the same word which is used in the 7th verse of the chapter where we read, "The mind of the flesh is enmity against God," where the thought is that not merely the thought of the flesh is against God, but the whole moral and intellectual life of the flesh is enmity against God.

(4) We now turn to a most remarkable passage—Rom. 15:30. "Now I beseech you, brethren, for the Lord Jesus Christ's sake, and for the love of the Spirit, that ye strive together with me in your prayers to God for me." What I wish you to notice in this verse are the words "The love of the Spirit." It is a wonderful thought. It teaches us that the Holy Spirit is not a mere blind influence or power, no matter how beneficent, that comes into our hearts and lives, but that He is a Divine Person, loving us with the tenderest love. I wonder how many of us have ever thought much regarding "the love of the Spirit." I wonder how many of us ministers who are here to-day have ever preached a sermon on the love of the Spirit. I wonder how many of you have ever heard a sermon on the love of the Spirit. Every day of your life you kneel down before God the Father, at least I hope you do, and say, "Heavenly Father, I thank thee for thy great love that led thee to give thy Son to come down to this world and die upon the cross of Calvary in my place." Every day of your life you kneel down and look up into the face of Jesus Christ the Son and say, "Thou blessed Son of God, I thank thee for that great love of thine that led thee to come down to this world in obedience to the Father and die in my place upon the cross of Calvary." But did you ever kneel down and look up to the Holy Spirit and say to him, "Holy Spirit, I thank thee for that great love

of thine"? And yet we owe our salvation as truly to the love of the Holy Spirit as we do to the love of the Father and the love of the Son. If it had not been for the love of God the Father to me, looking down upon me in my lost estate, yes, anticipating my fall and ruin and sending His Son down to this world to die upon the cross, to die in my place, I would have been in hell to-day. If it had not been for the love of Jesus Christ, the Son, coming down to this world in obedience to the Father to lay down His life, a perfect atoning sacrifice on the cross of Cavalry in my stead, I would have been in hell to-day. But if it had not been for the love of the Holy Spirit to me, coming down to this world in obedience to the Father and the Son, seeking me out in my lost condition, following me day after day, and week after week, and month after month, and year after year, when I would not listen to Him, when I deliberately turned my back upon Him, when I insulted Him, following me into places where it must have been agony for One so holy to go, following me day after day, week after week, month after month, year after year, until at last He succeeded in bringing me to my senses and bringing me to realise my utterly lost condition and revealed the Lord Jesus to me as just the Saviour I needed and induced me and enabled me to receive the Lord Jesus as my Saviour and my Lord; if it had not been for this patient, long-suffering, never-wearying love of the Spirit of God to me, I would have been in hell to-day.

(5) Turn now to a passage in the Old Testament. Neh. 9:20. "Thou gavest also thy good Spirit to instruct them, and withheldest not thy manna from their mouth, and gavest them water for their thirst." Here both intelligence and goodness are ascribed to the Holy Spirit. This passage does not add anything to the thought that we have already had: I brought it in simply because it is from the Old Testament. There are those who say that the doctrine of the Personality of the Holy Spirit is in the New Testament, but is not in the Old Testament; but here we find it as clearly in the Old Testament as in the New. Of course, we do not find it as frequently in the Old Testament as in the New, for this is the dispensation of the Holy Spirit: but the doctrine of the Personality of the Holy Spirit is there in the Old Testament. There are many who say that the doctrine of the Trinity is not in the Old Testament, that while it is in the New,

it is not in the Old. But it is in the Old, in the very first chapter of the Bible. In Gen. 1:26 we read, "And God said, let us make man in our image, after our likeness." Here the plurality of the persons in the Godhead comes out clearly. God did not say, "I will" or "Let me make man in my image." He said, "Let us make man in our image, after our likeness." The three persons of the Trinity are found in the first three verses of the Bible: "In the beginning God created the heaven and the earth." There you have God the Father. "And the earth was without form and void; and darkness was upon the face of the deep. And the Spirit of God moved upon the face of the waters." There you have the Holy Spirit. "And God said," there you have the Word, "Let there be light: and there was light." Here we have the three persons of the Trinity in the first three verses of the Bible. In fact the doctrine of the Trinity is found hundreds of times in the Old Testament. In the Hebrew Bible it occurs in every place where you find the word God in your English Bible, for the Hebrew word for God is a plural noun. Literally translated, it would be "Gods" and not God. In the very passage to which the Unitarians and the Jews, who reject the Deity of Christ, refer so often as proving conclusively that the Deity of Christ cannot be true, namely Deut. 6:4, the very doctrine that they are seeking to disprove is found; for Deut. 6:4 literally translated would read "Hear, O Israel: Jehovah our Gods is one Jehovah." Why did the Hebrews with their intense monotheism, use a plural name for God? This was the question that puzzled the Hebrew grammarians and lexicographers, and the best explanation they could arrive at was that the plural for God here used was the pluralis majestatis, the plural of majesty. The explanation is entirely inadequate, to say nothing of the fact that the pluralis majestatis in the Old Testament is a figure of very doubtful validity. There is another explanation far nearer at hand, and far more adequate and satisfactory, and that is that the Hebrew inspired writers use a plural name for God in spite of their intense monotheism, because there is a plurality of persons in the one Godhead.

(6) Now turn to Eph. 4:30. "And grieve not the Holy Spirit of God, whereby ye are sealed unto the day of redemption." Here grief is ascribed to the Holy Spirit. In other words, the Holy Spirit is not a mere blind impersonal influence or power that comes to

dwell in your heart and mine, but a person, a person who loves us, a person who is holy and intensely sensitive against sin, a person who recoils from sin in what we call its slightest forms as the holiest woman of earth never recoiled from sin in its grossest and most repulsive forms. And He sees whatever we do, He hears whatever we say, He sees our very thoughts, not a vagrant fancy is allowed a moment's lodgment in our mind but what He sees it. And if there is anything impure, unholy, immodest, untrue, false, censorious, or unChristlike in any way, He is grieved beyond expression. This is a wonderful thought and it is to me the mightiest incentive that I know to a Christian walk. How many a young man is kept back from doing things that he would otherwise do, by the thought that, if he did do that, his mother might hear of it and it would grieve her beyond expression. How many a young man has come to the great city and in some hour of temptation has been about to go into a place that no self-respecting man ought ever to enter, but just as his hand is on the doorknob and he is about to open the door, the thought comes to him, "If I should enter there mother might hear of it, and if she did, it would nearly kill her," and he has turned away without entering; but there is One holier than the holiest mother that any of us ever knew, One who loves us with a tenderer love than our own mother loves us, and Who sees everything we do, not only in the daylight but under the cover of night; Who hears every word we utter, every careless word that escapes our lips; Who sees every thought we entertain, yes, Who sees every fleeting fancy that we allow a moment's lodgment in our mind; and if there is anything unholy, impure, immodest, indecorous, unkind, harsh, censorious or unchristlike in any way in act or word or thought, He sees it and is grieved beyond expression. Oh, how often there has come into my mind some thought or imagination, I know not from what source, but that I ought not to entertain, and just as I was about to give it lodgment, the thought has come, "The Holy Spirit sees that and will be grieved by it," and the thought has gone. Bearing this thought of the Holy Spirit in our mind will help us to solve all the questions that perplex the young believer to-day. For example, the question, "Ought I as a Christian go to the theatre or the movies?" Well, if you go the Holy Spirit will go; for He dwells in the heart of every believer and goes wherever the believer goes. Were you ever at a theatre or at a moving picture show in your life where you thought the atmosphere of the place would be congenial to the Holy Spirit? If not, don't go. Ought I as a Christian go to the dance? Well, here again, if you go, the Holy Spirit will surely go. Were you ever at a dance in your life where you believed the atmosphere of the place would be congenial to the Holy Spirit? Shall I as a Christian play cards? Were you ever at a card party in all your life, even the most select little neighbourhood gathering, or even a home gathering to play cards, where you thought the atmosphere of the place would be congenial to the Holy Spirit? If not, don't play. So with all the questions that come up and that some of us find so hard to settle, this thought of the Holy Spirit will help you to settle them all, and to settle them right, if you really desire to settle them right and not merely to do the thing that pleases yourself.

2. The second line of proof of the personality of the Holy Spirit is that, many actions are ascribed to the Holy Spirit that only a person can perform. There are many illustrations of this in the Bible; but I will limit our consideration this morning to three instances.

(1) Turn again to the 2nd chapter of 1 Corinthians. In the 10th verse, we read, "But unto us, God revealed them through the Spirit: for the Spirit searcheth all things, yea, the deep things of God." Here the Holy Spirit is represented as searching the deep things of God. In other words, as we said under our previous heading, the Holy Spirit is not a mere illumination whereby our minds are made clear and strong to apprehend truth that they would not otherwise discover, but the Holy Spirit is a person Who Himself searches into the deep things of God and reveals to us the things which He discovers. Such words could only be spoken of a person.

(2) Now turn to Rom. 8:26 "And in like manner the Spirit also helpeth our infirmity: for we know not how to pray as we ought but the spirit himself maketh intercession for us with groanings that cannot be uttered." Here the Holy Spirit is represented as doing what only a person can do, praying. The Holy Spirit is not a mere influence that comes to impel us to prayer, and not a mere guidance to us in offering our prayers. He is a person who Himself prays. Every believer in Christ has two Divine Persons praying for Him.

First, the Son, our Advocate with the Father, who ever liveth to make intercession for us up yonder at the right hand of God in the place of power (John 2:1 and Heb. 7:25). Second, the Holy Spirit who prays through us down here. Oh, what a wonderful thought, that we have these two divine persons praying for us every day. What a sense it gives us of our security.

(3) Now turn to two other closely related passages. John 14:26. "But the comforter, even the Holy Spirit, whom the Father will send in my name, he shall teach you all things, and bring to your remembrance all that I have said unto you." Here the Holy Spirit is represented as doing what only a person could do, namely, teaching. We have the same thought in John 16:12-14. "I have yet many things to say unto you, but ye cannot bear them now. Howbeit when He, the Spirit of Truth, is come, He shall guide you into all the truth: for He shall not speak from Himself; but what things soever He shall hear, these shall He speak: and He shall declare unto you the things that are to come. He shall glorify me; for He shall take of mine, and shall declare it unto you." Here again the Holy Spirit is represented as a living personal teacher. It is our privilege to have the Holy Spirit as a living person to-day as our teacher. Every time we study our Bibles, it is possible for us to have this Divine Person the author of the Book, to interpret it to us and to teach us its meaning. It is a precious thought. How many of us have often thought when we heard some great human teacher whom God has especially blessed to us, "Oh, if I could only hear that man every day, then I might make some progress in my Christian life," but we can have a teacher more competent by far than the greatest human teacher that ever spoke for our teacher every day, the Holy Spirit.

3. The third line of proof of the personality of the Holy Spirit is that an office is predicated of the Holy Spirit that could only be predicated of a person. Look for example at John 14:16, 17. Here we read, "And I will pray the Father, and He shall give you another Comforter, that He may abide with you forever, even the Spirit of truth: whom the world cannot receive; for it seeth him not. Neither knoweth him: ye know him; for He abideth with you, and shall be in you." Here the Holy Spirit is represented as another Comforter who is coming to take the place of our Lord Jesus. Up to this time our

Lord Jesus had been the friend always at hand to help them in every emergency that arose. But now He was going and their hearts were filled with consternation, and He tells them that while He is going, another is coming to take His place. Can you imagine our Lord Jesus saying this if the other that was coming to take His place was a mere impersonal influence or power? Can you imagine our Lord Jesus saying what He says in John 16:7, "Nevertheless I tell you the truth, it is expedient for you that I go away; for if I go not away, the Comforter will not come unto you; but if I go, I will send him unto you," if that which was coming to take His place was not another person but a mere influence or power. In that case, is it for a moment conceivable that our Lord could say that it was expedient for Him, a Divine Person, to go and a mere influence or power, no matter how divine, come to take His place? No! No! What our Lord said was that He, one Divine Person, was going, but that another Person, just as Divine, was coming to take His place. This promise is to me one of the most precious promises in the whole Word of God for this present dispensation, the thought that during the absence of my Lord, until that glad day when He shall come back again, another Person, just as divine as He, is by my side, yes, dwells in my heart every moment to commune with me and to help me in every emergency that can possibly arise. I suppose you know that the Greek word translated Comforter in these verses means more than Comforter. It means Comforter plus a whole lot beside. The Greek word so translated is parakletos. This word is a compound word, compounded of the word para which means alongside, and kletos, one called, "One called to stand alongside another" to take his part and help him in every emergency that arises. It is the same word that is translated "advocate" in 1 John 2:1, "If any man sin, we have an advocate (parakleton) with the Father, Jesus Christ the righteous." But the word "Advocate" does not give the full force of the word. Etymologically it means about the same. Advocate is a Latin word transliterated into the English. The word is compounded of two words, ad, meaning to, and vocatus, one called, that is to say, one called to another to take his part, or to help him. But in our English usage it has obtained a restricted sense. The Greek word, as already said, means one called alongside another," and the thought is of a helper always at hand with his counsel and his strength and any form of help needed. Up to this time the Lord Jesus Himself had been their Paraclete, or friend always at hand to help. Whenever they got into any trouble they simply turned to Him. For example, on one occasion they were perplexed on the subject of prayer and they said to the Lord, "Lord teach us to pray." And He taught them to pray. On another occasion when Jesus was coming to them walking on the water, when their first fear was over and He had said, "It is I, be not afraid," then Peter said to Him, "Lord, if it be thou, bid me come unto thee upon the water." And the Lord said, "Come." Then Peter clambered over the side of the fishing smack and commenced to go to Jesus walking on the water. Seemingly he turned around, took his eyes off the Lord and looked at the fishing smack to see if the other disciples, John and James, and the rest, were noticing how well he was getting on, but no sooner had he got his eyes off the Lord than he began to sink, and he cried out saying, "Lord, save me," and Jesus reached out His hand and held him up. Just so, when they got into any other emergency they turned to the Lord and He delivered them. But now He was going, and consternation filled their hearts, and the Lord said to them, "Yes, I am going but another just as divine, just as able to help, is coming to take my place," and this other Paraclete is with us wherever we go, every hour of the day or night. He is always by our side. If this thought gets into your heart and stays there, you will never have another moment of fear no matter how long you live. How can we fear in any circumstances, if He is by our side? You may be surrounded by a howling mob. But what of it if He walks between you and the mob? That thought will banish all fear. I had a striking illustration of this in my own experience some years ago. I was speaking at a Bible Conference on Lake Kenka in New York State. I had a cousin who had a cottage four miles up the lake and I went up there and spent my rest day with him. The next day he brought me down in his steam launch to the pier where the Conference was held. As I stepped off the launch onto the pier he said to me, "Come back again to-night and spend the night with us," and I promised him that I would; but I did not realise what I was promising. That night, when the address was over as I went out of the hotel and started on my walk,

I found that I had undertaken a large contract. The cottage was four miles away, but a four mile walk or an eight mile walk was nothing under ordinary circumstances, but a storm was coming up, the whole heaven was overcast. The path led along a bluff bordering the lake, the path was near the edge of the bluff. Sometimes the lake was perhaps not more than ten or twelve feet below, at other times some thirty or forty feet below. I had never gone over the path before and as there was no starlight, I couldn't see the path at all. Furthermore, there had already been a storm that had gulleyed out deep ditches across the path into which one might fall and break his leg. I couldn't see these ditches except when there would be a sudden flash of lightning, and then I would see one and then it would be darker and I blinder than ever. As I walked along this path, so near the edge of the bluff with all the furrows cut through it, I felt it was perilous to take the walk and thought of going back; and then the thought came to me, "You promised that you would come to-night and they may be sitting up waiting for you." So I felt that I must go on. But it seemed creepy and uncanny to walk along the edge of that bluff on such an uncertain path that I couldn't see, and could only hear the sobbing and wailing and the moaning of the lake at the foot of the bluff as it rose in the fast approaching storm. Then the thought came to me, what was it you told the people there at the conference about the Holy Spirit being a Person always by our side? And I at once realised that the Holy Spirit walked between me and the edge of the bluff; and that four miles through the dark was four miles without a fear, a gladsome instead of a fearsome walk. I once threw this thought out in the Royal Albert Hall in London, one dark dismal February afternoon. There was a young lady in the audience who was very much afraid of the dark. It simply seemed impossible for her to go into a dark room alone. After the meeting was over she hurried home and rushed in to the room where her mother was sitting and cried, "O mother, I have heard the most wonderful address this afternoon about the Holy Spirit always being by our side as our ever-present helper and protector. I shall never be afraid of the dark again." Her mother was a practical English woman and said to her, "Well, let us see how real that is. Now go upstairs to the top floor, into the dark room, and shut the door and stay in there alone in the dark." The daughter went bounding up the stairs, went into the dark room, closed the door and it was pitch dark, and "Oh," she wrote me the next day, "it was dark, utterly dark, but that room was bright and glorious with the presence of the Holy Spirit."

In this thought is also the cure for insomnia. Did any of you ever have insomnia? I did. For two dark, awful years. Night after night, I would go to bed, almost dead, as it seemed to me, for sleep, and I thought I would certainly sleep as I could scarcely keep awake; but scarcely had my head touched the pillow when I knew I wouldn't sleep and I would hear the clock strike twelve, one, two, three, four, five, six, and then it was time to get up. It seemed as though I didn't sleep at all, though I have no doubt I did: for I believe that people who suffer from insomnia sleep more than they think they do, else we would die: but it seemed as if I didn't sleep at all, and this went on for two whole years, until I thought that if I couldn't get sleep I would lose my mind. And then I got deliverance. For years I would retire and fall asleep about as soon as my head touched the pillow. But one night I went to bed in the Bible Institute in Chicago where I was then stopping. I expected to fall asleep almost immediately, as had become my custom, but scarcely had my head touched the pillow when I knew I was not going to sleep. Insomnia was back. If you have ever had him you will always recognise him. It seemed as if Insomnia was sitting on the footboard looking like an imp, grinning at me and saying "I am back for two more years." "Oh," I thought, "two more years of this awful insomnia." But that very morning I had been teaching the students in the lecture room on the floor below on the Personality of the Holy Spirit, and the thought came to me almost immediately, "What was that you were telling the students down stairs this morning about the Holy Spirit being always with us?" And I said, "Why don't you practice what you preach?" And I looked up and said, "O thou blessed Holy Spirit of God, thou art here, if thou hast anything to say to me, I will listen." And He opened to me some of the sweet and precious things about Jesus Christ, filling my soul with calm and peace and joy, and the next thing I knew I was asleep and the next thing I knew it was tomorrow morning; and whenever Insomnia has come around since and sat on my footboard, I have done the same thing and it has never failed.

In this thought also is a cure for all loneliness. If the thought of the Holy Spirit as an Ever-present Friend always at hand, once enters your heart and stays there, you will never have another lonely moment as long as you live. My life for the larger part of the last sixteen years has been a lonely life. I have often been separated from all my family for months at a time. I have not seen my wife sometimes for two or three months at a time and for eighteen months I did not see any member of my family but my wife. One night I was walking the deck of a steamer in the South Seas between New Zealand and Tasmania. It was a stormy night. Most of the other passengers were below sick, none of the officers nor sailors could walk with me for they had their hands full looking after the boat. I had to walk the deck alone. Four of the five other members of my family were on the other side of the globe, seventeen thousand miles away by the nearest route that I could get to them, and the one member of my family who was nearer was not with me that night. As I walked the deck alone I got to thinking of the four children seventeen thousand miles away and was about to get lonesome, when the thought came to me of the Holy Spirit by my side, and that as I walked He took every step with me, and all loneliness was gone. I gave expression to this thought some years ago in the city of St. Paul, and at the close of the address a physician came to me and said, "I wish to thank you for that thought. I am often called at night to go out alone through darkness and storm far into the country, and I have been very lonely, but I will never be lonely again, for I will know that every step of the way the Holy Spirit is beside me in my doctor's gig."

In this same precious truth there is a cure for a broken heart. Oh, how many broken-hearted people there are in the world to-day, especially in these days of war and bloodshed and death! Many of us here have lost loved ones. Many more of us in all probability will during the months that are just ahead of us. But we need not have a moment's heartache if we only know the communion of the Holy Ghost. There is perhaps here to-day some woman who a year ago, or a few months ago, or a few weeks ago, or a few days ago, had by her side a man whom she dearly loved, a man so strong and wise that she was freed from all sense of responsibility and care; for all the burdens were upon him, and how bright and happy life was in his companionship! But the dark day came when that loved one was taken away, and how lonely and empty and barren, and full of burden and care, life is to-day! Listen! There is One who walks right by your side, wiser and stronger and more loving than the wisest and strongest and most loving husband that ever lived, ready to bear all the burdens and responsibilities of life, yes, ready to do far more: to come in and dwell in your heart and fill every nook and corner of your empty, aching heart, and thus banish all loneliness and heartache forever. I said this one afternoon in Saint Andrews Hall in Glasgow. At the close of the address, when I passed out into the reception room, a lady who had hurried along to meet me, approached me. She wore a widow's bonnet, her face bore the marks of deep sorrow, but now there was a happy look in her face. She hurried to me and said, "Doctor Torrey, this is the anniversary of my dear husband's death" (her husband was one of the most highly esteemed Christian men in Glasgow) "and I came to Saint Andrews Hall to-day saying to myself, 'Doctor Torrey will have something to say that will help me.' Oh," she continued, "you have said just the right word! I will never be lonesome again, never have a heartache again. I will let the Holy Spirit come in and fill every aching corner of my heart." Eighteen months passed; I was in Scotland again, taking a short vacation on the lochs of the Clyde on the private yacht of a friend. One day we stopped off a point, a little boat put off from the point and came alongside the steam yacht. The first one who clambered up the side of the yacht and onto the deck was this widow. Seeing me standing on the deck, she hurried across and took my hand in both of hers and with a radiant smile on her face she said, "Oh, Doctor Torrey, the thought you gave me in Saint Andrews Hall that afternoon stays with me still and I have not had a lonely or sad hour from that day to this."

But it is in our Christian work that the thought comes to us with greatest power and helpfulness. Take my own experience. I became a minister simply because I had to, or be forever lost. I do not mean that I am saved by preaching the Gospel; I am saved simply on the ground of Christ's atoning blood and that alone; but my becoming a Christian and accepting Him as my Saviour turned upon my preaching the Gospel. For six years I refused to come out as a Christian because I was unwilling to preach, and I felt that if I became a Christian I must preach. The night that I was converted I did not say, "I will accept Christ" or "I will give up my sins"; I said, "I will preach." But if there was ever a man who by natural temperament was unfitted to preach, it was I. I was one of these abnormally bashful boys. A stranger could scarcely speak to me without my blushing to the roots of my hair. Of all the tortures I endured at school there was none so great as that of reciting a piece. To stand up on the platform and have all the scholars looking at me, I could scarcely endure it, and when I had to recite and my own mother and father asked me to recite the piece before I went to school, I simply could not recite it before my own father and mother. Think of a man like that going into the ministry. Even after I was in Yale College,]when I would go home on a vacation and my mother would have callers and send for me to come in and meet them, I couldn't say a word. After they were gone my mother would say to me, "Archie, why didn't you say something to Mrs. S. or Mrs. D.?" and I would say, "Why, mother, I did!" and she would reply, "You didn't utter a sound." I thought I did, but it would come no further than my throat and there be smothered. I was so bashful that I never even spoke in a church prayer meeting until after I entered the theological seminary. Then I thought, if I was to be a preacher I must at least be able to speak in my own church prayer meeting. I made up my mind I would. I learned a piece by heart. I remember some of it now. I think I forgot some of it when I got up to speak that night. As soon as the meeting was thrown open I grasped the back of the settee in front of me and pulled myself up to my feet and held on to it lest I should fall. One Niagara went rushing up one side and another down the other, and I tremblingly repeated as much of my little piece as I could remember and then dropped back into the seat. At the close of the meeting a dear old maid, a lovely Christian woman, came to me and cheeringly said, "Oh, Mr. Torrey, I want to thank you for what you said to-night. It did me so much good. You spoke with so much feeling." Feeling! The only feeling I had was that I was scared nearly to death. Think of a man like that going into the ministry. My first years in the ministry were torture. I preached three times a day. I committed my sermons to memory and then I stood up and twisted the top button of my coat until I had twisted the sermon out and then when the third sermon was preached and finished, I dropped back into the haircloth settee back of the pulpit with a great sense of relief that that was over for another week. And then the thought would take possession of me, Well you have to begin to-morrow morning to get ready for next Sunday! But a glad day came when the thought I am trying to teach you this morning took possession of me, viz., that when I stood up to preach, that, though people saw me, that there was Another who stood by my side whom they did not see, but upon whom was all the responsibility for the meeting, and all that I had to do was to get as far back out of sight as possible and let Him do the preaching. From that day preaching has been the joy of my life. I would rather preach than eat. Sometimes when I rise to preach, before I have uttered a word, the thought of Him, standing beside me, able and willing to take charge of the whole meeting and do whatever needs to be done, has so filled my heart with exultant joy that I have felt like shouting. Just so in your Sunday School teaching. Some of you worry about your Sunday School classes for fear that you will say something that ought not to be said, or leave unsaid something that ought to be said, and the thought of the burden and responsibility almost crushes you. Listen! Always remember this as you sit there teaching your class: there is One right beside you Who knows just what ought to be said and just what ought to be done. Instead of carrying the responsibility of the class, let Him carry it, let Him do the teaching. One Monday morning I met one of the most faithful laymen I ever knew and a very gifted Bible teacher. He was deep in the blues, over his failure with his class the day before—at least, what he regarded as failure. He unburdened his heart to me. I said to him, "Mr. Dyer, did you not ask God to give you wisdom as you went before that class?" He said, "I did." I said, "Did you not expect Him to give it?" He said, "I did." Then I said, "What right have you to doubt that He did?" He replied, "I never thought of that before. I will never worry about my class again." Just so in personal work. When I or some one else urges you at the close of the meeting to go and speak to some one else, oh, how many of you want to go, but you don't stir. You think to yourself, "I might say the wrong thing." You will, if you say it. You will certainly say the wrong thing; but trust the Holy Spirit, He will say the right thing. Let Him have your lips to speak through. It may not appear the right thing at the time, but some time you will find out that it was just the right thing. One night in Launceston, Tasmania, as Mrs. Torrey and I came away from the meeting, my wife said to me, "Archie, I wasted my whole evening. I have been talking to the most frivolous girl. I don't think that she has a serious thought in her head." I replied, "Clara, how do you know? Did you not trust God to guide you?" "Yes." "Well, leave it with Him." The very next night at the close of the meeting the same seemingly utterly frivolous young woman came up to Mrs. Torrey, leading her mother by the hand, and said, "Mrs. Torrey, won't you speak to my mother? You led me to Christ last night, now please lead my mother to Christ."

4. But I must close. There is another line of proof of the personality of the Holy Spirit, but we have no time to dwell upon it. This line of proof is that a treatment is predicated of the Holy Spirit that could only be predicated of a person. In Isa. 63:10 we are taught that the Holy Spirit is rebelled against and grieved. You cannot rebel against or grieve a mere influence or power. Only a person can be rebelled against and grieved. In Heb. 10:29 we are taught that the Holy Spirit is "done despite unto," or "treated with contumely," insulted. You cannot treat an influence or power with contumely; only a person. In Acts 5:3 we are taught that the Holy Spirit is lied to. You can only lie to a person. In Matt. 12:31 we are taught that the Holy Spirit is blasphemed against. We are told that the blasphemy against the Holy Ghost is more serious than the blasphemy against the Lord Jesus, and this certainly could only be said of a person and a Divine Person.

To sum it all up, the Holy Spirit is a Person. Theoretically we probably all believed this before, but do we in our real thought of Him, in our practical attitude toward Him, treat Him as a person? Do we really regard Him as real a person as Jesus Christ is, as loving, as wise, as strong, as worthy of our confidence and love, and surrender as He? A Divine Person always by our side? The Holy Spirit came into this world to be to the disciples of our Lord after our Lord's own departure, and to be to us, what Jesus Christ had been to them during the days of His personal companionship with them. Is He that to you to-day? Do you know the "communion of the Holy Spirit?" the companionship of the Holy Spirit, the partnership of the Holy Spirit, the fellowship of the Holy Spirit, the comradeship of the Holy Spirit? To put it into a single word, the whole object of this address this morning, I say it reverently, is to introduce you to my Friend, the Holy Spirit.

VII

The Deity of the Holy Spirit and the Distinction Between the Father, Son and Holy Spirit

I spoke in a previous chapter on the personality of the Holy Spirit. We saw clearly that the Holy Spirit was a person. Incidentally I referred to His Deity in passing, but did not dwell upon it, so the question remains, Is the Holy Spirit a Divine person? and still another question, If the Holy Spirit is a Divine person, is He a separate and distinct personality from the Father and the Son? We shall consider this morning what the Bible teaches upon these points.

I. THE DEITY OF THE HOLY SPIRIT

We take up first the question of the Deity of the Holy Spirit. The fact that the Holy Spirit is a person does not prove that He is divine. There are spirits who are persons but who are not God. There are five distinct lines of proof of the Deity of the Holy Spirit, that the Holy Spirit is God.

1. The first line of proof of the Deity of the Holy Spirit is that each of the four distinctively Divine attributes are ascribed to the Holy Spirit in the Bible. There are four distinctively divine attributes; that is to say, there are four attributes which God alone possesses, and any person who has these attributes must therefore be God. The four distinctively divine attributes are omnipotence, omniscience, omnipresence and eternity.

(1) First of all, omnipotence is ascribed to the Holy Spirit, for example, in Luke 1:35: "And the angel answered and said unto her, the Holy Spirit shall come upon thee, and the power of the most high shall overshadow thee: wherefore also that which is to be born shall be called holy, the Son of God." This passage plainly declares that the Holy Spirit has the power of the Most High, that He is omnipotent.

(2) In the next place, omniscience is ascribed to the Holy Spirit. This is done, for example, in I Corinthians 2:10, 11: "But unto us God revealed them through the Spirit: for the Spirit searcheth all things, yea, the deep things of God. For who among men knoweth the things of a man, save the Spirit of the man, which is in him? Even so the things of God none knoweth, save the Spirit of God." Here we are distinctly told that the Holy Spirit searcheth all things and knoweth all things, even the deep things of God. We find the same thought again in John 14:26: "But the Comforter, even the Holy Spirit, whom the Father will send in my name, He shall teach you all things, and bring to your remembrance all that I said unto you." Here we are distinctly told that the Holy Spirit teaches all things, and therefore must know all things. This is stated even more explicitly in John 16:12-13: "I have yet many things to say unto you, but ye cannot bear them now. Howbeit when He, the Spirit of Truth, is come, He shall guide you into all the truth." In all these passages it is either directly declared or unmistakably implied that the Holy Spirit knows all things, that He is omniscient.

(3) In the third place, omnipresence is ascribed to the Holy Spirit. We find this in Psalms 139:7-10: "Whither shall I go from thy Spirit? or whither shall I flee from thy presence? If I ascend up into heaven, thou art there: if I make my bed in Sheol, behold, thou art there. If I take the wings of the morning, and dwell in the uttermost parts of the sea; even there shall thy hand lead me, and thy right hand shall hold me." Here we are told in the most explicit and unmistakable way that the Spirit of God, the Holy Spirit, is everywhere; that there is no place in heaven, earth or hades whither we can go from His presence.

(4) Eternity is also ascribed to the Holy Spirit. This we find in Hebrews 9:14, where we read: "How much more shall the blood of Christ, who through the Eternal Spirit offered himself without blemish unto God, cleanse your conscience from dead works to serve the living God?" Here we find the words "the Eternal Spirit" just as elsewhere we find the words "the Eternal God" (e.g., Deut. 33:27): Putting these different passages together, we see clearly that each of the four distinctively divine attributes, the four attributes

that no one but God possesses, are ascribed to the Holy Spirit.

2. The second line of proof of the true Deity of the Holy Spirit is found in the fact that three distinctively divine works are ascribed to the Holy Spirit—that is to say, the Holy Spirit is said to do three things which God alone can do.

(1) The first of these distinctively divine works that are ascribed to the Holy Spirit is the work which we always think of first when we think of God and His work—that is to say, the work of creation. We find creation ascribed to the Holy Spirit in Job 33:4: "The Spirit of God hath made me, and the breath of the Almighty giveth me life." We find the same thing implied in Psalms 104:30: "Thou sendest forth thy Spirit, they are created; and thou renewest the face of the ground." In these two passages creation, the most distinctively divine of all works, is ascribed to the Holy Spirit.

(2) The impartation of life is ascribed to the Holy Spirit. This we find, for example, in John 6:63: "It is the Spirit that quickeneth; the flesh profiteth nothing." We find the same thing again in Romans 8:11: "But if the Spirit of him that raised up Jesus from the dead dwell in you, He that raised up Christ from the dead shall also quicken your mortal bodies by His Spirit that dwelleth in you." In this passage we have not merely impartation of life to the spirit of man, but the impartation of life to the body in the resurrection of the body ascribed to the Holy Spirit. Man's creation and the impartation of life to man are ascribed to the operation of the Holy Spirit in the first book in the Bible, where we read in Genesis 2:7: "And Jehovah God formed man of the dust of the ground, and breathed into his nostrils the breath of life; and man became a living soul." Here we are told that man was created and became a living soul through God's breathing into him the breath of life. This clearly implies that it was through the instrumentality of the Holy Spirit; for the Holy Spirit is the breath of God going out in a personal way.

(3) The third divine work ascribed to the Holy Spirit is the authorship of divine prophecies. We find this, for example, in II Peter 1:21: "For no prophecy ever came by the will of man: but men spake from God, being moved by the Holy Spirit." Here we are distinctly told that it was through the operation of the Holy Spirit

that men were made the mouthpiece of God and uttered God's truth. We find this same thought also in the Old Testament in II Samuel 23:2, 3: "The Spirit of Jehovah spake by me, and His word was upon my tongue. The God of Israel said, the Rock of Israel spake to me." In this passage, also, the authorship of God's prophecies is ascribed to the Holy Spirit. Taking these passages together, we see that three distinctively divine works are ascribed to the Holy Spirit.

3. The third line of proof of the Deity of the Holy Spirit is found in the fact that passages which refer to Jehovah in the Old Testament are taken to refer to the Holy Spirit in the New Testament. There are numerous instances of this, not as numerous as in the case of Jesus Christ, the Son, and yet enough to make it perfectly clear that the Holy Spirit occupies the same place in New Testament thought which Jehovah occupies in Old Testament thought.

(1) A striking illustration of this is found in Isaiah 6:8-10; cf. Acts 28:25-27. In Isaiah 6:8-10, we read: "And I heard the voice of the Lord, saying, whom shall I send, and who will go for us? Then I said, here am I; send me. And he said, go, and tell this people, hear ye indeed, but understand not; and see ye indeed, but perceive not. Make the heart of this people fat, and make their ears heavy, and shut their eyes; lest they see with their eyes, and hear with their ears, and understand with their heart, and turn again, and be healed." Here we are distinctly told it is the "Lord," and the context shows that the Lord is the Lord Jehovah who is speaking, but when we turn to Acts 28:25-27, we read these words: "And when they agreed not among themselves, they departed after that Paul had spoken one word, well spake the Holy Spirit through Isaiah the prophet unto your fathers" (notice that in the passage in Isaiah we [150]are told it is the Lord Jehovah who spoke, and here we are told by Paul that it is the Holy Spirit who spake through the prophet), "saying, go thou unto this people, and say, by hearing ye shall hear, and shall in no wise understand; and seeing ye shall see, and shall in no wise perceive: for this people's heart is waxed gross, and their ears are dull of hearing, and their eyes they have closed; lest haply they should perceive with their eyes, and hear with their ears, and understand with their heart, and should turn again, and I should heal

them." In the one place, the place in the Old Testament, we are told that the Lord Jehovah is the speaker; in the other place, in the New Testament, we are told that the Holy Spirit is the speaker; that is to say, the Holy Spirit occupies the place in New Testament thought that the Lord Jehovah occupies in Old Testament thought. It is noticeable that this same passage in another place is applied to Jesus Christ (John 12:39-41). May it not be that in the threefold "Holy" in the seraphic cry recorded in this chapter in Isaiah (Isaiah 6:3) we have a hint of the tri-personality of Jehovah of Hosts, and hence the propriety of the threefold application of the vision?

(2) Another illustration of a statement, which in the Old Testament is given as referring to Jehovah, being applied to the Holy Spirit in the New Testament, is found by a comparison of Exodus 16:7 with Hebrews 3:7-9. In Exodus 16:7 we read: "And in the morning, then shall ye see the glory of Jehovah; for that he heareth your murmurings against Jehovah: and what are we, that ye murmur against us?" Here we are told that the murmuring and provocation of the children of Israel in the wilderness were against Jehovah, but in Hebrews 3:7-9, we read: "Wherefore, even as the Holy Spirit saith, to-day if ye shall hear his voice, harden not your hearts, as in the provocation, like as in the day of the trial in the wilderness, where your fathers tried me by proving me, and saw my works forty years." In this New Testament passage we are told that it was the Holy Spirit that they provoked in the wilderness, making it clear that the Holy Spirit occupies here in New Testament thought the position Jehovah occupied in Old Testament thought in Exodus 16:7.

To sum up the passages under this head, we see that statements which in the Old Testament distinctly name the Lord, God or Jehovah, as their subject, are applied to the Holy Spirit in the New Testament. That is to say, the Holy Spirit occupies the position of Deity in New Testament thought.

4. The fourth way in which the Deity of the Holy Spirit is clearly taught in the New Testament is that the name of the Holy Spirit is coupled with that of God the Father in a way that it would be impossible for a reverent and thoughtful mind to couple the name of any finite being with that of Deity. There are numerous illustrations

of this. Three will answer for our present purpose.

(1) We read, for example, in I Corinthians 12:4-6: "Now there are diversities of gifts, but the same Spirit. And there are diversities of ministrations, and the same Lord. And there are diversities of workings, but the same God, who worketh all things in all." In this passage we see the name of the Holy Spirit coupled with that of God and of the Lord in a way in which it would be impossible for an intelligent worshipper of God to couple the name of any finite being with that of the Deity.

(2) We see the same thing again in Matthew 28:19: "Go ye therefore, and make disciples of all the nations, baptising them into the name of the Father and of the Son and of the Holy Spirit." If the Holy Spirit is not God, it would be shocking to couple His name in this way with that of God, the Father, and of the Lord Jesus, His Son.

(3) Another striking illustration of this is found in II Corinthians 13:14: "The grace of the Lord Jesus Christ, and the love of God, and the communion of the Holy Spirit, be with you all." Here the name of the Holy Spirit is coupled on a ground of equality with that of the Father and of the Son. In all these passages, the name of the Holy Spirit is coupled with that of God in a way in which it would be impossible for a reverent, thoughtful mind to couple the name of any finite being with that of Deity.

The fifth and last, and, if possible, more decisive way in which the Deity of the Holy Spirit is taught in the Bible is that the Holy Spirit in so many words is called God. This we find in Acts 5:3, 4: "But Peter said, Ananias, why hath Satan filled thy heart to lie to the Holy Spirit, and to keep back part of the price of the land? While it remained, did it not remain thine own? And after it was sold, was it not in thy power? How is it that thou hast conceived this thing in thy heart? Thou hast not lied unto men, but unto God." In the third verse we are distinctly told that it was to the Holy Spirit to Whom Ananias lied, and in the fourth verse we are told that it was to God that Ananias lied. Putting the two statements together, it is evident that the Holy Spirit is God.

To sum up all that we have said under the head of the Deity of the Holy Spirit, we see that by the ascription of all the distinctively divine attributes, and several distinctively divine works, by referring statements which in the Old Testament distinctly named Jehovah, the Lord or God, as their subject, to the Holy Spirit in the New Testament, by coupling the name of the Holy Spirit with that of God in a way in which it would be impossible to couple the name of any finite being with that of Deity, by calling the Holy Spirit "God," in all these unmistakable ways God in His Word distinctly proclaims that the Holy Spirit is a Divine Person. It is absolutely impossible for any one to go to the Bible to find out what it actually teaches, [154] and not merely to twist and distort it to fit into his own preconceived notions, and come to any other conclusion but that the Holy Spirit is a Divine Person, that He is God.

II. THE DISTINCTION BETWEEN THE FATHER, THE SON AND THE HOLY SPIRIT

But now we come to the question, Is the Holy Spirit a distinct personality from the Father and from the Son? He might be a person, as we have clearly seen that He is, and He might be a divine person, as we have just seen that He is, and at the same time He might be only the same person who manifested Himself at times as the Father and at other times as the Son, and in that case there would not be three divine Persons in the Godhead, but one divine Person, who variously manifested Himself as Father, Son and Holy Spirit. So the question that now confronts us is, Is the Holy Spirit a distinct personality separate and distinct from the Father and from the Son? This question is plainly answered in various passages in the New Testament.

1. We find this question answered in the first place in John 14:26 and John 15:26. In John 14:26 we read: "But the Comforter, even the Holy Spirit, whom the Father will send in my name, He shall teach you all things, and bring to your remembrance all that I said unto you." In John 15:26 we read: "But when the Comforter is come, whom I will send unto you from the Father, even the Spirit of Truth, which proceedeth from the Father, he shall bear witness of me." In both of these passages we are told that the Holy Spirit is an

entirely distinct personality from the Father and the Son, that He is sent from the Father by the Son. We are elsewhere taught that Jesus Christ was sent by the Father (John 6:29; 8:29, 42). It is as clear as language can make it in these passages that Father, Son and Holy Spirit are not one and the same Person manifesting Himself in three different forms, but that they are three distinct personalities.

2. We find clear proof that the Father, Son and Holy Spirit are three distinct personalities in John 16:13, where we read: "Howbeit when He, the Spirit of Truth, is come, he shall guide you into all the truth: for He shall not speak from Himself; but what things soever He shall hear, these shall He speak: and He shall declare unto you the things that are to come." In this passage the clearest possible distinction is drawn between the Holy Spirit who speaks and the One from whom He speaks, and we are told in so many words that this One from whom He speaks is not Himself, but another.

3. In the next verse the same thought is brought out in still another way. In this verse, John 16:14, we read: "He shall glorify me: for He shall take of mine, and shall declare it unto you." Here the clearest distinction is drawn between He, the Holy Spirit, and Me, Jesus Christ. It is the work of the Holy Spirit not to glorify Himself, but another, and this Other is Jesus Christ, and He takes what belongs to another; that is, to Christ, and declares it unto believers. It would be impossible to express in human language a distinction between two personalities more plainly than the distinction between the Son and the Holy Ghost is expressed in this verse.

4. The distinction between the Father and the Son and the Holy Spirit is very clearly brought out in Luke 3:21, 22: "Now it came to pass, when all the people were baptised, that, Jesus also having been baptised, and praying, the heaven was opened, and the Holy Spirit descended in a bodily form, as a dove, upon him, and a voice came out of heaven, thou art my beloved Son; in thee I am well pleased." Here a clear distinction is drawn between Jesus Christ who was on the earth, and the Father who spake to Him from heaven, and the Holy Spirit who descended in bodily form as a dove from the Father upon the Son.

5. Still another striking illustration is found in Matthew 28:19:

"Go ye therefore, and make disciples of all the nations, baptising them into the name of the Father and of the Son and of the Holy Spirit." Here a clear distinction is drawn between the name "of the Father," and the name "of the Son," and the name "of the Holy Spirit."

6. A very striking setting forth of a clear distinction between the Father, Son and Holy Spirit [157]is found in John 14:16, 17: "And I will pray the Father, and He shall give you another Comforter that He may be with you for ever, even the Spirit of truth." Here the clearest possible distinction is drawn between the Son who prays, and the Father to whom He prays, and "another Comforter," who is given in answer to His prayer. Nothing could possibly be plainer than the distinction that Jesus Christ draws in this passage between Himself and the Father and the Holy Spirit.

7. We find the same thing again in John 16:7: "Nevertheless I tell you the truth: it is expedient for you that I go away; for if I go not away, the Comforter will not come unto you; but if I go, I will send Him unto you." Here the Lord Jesus Himself draws a clear distinction between Himself, who is about to go away, and the Holy Spirit, the other Comforter who is coming to take His place after He has gone away.

8. The same thing is brought out again in Peter's sermon on the day of Pentecost in Acts 2:33, where Peter is recorded as saying: "Being therefore by the right hand of God exalted, and having received of the Father the promise of the Holy

We have seen that the Bible makes it plain that the Holy Spirit is a Divine Person and that He is an entirely separate personality from the Father and from the Son. In other words, that there are three divine Persons in the Godhead. It has oftentimes been said that the doctrine of the Trinity is not taught in the Bible. It is true that the doctrine of the Trinity is not directly taught in the Bible in so many words, but the doctrine of the Trinity is simply the putting together of truths that are clearly and unmistakably taught in the Bible. It is clearly taught in the Bible that there is but one God (Deuteronomy 6:4). But it is taught with equal clearness, as we have seen to-day, that there are three Divine Persons, the Father, the Son and the Holy

Ghost; and the doctrine of the Trinity is the putting together of these truths which are taught with equal plainness.

But, some one may ask, How can God be three and one at the same time? The answer to this question is very simple and easily understandable. He cannot be three in one in the same sense, nor does the Bible teach that He is. But in what sense can He be one and three? A perfectly satisfactory answer to this question is manifestly impossible from the very nature of the case—first, because God is Spirit and numbers belong primarily to the physical world, and difficulty must always arise when we attempt to conceive of spiritual being in the forms of physical thought. In the second place, a perfectly satisfactory answer to the question is impossible because God is infinite and we are finite. "God dwells in the light that no man can approach unto," and our attempts at a philosophical explanation of the Trinity of God is an attempt to put the facts of infinite being into the forms of finite thought, and of necessity such an attempt can at the very best be only partially successful. This much we know, that God is essentially one, and also that there are three Persons in this one Godhead. There is but one God, but this one God makes Himself known to us as three distinct Persons—Father, Son and Holy Spirit. There is one God, eternally existing, and manifesting Himself in three Persons—Father, Son and Holy Spirit. If we were to go into the realm of philosophy, it could be shown that from the very necessities of the case, that if God were to be God, there must be in the eternal Godhead before the creation of finite beings a multiplicity of persons; for otherwise God could not love, for there would be no one to love, and therefore God could not be God. The ease with which one can grasp the Unitarian conception of God is not in its favour but against it. Any god who could be thoroughly comprehended by a finite mind would not be an infinite God. It would be impossible for a thoroughly intelligent mind to really worship a god whom he could thoroughly understand. If God is to be really God, He must be beyond our complete understanding.

The doctrine of the Trinity is not merely a speculative doctrine. It is a doctrine of tremendous daily practical importance. It enters into the very warp and woof of our experience, if our experience is a truly Christian experience. For example, in our prayer we need God, the Father, to Whom we pray, we need God, the Son, through Whom we pray, and we need God, the Holy Spirit, in Whom we pray. So also in our worship we need God, the Father, the very centre of our worship, we need the Son, through Whom we approach Him in our worship, and we need to worship by the Holy Spirit. But all three—Father, Son and Holy Spirit—are the objects of our worship. The long metre doxology is thoroughly Christian in its worship when it sings:

"Praise God from whom all blessings flow,

Praise Him all creatures here below,

Praise Him above, ye heavenly hosts,

Praise Father, Son and Holy Ghost."

And so, also, is the Gloria Patri, the words of which we so often sing, but the thought of which we so seldom grasp:

Glory be to the Father, and to the Son, and to the Holy Ghost, as it was in the beginning, is now, and ever shall be, world without end, Amen.

VIII

The Atonement: God's Doctrine of the Atonement vs. Unitarian and Christian Science Doctrines of the Atonement

"Apart from the shedding of blood there is no remission."—Hebrews 9:22.

Our subject in this chapter is "God's Doctrine of the Atonement vs. the Unitarian and Christian Science Doctrines of the Atonement." One of the most fundamental, central and vital doctrines of the Christian faith is the Christian doctrine of the Atonement. Without the Bible Doctrine of the Atonement you have no Christianity, but the Devil's substitute for Christianity. Without the Bible Doctrine of the Atonement you have no real gospel, but an utterly false and soul-destroying philosophy. In speaking on the doctrine of the Deity of Christ I said: "If a man really holds to right views concerning the person of Jesus Christ he will sooner or later get right views on every other question, but if he holds a wrong view concerning the person of the Lord Jesus Christ he is pretty sure to go wrong on everything else sooner or later." The same is true regarding the doctrine of the Atonement: If a man really holds to right views concerning the Atonement made by our Lord and Saviour Jesus Christ on the Cross of Calvary, he will sooner or later get right on every other question; but if he holds a wrong view regarding the Atonement made by our Lord and Saviour Jesus Christ, he is pretty sure to go wrong on everything else sooner or later. There is a great need in this day of teaching on this subject that is definite, clear, accurate, exact, complete; because not only in Unitarian and Christian Science circles, but also in circles that are nominally orthodox, in professedly Christian colleges, seminaries, pulpits, Sunday School classes, and religious papers, magazines, pamphlets, books, there is much teaching to-day that is vague, inaccurate, misleading, unscriptural, and oftentimes utterly false and devilish, teaching that is essentially Unitarian or Eddyistic. Men and women use the old words with a new meaning; so as to deceive, if it were possible, the very elect. Even the Christian Scientist will tell you he believes in the Atonement, and that Mrs. Eddy taught the Atonement. But when you begin to ask direct and pointed questions regarding his belief and teaching you will find that by Atonement he meant, and that Mrs. Eddy meant, something utterly different from what you mean and what the Bible teaches. Paul tells us that the Devil camouflages as an angel of light (II Cor. 11:14), but never has he done it more successfully and dangerously than in the teaching regarding the Atonement which he has inspired in Mrs. Eddy and in Unitarian teachers, and also in the teachers in many supposedly orthodox pulpits, in many Congregational pulpits, in some Methodist pulpits, in many Baptist pulpits, and even in some Presbyterian pulpits. Some years ago in teaching a Bible class in Minneapolis, attended by people from all the churches, I remarked incidentally that Christian Science denied the doctrine of the Atonement through the shed blood of Jesus Christ. A very intelligent lady, a lady perfect in her manners, came to me at the close of the class and said: "Mr. Torrey, you ought not to have said what you said to-day about Christian Science; for you do not understand its teachings. They do teach the Atonement." I replied: "I said that Christian Science denies the Doctrine of the Atonement through the shed blood of Jesus Christ. Do you believe that Jesus Christ bore your sins in His own body on the cross?" She answered: "I think Christian Science is a beautiful system of teaching." I said: "That is not what I asked you. Do you believe that Jesus Christ bore your sins in His own body on the cross?" She replied: "Christian Science has done me a great deal of good." "That is not what I asked you. Do you believe that Jesus Christ bore your sins in His own body on the cross?" "I think that Jesus Christ's life was the most beautiful life ever lived here on earth." "That is not what I asked you. Do you believe Jesus Christ bore your sins in His own body on the cross?" "The Christian Scientists are lovely people." "That is not what I asked you. Do you believe that Jesus Christ bore your sins in His own body on the cross?" "I believe in following the Lord Jesus Christ."

"Do you believe that Jesus Christ bore your sins in His own body on the cross?" "Oh," she said, "that is a doctrinal question." "Now," I said, "you are yourself an illustration of the truth of the very thing I said. You do not believe in the Atonement through the shed blood of Jesus Christ." The Christian Scientist uses the word "atonement," but he means something entirely different from what the Bible teaches regarding the atoning death of Jesus Christ. So does the Unitarian. So do many of the ministers supposedly of orthodox denominations. The pastor of a Congregational church in this city said recently: "I have my own kind of religion; it answers for me, but I hope I have sense enough to see that it would not answer for everybody. I imagine the Salvation Army captain preaching my kind of religious doctrine, without a devil, without a hell, without an atonement of blood and recompense, without an infallible Bible—and I see his audience melting away like snow in the rain. Is his doctrine truer than mine, or is mine truer than his? Why, neither; his is true for him and mine for me—that is all—each after his own kind." Now this may sound tolerant and lovely, but it is utter nonsense. Any doctrine which is not true for everybody is not for anybody true, and any doctrine which is true is true for everybody. If a doctrine that leaves out "an atonement of blood" is not true for the Salvation Army—and it certainly is not—it is not true for anybody else. Truth is not relative; it is absolute. What is true is true, and what is false is false. So we come face to face with the question, What does the Bible teach on this great fundamental doctrine?

I. THE NECESSITY AND IMPORTANCE OF HIS DEATH

The first thing that the Bible plainly teaches on this question is the absolute necessity and fundamental importance of the death of Jesus Christ, the absolute necessity and fundamental importance of the shedding of His blood. The tendency of our day in Unitarian circles, and in orthodox circles that have been leavened by the corrupting leaven of Unitarianism, is to minimise the importance of the death of our Lord Jesus Christ. The tendency is to make His life and character, His teaching and leadership, the main thing. Christian Science even goes so far as to deny the fact of His death. To them

His supposed death is "an illusion," it is "only mortal thought," but the Bible puts the emphasis upon His atoning death.

1. The death of Jesus Christ is mentioned directly more than 175 times in the New Testament. Besides this there are very many prophetic and typical references to the death of Jesus Christ in the Old Testament. When Mr. Alexander and I were holding our meetings in the Royal Albert Hall in London, some one took away one of our hymn books and went through it and cut out every reference to the blood, and then sent it back to me through the mail, saying, "I have gone through your hymn book and cut out every reference to the blood. These references to the blood are foolish. Now sing your hymns with the blood left out and there will be some sense in them." If any of you should take your Bible and go through it in that way and cut out of the New Testament and the Old Testament every passage that referred to the death of Christ, or to His atoning blood, you would have only a sadly torn and tattered Bible left, a Bible without a heart and a Gospel without saving power. If I were a member of a church where the pastor said that he preached a system of "religious doctrine, without a devil, without a hell, without an atonement of blood and recompense, without an infallible Bible," to use his own language, he would see his audience "melting away like snow in the rain" as far as I was concerned. I would either take my hat and get out of that church, or else the pastor would take his hat and get out of the pulpit; for I should know that he was not preaching God's pure, saving gospel, but the Devil's poisonous substitute for the gospel.

2. Not only are the references to the death of Christ so numerous in Old Testament and New Testament, but we are taught distinctly in Hebrews 2:14 that Jesus Christ became a man for the specific purpose of dying, that He became a partaker of flesh and blood in order that He might die. In this passage we read, "For as much as the children are partakers of flesh and blood, He also Himself likewise took part of the same; that through death He might destroy him that had the power of death, that is the Devil" (Heb. 2:14). The meaning of these words is as plain as day. They tell us that the incarnation was for the purpose of the death. They tell us that Jesus Christ's death was not a mere accident or incident of His human life (as many would have us believe), but that it was the supreme purpose

of it. He became man in order that He might die as man and for man. This is the doctrine of the Bible, and it is true for anybody and for everybody.

3. Furthermore, He died for a specific purpose, as a ransom for us. He Himself said so. In Matt. 20:28 He says, "The Son of man came not to be ministered unto, but to minister, and to give His life a ransom for many."

4. One of the most remarkable scenes recorded in the New Testament is that of the transfiguration, when Moses and Elijah came back from the other world to commune with Jesus. And what did they talk about in that great moment of human history? Luke tells us in the 9th chapter of his Gospel, the 30th and 31st verses, "And behold, there talked with Him (i.e., with Jesus) two men, which were Moses and Elijah: who appeared in glory, and spake of His decease which He was about to accomplish at Jerusalem." His atoning death was the one subject that engrossed the attention of these two who came back from the glory world. We are also told in I Peter 1:10-12 that the death of Jesus Christ is a subject of intensest interest and earnest inquiry on the part of the angels.

5. The death of Christ is the central theme of heaven's song. Rev. 5:8-12 gives us a picture of heaven with its wonderful choir of ten thousand times ten thousand and thousands of thousands, and this is the description of the song they sing: "And when he had taken the book, the four living creatures and the four and twenty elders fell down before the Lamb, having each one a harp, and golden bowls full of incense, which are the prayers of the saints. And they sing a new song, saying, Worthy art thou to take the book and to open the seals thereof: for thou wast slain, and didst purchase unto God with thy blood men of every tribe, and tongue, and people, and nation, and madest them to be unto our God a kingdom and priests; and they reign upon the earth. And I saw, and I heard a voice of many angels round about the throne and the living creatures and elders; and the number of them was ten thousand times ten thousand, and thousands of thousands; saying with a great voice, Worthy is the Lamb that was lslain to receive the power, and riches, and wisdom, and might, and honour, and glory, and blessing. And every created thing which is in the heaven, and on the earth, and under the earth, and on the sea, and

all things that are in them, heard I saying, Unto him that sitteth on the throne, and unto the Lamb, be the blessing, and the honour, and the glory, and the dominion, for ever and ever" (Rev. 5:8-12). So it is evident that the great central theme of heaven's song is the atoning death of Jesus Christ, and the shed "blood" by which He redeemed "men of every tribe, and tongue, and nation." If the Unitarian or the Christian Scientist or the New Theologian should get to heaven they would have no song to sing. The glorious song of that wondrous choir would sound to him like a song "of the shambles." He would be very lonesome and feel that he had got into the wrong pew.

II. THE PURPOSE OF THE DEATH OF JESUS CHRIST

So much for the fundamental and central importance of His death, or of the shedding of His blood. But what was the purpose of the shedding of His blood?

1. First of all, the Bible distinctly and repeatedly tells us by direct statement, and by countless typical reference in the Old Testament, that He died as a vicarious offering for sin; that is, that He, an absolutely perfect, righteous one, who [171]deserved to live, died in the place of unjust men who deserved to die. For example, we read in Isa. 53:5, "But He was wounded for our transgressions, He was bruised for our iniquities; the chastisement of our peace was upon Him; and with His stripes we are healed." And in the eighth verse we read, "By oppression and judgment He was taken away; and as for His generation, who among them considered that He was cut off out of the land of the living for the transgression of my people to whom the stroke was due?" And in the 11th and 12th verses we read, "He shall see of the travail of His soul, and shall be satisfied: by the knowledge of Himself shall my righteous servant justify many; and He shall bear their iniquities. Therefore will I divide Him a portion with the great, and He shall divide the spoil with the strong; because He poured out His soul unto death, and was numbered with the transgressors: yet He bare the sin of many. And made intercession for the transgressors." In I Peter, 3:18 we read, "Christ also suffered for sins once, the righteous for the unrighteous, that He might bring us to God; being put to death in the flesh, but made alive in the spirit." And in 1 Peter 2:24 we read,

"Who His own self bare our sins in His own body upon the tree, that we, having died unto sins, might live unto righteousness; by whose stripes ye were healed." Now the meaning of these verses and many other verses, is inescapable. They teach in language the meaning of which no one can misunderstand (unless he is determined not to see) that the death of Jesus Christ was a vicarious atonement, that is, a just one, who deserved to live, dying in the place of unjust ones who deserved to die. It was, to use the language of the Los Angeles minister who denied his belief in it, "an atonement of blood and recompense." This is God's doctrine of the Atonement versus the Unitarian and Christian Science doctrine of the Atonement.

2. But this is not all. We are further taught that He died as a ransom, that is, His death was the price paid to redeem others from death. He Himself says so. His own words are, "The Son of man came not to be ministered unto, but to minister, and to give his life a ransom for many." If His life was not a ransom, that is to say, if He did not redeem others from death by dying in their place, then He was the greatest fool in the whole history of this universe. Was He a fool or was He a ransom? No one who in any real sense can be said to believe on the Lord Jesus Christ can hesitate as to his answer.

3. But even this is not all. The Bible distinctly tells us that He died as a sin offering, i.e., it was on the ground of His death, and on this ground alone, that forgiveness of sin is made possible for and offered to sinners. This we are told in the 53rd chapter of Isaiah, to which reference has already been made. In the 10th verse it is written, "Yet it pleased Jehovah to bruise him; He (i.e., Jehovah) hath put him to grief (literally, made him sick): when thou shalt make his soul an offering for sin, he shall see his seed, he shall prolong his days, and the pleasure of Jehovah shall prosper in his hand." Now the meaning of "offering for sin" is unquestionable to any one who has studied the Old Testament offerings. An "offering for sin" or a "guilt offering," which is the exact force of the Hebrew word translated "an offering for sin," was a death of a sacrificial victim on the ground of which pardon was offered to sinners (Lev. 6:6-10, R. V.). The Holy Spirit says expressly in Heb. 9:22, in words the meaning of which is unmistakable, and the force of which is inescapable, "Apart from shedding of blood there is no remission,"

and the whole context in which the passage is found shows that the blood, to which all the blood of the Old Testament types as sacrifices pointed forward, was the blood of Jesus Christ. So then the Word of God declares that apart from the shedding of the blood of Jesus Christ there is absolutely no pardon for sin. There is absolutely no forgiveness outside the atoning blood of Christ. Without Christ's atoning blood every member of the human race must have perished forever.

4. Fourth and further yet, the Bible teaches that Jesus Christ died as a propitiation for our sins. God the Father gave Christ the Son to be a propitiation by His blood. That is to say that Jesus Christ, through the shedding of His blood, is that by which God's holy wrath at sin is appeased. We read in 1 John 4:10, "Herein is love, not that we loved God, but that He loved us, and sent His Son to be the propitiation for our sins." And we read in Rom. 3:25, 26, "Whom God set forth to be a propitiation, through faith, in His blood, to show His righteousness because of the passing over of the sins done aforetime, in the forbearance of God; (26) for the showing, I say, of His righteousness at this present season: that He might Himself be just, and the justifier of Him that hath faith in Jesus." The meaning of these words also is as plain as day. The two Greek words in these two passages are not exactly the same words (hilasmos and hilasterion) but are from the same root. The word used in 1 John 4:10 is hilasmos and the word used in Rom. 3:25 is hilasterion. The definition given of the first in Thayer's Dictionary of New Testament Greek, the standard work, is "a means of appeasing." The definition given in the same lexicon of the second word is "an expiatory sacrifice." So the thought that is in both passages is that the death of Jesus Christ was a "propitiation," "an expiatory sacrifice," the "means of appeasing" God's holy wrath at sin, or in other words, that Jesus, through the shedding of His blood, is that by which the wrath of God against us as sinners is appeased. God's holiness and consequent hatred of sin, like every other attribute of His character, is real and must manifest itself. His wrath at sin must strike somewhere, either on the sinner himself or upon a lawful substitute. It struck upon Jesus Christ, a lawful substitute. As we read in Isa. 53:6, "All we like sheep have gone astray; we have turned every one to his own way; and Jehovah hath

laid on Him the iniquity of us all." The word translated "hath laid," according to the margin of the Revised Version, means literally, "hath made to light." More literally still it means, "hath made to strike." Reading it this way, what God says is, "All we like sheep have gone astray; we have turned every one to his own way; and Jehovah hath made to strike on him (i.e., on the Lord Jesus) the iniquity of us all." And in the eighth verse of the same chapter we are taught that "the stroke due" to others fell upon Him, and He was consequently "cut off out of the land of the living." The death of Jesus Christ has its first cause in the demands of God's holiness. This is the Bible doctrine versus the Unitarian and Christian Science doctrine of atonement. The doctrine is often misrepresented and caricatured as being that "God, a holy first person, took the sins of man, the guilty second person, and put them on Jesus Christ, an innocent third person," and it is objected that this would not be just. No; this would not be just, and it is not for a moment the doctrine of the Bible, for the Bible clearly teaches that Jesus Christ was not "a third person," but was Himself God, and that He was Himself man, so He is not a third person at all, but both the first person and the second person, and the doctrine is that God Himself, the offended first person, substitutes His atoning action whereby He expresses His hatred against sin, for His punitive action whereby He would express the same thing; that God, instead of visiting the sins of the sinner upon the sinner, takes the punishment upon Himself. This certainly is something more than just, it is wondrous love.

5. Further yet, the Bible teaches us that Jesus Christ died to redeem us from the curse of the law by bearing that curse Himself. We read in Gal. 3:10, "As many as are of the works of the law are under a curse, for it is written: Cursed is every one who continueth not in all things that are written in the Book of the Law, to do them." So then, every one of us is under the curse of the broken law, for not one of us has continued "in all things that are written in the book of the law, to do them." But we read in the 13th verse, "Christ redeemed us from the curse of the law, having become a curse for us (literally, in our behalf): for it is written, Cursed is every one that hangeth on a tree." By His death by crucifixion He redeemed us from the curse which we deserved by taking that curse upon Himself. This certainly

is "an atonement of blood and recompense."

6. The Bible puts essentially the same truth in still another form, viz., that Jesus Christ died as our Passover sacrifice—that is, that His shed blood might serve as a ground upon which God would pass over and spare us. We read in 1 Cor. 5:7, "For our passover also hath been sacrificed, even Christ." Now what a passover sacrifice was and signified we learn from Ex. 12:12, 13, where our Lord told the children of Israel at the inauguration of the passover, "For I will go through the land of Egypt in that night, and will smite all the firstborn in the land of Egypt, both man and beast; and against all the Gods of Egypt I will execute judgment: I am Jehovah, and the blood shall be to you for a token upon the houses where ye are: and when I see the blood, I will pass over you, and there shall be no plague upon you to destroy you, when I smite the land of Egypt." And again we read in the 23rd verse of the same chapter, "For Jehovah will pass through to smite the Egyptians; and when He seeth the blood upon the lintel, and on the two side-posts, Jehovah will pass over the door, and will not suffer the destroyer to come in unto your houses to smite you." Paul wrote his words with all this in mind, and in saying that Christ is our Passover sacrifice beyond a question he meant that the shed blood of Jesus Christ serves as a ground, and the only ground, upon which God passes over and spares us.

III. THE RESULTS OF THE ATONING DEATH

We have seen then the gracious and glorious purposes of the Atoning Death of Jesus Christ. What are the results of that death? They are even more glorious. I can speak of them this morning only in part.

1. The first result of the atoning death of Jesus Christ is that a propitiation is provided for the whole world. We read in 1 John 2:2, "He is the propitiation for our sins; and not for ours only, but also for the whole world." This plainly means that by the death of Jesus Christ a basis is provided upon which God can deal in mercy and does deal in mercy with the whole world. All of God's dealings in mercy with any man are on the ground of Christ's death. Only on the ground of Christ's death could God deal in mercy with any man. God's dealings in mercy with the rankest blasphemer or the most

blatant atheist is on the ground of the atoning death of Jesus Christ.

2. In the second place through the atoning death of Jesus Christ all men obtain resurrection from the dead. We read in Rom. 5:18, "So then as through one trespass (i.e., the trespass of Adam) the judgment came unto all men to condemnation; even so through one act of righteousness (i.e., through Christ's righteous act in dying on the cross in obedience to the will of God) the free gift came unto all men to justification of life." And we are told in 1 Cor. 15:22, "As in Adam all die, so also in Christ shall all be made alive." The Apostle Paul in the whole chapter is speaking about the resurrection of the body, not about eternal life, and he here distinctly teaches that as every child of Adam loses life (physical life—see Gen. 3:19) in the first Adam, so also in Jesus Christ, the second Adam, he obtains resurrection from the dead, through the atoning death of Jesus Christ. Every man, the rankest infidel as well as the most devout believer, will some day be raised from the dead because Christ died in his place. Whether the resurrection which he obtains through the death of Jesus Christ shall be a "resurrection of life" or a "resurrection of condemnation," "shame and everlasting contempt" (John 5:28, 29; Dan. 12:2) depends entirely upon what attitude the individual takes toward the Christ in whom he gets the resurrection.

3. By the atoning death of Jesus Christ all believers in Jesus Christ have forgiveness of all their sins. We read in Eph. 1:7, "In whom (i.e., in Jesus Christ) we have our redemption through His blood, the forgiveness of our trespasses, according to the riches of His grace." Because Jesus Christ died as a full satisfaction for our sins, forgiveness of sin is not something which believers are to do something to secure, it is something which the blood of Jesus Christ has already secured and which our faith has already appropriated to ourselves; "we have forgiveness," we are forgiven. Every believer in Jesus Christ is forgiven every sin he ever committed or ever shall commit, because Jesus Christ shed His blood in his place. Through Christ's atoning death all believers in Him, although they once "were enemies," are now "reconciled to God by the death of His Son." As we read in Rom. 5:10, "While we were enemies, we were reconciled to God through the death of His Son." That is to say, the enmity between God and the sinner is done away with, or, as Paul

puts it in Col. 1:20, Christ has "made peace through the blood of His cross," or, as he puts it in the next verse but one, Col. 1:22, Christ "hath reconciled" believers "in the body of His flesh through death." The story is told of a faithful vicar in England who was told that one of his parishioners was dying. She was a good woman, but he hurried to her side to talk with her. As he sat down by the side of the dying woman he said to her very gently but solemnly, "They tell me you have not long to live." "No," she replied, "I know I have not." "They tell me you will probably not live through the night." "No," she replied, "I do not expect to live through the night." Then he said very earnestly, "Have you made your peace with God?" She replied, "No, I have not." "And are you not afraid to meet God without having made your peace with Him?" "No, not at all," she calmly replied. Again he said to her, "Do you understand what I am saying? Do you realise that you are at the point of death?" "Yes." "Do you realise you will probably not live through the night?" "Yes." "And you have not made your peace with God?" "No." "And you are not afraid to meet God?" "No, not at all." There was something about the woman's manner that made him feel there was something back of her words, and he said to her, "What do you mean?" She replied, "I know I am dying. I know I am very near death. I know I shall not live through the night. I know I must soon meet God, and I am not at all disturbed, for I know that I did not need to make my peace with God, because Jesus Christ made peace with God for me more than eighteen hundred years ago by His death on the cross of Calvary, and I am resting in the peace that Jesus Christ has already made." The woman was right: no man needs to make his peace with God, Jesus Christ has already made peace by His atoning death, and all we have to do is to enter into the peace which Jesus Christ has made for us, and we enter into that peace by simply believing in the One who made peace by His death upon the cross. Jesus Christ's work was a complete and perfect work. There is nothing to be added to it. We cannot add anything to it, and we do not need to add anything to it. Jesus Christ has "made peace through the blood of His cross."

4. The fourth result of the atoning death of Jesus Christ is that because of the atoning death of Jesus Christ all believers in Him are justified. We read in Rom. 5:9, "Being now justified by His blood."

Justification is more than forgiveness. Forgiveness is negative, the putting away of our sins, manifested in God's treating us as if we never had sinned. Justification is positive, the reckoning of us positively righteous, the imputing to us the perfect righteousness of God in Jesus Christ, not merely the treating us as if we had never sinned, but the reckoning us clothed upon with perfect righteousness. By reason of Jesus Christ's atoning death there is an absolute interchange of position between Jesus Christ and His people. In His death upon the cross Jesus Christ took our place of condemnation before God, and the moment we accept Him we step into His place of perfect acceptance before God. As Paul puts it in 2 Cor. 5:21, "Him who knew no sin He made to be sin on our behalf; that we might become the righteousness of God in Him." Jesus Christ stepped into our place in the curse and rejection, and the moment we accept Him we step into His place of perfect acceptance, or as it has been expressed by another:

"Near, so very near to God,
Nearer I cannot be;
For in the person of His Son,
I'm just as near as He.
Dear, so very dear to God,
Dearer I cannot be;
For in the person of His Son,
I'm just as dear as He."

5. Furthermore, because of the full atonement that Jesus Christ has made by the shedding of His blood, by His atoning death on the cross, every believer in Him can enter boldly into the holy place, into the very presence of God. As it is put in Heb. 10:19, 20, "Having therefore, brethren, boldness to enter into the holy place (i.e., into the very presence of God) by the blood of Jesus, by the way which He dedicated for us, a new and living way, through the veil, that is to say, His flesh; and having a great priest over the house of God; let us draw near with a true heart in fullness of faith." Oh, how some of us hesitate to come into the presence of God when we think of the greatness and the number of our sins, and when we think how holy God is, how the very seraphim (the "burning ones," burning in their own intense holiness) veil their faces and feet in His presence and

unceasingly cry "Holy, holy, holy, is Jehovah of Hosts" (Isa. 6:2, 3). "God is Holy," we think. "Yes." "And I am a sinner." "Yes." But by the wondrous offering of Christ "once for all" I am "perfected forever," and on the ground of that blood so precious and so sufficient unto God, I can march boldly into the very presence of God, look up with unveiled face into His face and call Him "Father," and pour out before Him every desire of my heart. Oh, wondrous blood!

6. But this is not all. Because of the atoning death of Jesus Christ those who believe in Him shall ever live with Him. How plainly Paul puts it in 1 Thess. 5:10, "Who died for us, that, whether we wake or sleep, (i.e., at His coming), we should live together with Him."

7. Further yet, because of the atoning death of Jesus Christ, all those who believe on Him receive the promise of the eternal inheritance. This is what we are told in Heb. 9:15, "And for this cause He is the mediator of a new covenant, that a death having taken place for the redemption of the transgressions that were under the first covenant, they that have been called may receive the promise of the eternal inheritance." I wish I had time to dwell upon that.

8. There are other results of the atoning death of Jesus Christ as regards the Devil and his angels, into which we have no time to go. Just one more thing as regards the results of the atoning death of Jesus Christ as it relates to the material universe. God teaches us that through the death of Jesus Christ the material universe—"all things, whether they be things in earth, or things in heaven"—is reconciled unto God. These are His words, "For it was the good pleasure of the Father that in Him (i.e., in Jesus Christ) should all the fullness dwell and, having made peace through the blood of His cross, by Him to reconcile all things unto Himself; by Him, I say, whether they be things in earth, or things in Heaven" (Col. 1:19, 20). These are wonderful words. They tell us that the death of Jesus Christ has a relation to the material universe, to things on earth and to things in heaven, as well as to us and our sins. The material universe has fallen away from God in connection with sin (Rom. 8:20, R. V.; Gen. 3:18). Not only earth but heaven has been invaded and polluted by sin (Eph. 6:12, R. V.; Heb. 9:23, 24). Through the death of Jesus Christ this pollution is put away. Just as the blood of the Old Testament

sacrifice was taken into the most holy place, the type of heaven, so Christ has taken the blood of the better sacrifice into heaven itself and cleansed it. "All things . . . whether they be things in earth or things in heaven" are now reconciled to God. "The creation itself also shall be delivered from the bondage of corruption into the liberty of the glory of the children of God" (Rom. 8:21). "We look for new heavens and a new earth, wherein dwelleth righteousness" (2 Peter 3:13). The atonement of Jesus Christ has an immense sweep—far beyond the reach of our human philosophies. We have just begun to understand what the blood that was spilled on Calvary means. Sin is a far more awful, ruinous, and far-reaching evil than we have been wont to think, but the blood of Christ has a power and efficiency, the fullness of which only eternity will disclose.

IX

The Distinctive Doctrine of Protestantism: Justification by Faith

"Be it known unto you therefore, brethren, that through this man is proclaimed unto you, remission of sins: and by him every one that believeth is justified from all things, from which he could not be justified by the law of Moses."—Acts 13:38, 39.

"But to him that worketh not, but believeth on him that justifieth the ungodly, his faith is reckoned for righteousness."—Rom. 4:5.

These are two remarkable passages and this chapter will be occupied with an exposition of them. Our subject this morning is, The Distinctive Doctrine of Protestantism: Justification by Faith. The doctrine of Justification by Faith was the doctrine that made the Reformation. It is to-day one of the cardinal doctrines of the Evangelical Faith. This doctrine, though first fully expounded and constantly emphasised by Paul, runs throughout the entire Bible from Genesis to Revelation. It is in the first book of the Bible, the book of Genesis, that we read, "Abraham believed in the Lord; and he counted it to him for righteousness." (Gen. 15:6.) In these words in the very first book in the Bible we have the germ of the whole gracious and precious doctrine of Justification by Faith.

I. WHAT IS JUSTIFICATION?

The first thing for us to understand clearly is just what justification is. It is at this point that many go astray in their study of this great truth. There are two fundamentally different definitions of the meaning of the words "justify" and "justification." The one definition of Justify is, to make righteous, and of Justification, the being made righteous. The other definition of "justify" is, to reckon, declare, or show to be righteous, and of "justification," the being declared or reckoned righteous. On these two different definitions two different schools of thought depart from one another. Which is the true definition? The way to settle the meaning of any word in the Bible is by an examination of all the passages in which that word and its derivatives is found. If any one will go through the Bible, the Old Testament and the New, and carefully study all the passages in which the word "justify" and its derivatives is found, he will discover that beyond a question, in Biblical usage, to "justify" means, not to make righteous, but to reckon righteousness, declare righteous, or show to be righteous. A man is justified before God when God reckons him righteous. This appears, for example, in the fourth chapter of Romans, 2nd to 8th verses, R. V. "For if Abraham was justified by works, he hath whereof to glory; but not toward God. For what saith the scripture? And Abraham believed God and it was reckoned unto him for righteousness. Now to him that worketh, the reward is not reckoned as of grace, but as of debt. But to him that worketh not, but believeth on him that justifieth the ungodly, his faith is reckoned for righteousness even as David also pronounced blessing upon the man unto whom God reckoneth righteousness apart from works, saying, blessed are they whose iniquities are forgiven, and whose sins are covered, blessed is the man to whom the Lord will not reckon sin." It is plain from this passage, as from many other passages, that a man is justified when God reckons him righteous, no matter what his principles of character and of conduct may have been. We shall see later that justification means more than mere forgiveness.

II. HOW ARE MEN JUSTIFIED?

We come now to the second question, and the all-important question, How are men justified? In general there are two opposing views of justification: one that men are justified by their own works, i.e., on the ground of something which they do themselves. This view may be variously expressed. The good works that men speak of as a ground of their justification may be their good moral conduct, or their keeping the Golden Rule, or something of that sort. Or they may be works of religion, such as doing penance, saying prayers, joining the church, going to church, being baptised, or partaking of the Lord's Supper, or the performance of some other religious duties. But these all amount to the same thing: it is something that we ourselves do that brings justification, some works of our own, some works that we do, are taken as the ground of our justification. The other view of justification is that we are justified, not by our own works in any sense, but entirely by the work of another, i.e., by the atoning death of Jesus Christ on the cross of Calvary, that our own works have nothing to do with our justification, but that we are justified entirely by Christ's finished and complete work of atonement, by His death for us on the Cross, and that all that we have to do with our justification is merely to appropriate it to ourselves by simply trusting in Him who made the atonement. Which is the correct view? We shall go directly to the Bible for the answer to this all-important question.

1. The first part of the answer we will find in Rom. 3:20, "Therefore by the deeds of the law there shall no flesh be justified in his sight: for through the law cometh the knowledge of sin." It is here very plainly stated that we are not justified by keeping the law of God, either the Mosaic law or any other law, and that the law is given, not to bring us justification, but to bring us a knowledge of sin, i.e., to bring us to the realisation of our need of justification by grace. It is plainly stated here that no man is justified by works of the law. The same great truth is found in Gal. 2:16: "Knowing that a man is not justified by the works of the law, save through faith in Jesus Christ, even we believed on Christ Jesus, that we might be justified by faith in Christ, and not by the works of the law: for by the works of the law shall no flesh be justified." Justification by any works of our own is an impossibility. It is an impossibility because to be justified by works of the law, or by anything we can do, we must perfectly keep the law of God. The law demands perfect obedience as a ground of justification. It says, "Cursed is every one that continueth not in all things that are written in the book of the law to do them." (Gal. 3:10.). But not one of us has perfectly kept the law of God, and the moment we break the law of God at any point, justification by works becomes an absolute impossibility. So as far as the law of God is concerned, every one of us is "under the curse," and if we are justified at all we must find some other way of justification than by keeping the law of God. God did not give man

the law with the expectation or intention that he would keep it and be justified thereby. He gave them the law to produce conviction of sin, to stop men's mouths, and to lead them to Christ. Or, as Paul puts it in Rom. 3:19, 20, "Now ye know that what things soever the law saith, it speaketh to them that are under the law; that every mouth may be stopped, and all the world may be brought under the judgment of God: because by the works of the law shall no flesh be justified in his sight: for through the law cometh the knowledge of sin." As plain as these words of God are, strangely enough there are many to-day who are preaching the law as a way of salvation. But when they so preach they are preaching another way of salvation than that laid down in God's own word.

2. The second part of the answer to the question as to how we are justified we find in Rom. 3:24. "Being justified freely by his grace through the redemption that is in Christ Jesus." The word translated "freely" in this passage means, as a free gift, and the verse tells us that men are justified as a free gift by God's grace (i.e., God's unmerited favour) through (i.e., on the ground of) the redemption that is in Christ Jesus. In other words, justification is not on the ground of any desert there is in us, not on the ground of anything that we have done, we are not justified by our own doing nor by our own character. Justification is a free gift that God bestows absolutely without pay. The channel through which this free gift is bestowed is the redemption that is in Christ Jesus. We shall see later that this means through the purchase price that Christ paid for our redemption, i.e., the shedding of His blood on the cross of Calvary.

3. This leads us to the third part of the answer to the question, how men are justified. We find this third part of the answer in Rom. 5:9, "Much more then, being now justified by his blood, shall we be saved from the wrath of God through Him." Here we are told in so many words that we are justified, or counted righteous "by," or more literally, "in," Christ's blood, i.e., on the ground of Christ's propitiatory death. We were all under the curse of the broken law of God, for we had all broken it, but by dying in our stead on the cross of Calvary our Lord Jesus "Christ redeemed us from the curse of the law, having become a curse for us; for it is written, cursed is every one that hangeth on a tree." (Gal. 3:13.) Or, as Peter puts it in

1 Pet. 2:24, "Who his own self bare our sins in his own body upon the tree." Or as Paul puts it again in 2 Cor. 5:21, "Him who knew no sin he (God) made to be sin on our behalf; that we might become the righteousness of God in Him." We shall have occasion to come back to this passage later. All that I wish you to notice in it at this time is that it is on the ground of Jesus Christ becoming a substitute for us, on the ground of His taking the place we deserved; on the cross, that we are reckoned righteous. The one and only ground of justification is the shed blood of Jesus Christ. Of course, this doctrine is entirely different from the teaching of Christian Science, and entirely different from the teaching of much that is called New Theology, and entirely different from the teaching of New Thought and Theosophy, and entirely different from the teaching of Unitarianism, but it is the teaching of the Word of God. We find this same teaching clearly given by the prophet Isaiah seven hundred years before our Lord was born, in Isaiah 53:6, where he says, "All we like sheep have gone astray; we have turned every one to his own way, and the Lord hath laid (literally, made to strike) on him (i.e., on the Lord Jesus) the iniquity of us all." Get this point clearly settled in your mind, that the sole but all-sufficient ground upon which men are justified before God is the shed blood of Jesus Christ, offered by Jesus Christ as an atonement for our sins and accepted by God the Father as an all-sufficient atonement.

4. The fourth part of the answer to the question how men are justified we find in Rom. 3:26, "For the showing, I say, of his (i.e., God's) righteousness at this present season: that he (i.e., God) might himself be just, and the justifier of him that hath faith in Jesus." Here we are taught that men are justified on the condition of faith in Jesus. If possible, Rom. 4:5 makes this even more plain, "But to him that worketh not but believeth on him that justifieth the ungodly, his faith is reckoned for righteousness." Here the Holy Spirit, speaking through the Apostle Paul, tells us that to those who believe in Jesus their faith is counted for righteousness. In other words, faith makes ours the shed blood which is the ground of justification, and we are justified when we believe. All men are potentially justified by the death of Christ on the cross, but believers are actually justified by appropriating to themselves what there is of justifying value in the

shed blood of Christ by simple faith in Him. In other words, the shed blood of Christ is the sole and all-sufficient ground of justification: simple faith in Jesus Christ who shed the blood is the sole condition of justification. God asks nothing else of the sinner than that he should believe on His Son, Jesus Christ, and when he does thus believe he is justified. When we believe we are justified, whether we have any works to offer or not; or, as Paul puts it in Rom. 3:28, "We reckon therefore that a man is justified by faith apart from works of the law." Or, as it is put in the verse already quoted, Rom. 4:5, "But to him that worketh not, but believeth on him that justifieth the ungodly, his faith is reckoned for righteousness." A man is justified entirely apart from works of the law, i.e., he is justified on condition that he believes on Jesus Christ, even though he has no works to offer as the ground upon which to claim justification. When we cease to work for justification and simply "believe on Him who justifieth the ungodly," that faith is reckoned to us for righteousness, and therefore we are counted righteous. The question then is not, have you any works to offer, but do you believe on Him who justifies the ungodly. Works have nothing to do with justification except to hinder it when we trust in them. The blood of Jesus Christ secures it, faith in Jesus Christ appropriates it. We are justified not by our works, but by His work. We are justified upon the simple and single ground of His shed blood and upon the simple and single condition of our faith in Him Who shed the blood. So great is the pride of the natural heart that it is exceedingly difficult to hold men to this doctrine of justification by faith alone apart from works of law. We are constantly seeking to bring in our works somewhere.

5. But we have not as yet completely answered the question of how men are justified. There is another side to the truth and if our doctrine of justification is to be complete and well-balanced, we must look at that other side. You will find part of this other side in Rom. 10:8, 10, "If thou shalt confess with thy mouth Jesus as Lord, and shalt believe in thy heart that God raised him from the dead, thou shalt be saved; for with the heart man believeth unto righteousness; and with the mouth confession is made unto salvation." God here tells us that the faith that appropriates justification is a faith with the heart, i.e., a faith that is not a mere notion, or opinion, but a faith

that leads to action along the line of that faith, and it is therefore a faith that leads to open confession with the mouth, of Jesus as our Lord. If some one has some kind of faith, or what he calls faith, that does not lead him to an open confession of Christ, he has a faith that does not justify; for it is not a faith with the heart. Our Lord Jesus Christ Himself tells us that heart faith leads to open confession; for He says in Matt. 12:34, "Out of the abundance of the heart the mouth speaketh." Faith in Jesus Christ in the heart leads inevitably to a confession of Jesus as Lord with the mouth, and if you are not confessing Jesus as your Lord with your mouth you have not justifying faith and you are not justified.

6. The rest of the other side of the truth about being justified by faith, you will find in Jas. 2:14, 18-24, R. V. "What doth it profit, my brethren, if a man say he hath faith but have not works? Can that faith save him?" We see here that a faith that a man merely says he has, but that does not lead to works along the line of that which he claims to believe, cannot justify, but to go on, verses 18-24, "Yea, a man will say, thou hast faith, and I have works, show me thy faith apart from thy works, and I by my works will show thee my faith. Thou believest that God is one; thou doest well: the devils also believe and shudder. But wilt thou know, O vain man, that faith apart from works is barren? Was not Abraham our father justified by works, in that he offered up Isaac his son, upon the altar? Thou seest that faith wrought with his works, and by works was faith made perfect (i.e., in the works to which Abraham's faith led, faith had its perfect manifestation); and the scripture was fulfilled which saith, and Abraham believed God, and it was reckoned unto him for righteousness; and he was called the friend of God. Ye see that by works a man is justified, and not only by faith." Some see in these words a contradiction between the teaching of James and the teaching of Paul, but there is no contradiction whatever. But James here teaches us an important truth, namely, that the faith that one says he has, but which does not manifest itself in action along the line of the faith professed, will not justify. The faith that justifies is real faith that leads to action accordant with the truth we profess to believe. It is true that we are justified simply upon faith apart from the works of the law, but it must be a real faith, otherwise it does

not justify. As some one has put it, "We are justified by faith without works, but we are not justified by a faith that is without works." The faith which God sees and upon which He justifies, leads inevitably to works which men can see. God saw the faith of Abraham the moment Abraham believed, and before there was any opportunity to work, and counted that faith to Abraham for righteousness. But the faith that God saw was a real faith and led Abraham to works that all could see, and these works proved the reality of his faith. The proof to us of the faith is the works, and we know that he that does not work has not justifying faith.

We must not lose sight on the one side of the truth which Paul emphasises against legalism, namely, that we are justified on the single and simple condition of a real faith in Christ; but on the other side we must not lose sight of the truth which James emphasises against antinomianism, namely, that it is only a real faith that proves its genuineness by works, that justifies. To the legalist who is seeking to do something to merit justification we must say, "Stop working and believe on Him that justifieth the ungodly" (Rom. 4:5). To the antinomian, i.e., to the one who thinks he can live a lawless, careless, unseparated, sinful life and still be justified, the one who boasts that he has faith and is justified by it, but who does not show his faith by his works, we must say, "What doth it profit, if a man say he have faith, but have not works? Can that faith save him?" (Jas. 2:14, R. V.) We are justified by faith alone, but we are not justified by a faith that is alone, but a faith that is accompanied by works.

III. THE EXTENT OF JUSTIFICATION

I think we have made it plain just how one is justified, and now we come to another question and that is, the extent of justification. To what extent is a man who believes in the Lord Jesus justified? This question is very plainly answered and wonderfully answered, and gloriously answered in Acts 13:38, 39, "Be it known unto you therefore, brethren, that through this man is proclaimed unto you remission of sins: and by him every one that believeth is justified from all things, from which he could not be justified by the law of Moses." These words very plainly declare to us that every believer in Jesus Christ is justified "from all things." In other words, the old account against the believer is all wiped out. No matter how bad and how black the account is, the moment a man believes in Jesus Christ, the account is wiped out. God has absolutely nothing which He reckons against the one who believes in Jesus Christ. Even though he is still a very imperfect believer, a very young man and immature Christian, he is perfectly justified. As Paul puts it in Rom. 8:1, "There is therefore now no condemnation to them that are in Christ Jesus." Or, as he puts it further down in the chapter, verses 33, 34, "Who shall lay anything to the charge of God's elect? It is God that justifieth; who is he that shall condemn? It is Christ Jesus that died, yea rather, that was raised from the dead, who is at the right hand of God, who also maketh intercession for us." If the vilest murderer or sinner of any kind on earth should come in here this morning and right here now, hearing the gospel of God's grace, should believe in the Lord Jesus Christ, put confidence in Him as his Saviour, and accept Him as such, surrendering to Him and confessing Him as His Lord, the moment he did it every sin he ever committed would be blotted out and his record would be as white in God's sight as that of the purest angel in heaven. God has absolutely nothing that He reckons against the believer in Jesus Christ. But even that is not all. Paul goes even beyond this in 2 Cor. 5:21, "He who knew no sin he (God) made to be sin on our behalf; that we might become the righteousness of God in him." Here we are explicitly told that the believer in Jesus Christ is made the righteousness of God in Christ. In Phil. 3:9, R. V. we are told that when one is in Christ he has a righteousness not of his own, but a "righteousness which is of God upon faith." In other words, there is an absolute interchange of positions between Christ and the justified believer. Christ took our place, the place of the curse on the cross (Gal. 3:13). He was "made to be sin on our behalf" (2 Cor. 5:21). God reckoned Him a sinner and dealt with Him as a sinner, so that in the sinner's place, as He died, He cried, "My God, my God, why hast thou forsaken me?" And when we are justified we step into His place, the place of perfect acceptance before God, or to use the exact words of Scripture, we "Become the righteousness of God in him." To be justified is more than to be forgiven! Forgiveness is negative, the putting away of sin; Justification is positive, the reckoning of positive and perfect righteousness to the one justified. Jesus Christ is so united to the believer in Him that God reckons our sins to Him. The believer, on the other hand, is so united to Christ that God reckons His righteousness to us. God sees us, not as we are in ourselves, but as we are in Him and reckons us as righteous as He is. When Christ's work in us is completed we shall be in actual fact what we are already in God's reckoning, but the moment one believes, as far as God's reckoning is concerned, he is as absolutely perfect as he ever shall be. Our present standing before God is absolutely perfect, though our present state may be very imperfect. To use again the familiar couplet:

"Near, so very near to God,
Nearer I cannot be;
For in the person of His Son,
I am just as near as He.
Dear, so very dear to God,
Dearer I cannot be;
For in the person of His Son,
I am just as dear as He."

IV. THE TIME OF JUSTIFICATION

There remains one question still to consider, though we have really answered it in what has already been said, and that is, the time of justification, or when a believer is justified. When is a believer justified? This question is answered plainly in one of our texts, Acts 13:39, "And by him every one that believeth is justified from all things, from which he could not be justified by the law of Moses." What I wish you to notice particularly now in this verse is the word Is, "Everyone that believeth is justified from all things." This answers plainly the question as to when a believer is justified. In Christ Jesus every believer in Him is justified from all things the moment he believes. The moment a man believes in Jesus Christ that moment he becomes united to Christ, and that moment God reckons the righteousness of God to him. I repeat again, if the vilest murderer or sinner of any kind in the world should come into this room this morning while I am preaching and should here and now believe in the Lord Jesus Christ, the moment that he did it, not only would every sin he ever committed be blotted out, but all the perfect righteousness of God in Christ would be put to his account, and his standing before God would be as perfect as it will be when he has been in heaven ten million years. Let me repeat to you again the incident I told you one Sunday night some weeks ago. I was preaching one Sunday morning in the Moody church in Chicago on Rom. 8:1, "There is therefore now no condemnation to them that are in Christ Jesus," and in the course of my preaching I said, "If the vilest woman there is in Chicago should come into the Chicago Avenue church this morning, and should here and now accept Jesus Christ as her Saviour, the moment she did it every sin she ever committed would be blotted out and her record would be as white in God's sight as that of the purest woman in the room." Unknown to me, one of the members of my congregation that very morning had gone down into a low den of iniquity near the river and had invited a woman who was an outcast to come and hear me preach. The woman replied, "I never go to church. Church is not for the likes of me. I would not be welcome at the church if I did go." The woman who was a saint replied, "You would be welcome at our church," which, thank God, was true. But, "No," the woman urged, "it would not do for me to go to church, church is not for the likes of me." But the woman who was a saint urged the woman who was a sinner to go. She offered to accompany her to the church, but the other said, "No, that would never do. The policemen know me and the boys on the street know me and sometimes throw stones at me, and if they saw you going up the street with me they would think you such as I am." But the woman who was a saint had the Spirit of the Master and said, "I don't care what they think of me. If you will accompany me to hear Mr. Torrey preach I will go along with you." The other woman refused. But the saved woman was so insistent that the woman who was an outcast finally said, "If you will go up the street a few steps ahead I will follow you up the street." So up La Salle Avenue they came, the woman who was a saint a few steps ahead and the woman who was a sinner a few steps behind. Block after block they came until they reached the corner of La Salle and Chicago Avenues. The woman who was a saint entered the tower door at the corner, went up the steps, entered the church, and the woman who was a sinner followed her. On reaching the door the woman who was a sinner looked in, saw a vacant seat under the gallery in the very last row at the back, and slipped into it, and scarcely had she taken the seat when I made the remark that I just quoted, "If the vilest woman there is in Chicago should come into the Chicago Avenue church this morning and should here and now accept Jesus Christ as her personal Saviour, the moment she did it every sin she ever committed would be blotted out and her record would be as white in God's sight as that of the purest woman in the room." My words went floating down over the audience and dropped into the heart of the woman who was a sinner. She believed it, she believed that Jesus died for her, she believed that by the shedding of His blood she could be saved, she believed, and found pardon and peace and justification then and there. And when the meeting was over she came up the aisle to the front as I stepped down from the pulpit, tears streaming down her face, and thanked me for the blessing that she had received. And I repeat it here this morning, not knowing who may be here, not knowing what may be the secret life of any one of you who is here, not knowing what may be the sins that may be hidden in your heart, if the vilest man or woman on earth should come into the Church of the Open Door this morning and should here and now put their trust in Jesus Christ, the moment you did it every sin you ever committed would be blotted out and in an instant your record would be as white in God's sight, not only as that of the [urest woman in the room, but as that of the purest angel in heaven, and not only that, but all the perfect righteousness of God that clothed our Lord Jesus Christ would be put to your account and you would be just as near and just as dear to God as the Lord Jesus Christ Himself is. That is the doctrine of justification by faith. Wondrous doctrine! Glorious doctrine!

The New Birth

"Jesus answered and said unto him, verily, verily, I say unto thee, except a man be born anew, he cannot see the kingdom of God. . . . Jesus answered, Verily, verily, I say unto thee, except a man be born of water and the Spirit, he cannot enter into the kingdom of God."—John 3:3, 5.

Our subject in this chapter is Regeneration, or the New Birth. I spoke on this subject a year or so ago, but I am going to treat it in an entirely different way in this chapter and furthermore no course of sermons on the Fundamental Doctrines of the Christian Faith would be complete without a sermon on the New Birth. What we have to say in this chapter will come under four heads: I. What Is the New Birth? II. The Results of the New Birth, III. The Necessity of the New Birth, IV. How One Is Born Again.

I. What is the New Birth?

The first question that confronts us is, What is the New Birth? Many speak of the New Birth or of Regeneration without any definite conception of just what the New Birth is, and so are never sure whether they themselves have been born again or not.

As plain and clear a definition of the New Birth as we can find in the Word of God is given in 2 Pet. 1:4, "Whereby he hath granted unto us his precious and exceeding great promises; that through these ye may become partakers of the divine nature, having escaped from the corruption that is in the world by lust." From these words of Peter it is evident that the New Birth is the impartation to the one who is born again, of a new nature, God's own nature. By being born again we become actual partakers of the Divine nature. We are all born into this world with a corrupted intellectual and moral nature. The natural man, or unregenerate man, is intellectually blind, blind to the truth of God, "the things of the Spirit" he cannot see or receive. "They are foolishness unto him, and he cannot know them" (1 Cor. 2:14). His affections are corrupt, he loves the things he ought to hate and hates the things he ought to love. A definite description of the affections and tastes and desires of the unregenerate man is found in Gal. 5:19, 20, 21. He is also perverse in his will, as Paul puts it in Rom. 8:7, "The mind of the flesh is enmity against God; for it is not subject to the law of God, neither indeed can be." This state of intellectual spiritual blindness and moral corruption is the condition of every unregenerate man. No matter how cultured or refined or moral he may be outwardly, his inner life is radically wrong. In the New Birth God imparts to the one who is born again His own wise and holy nature, a nature that thinks as God thinks ("He is renewed in knowledge after the image of him that created him"—Col. 3:10); he feels as God feels, loves the things that God loves, hates the things that God hates, wills as God wills (1 John 3:14; 4:7, 8). It is evident then that regeneration is a deep thorough-going change in the deepest springs of thought, feeling and action. A change so thorough-going that Paul says in 2 Cor. 5:17, "If any man is in Christ, he is a new creature (more exactly, Creation): the old things are passed away; behold they are become new." To use the inspired language of the Apostle John, regeneration is a passing "out of death into life." John says in 1 John 3:14, "We know that we have passed out of death into life." Until we are thus born again we are in a condition of moral and spiritual death. When we are born again we are "quickened" (or made alive), we who "were dead through our trespasses and sins." (Eph. 2:1). There is a profound contrast between regeneration and mere conversion. Conversion is an outward thing, a turning around. One is faced the wrong way, faced away from God; he turns around and faces toward God. That is conversion. But regeneration is not a mere outward change, but a thorough-going change in the deepest depths of one's being, that leads to a genuine conversion or genuine outward change. Many an apparentlythorough conversion is a temporary thing because it did not go deep enough, but regeneration is a permanent thing. When

God imparts His nature to a man, that nature abides in the man. When he is born again he cannot be unborn, or as John puts it in 1 John 3:9, "Whosoever is begotten of God doth no sin, because his (God's) seed abideth in him." A man may be converted a thousand times, he can be regenerated but once.

II. RESULTS OF THE NEW BIRTH

We now come to the second question, closely related to the first, and it will help us to understand even more clearly what the New Birth is. What are the results that follow when one is born again? They are numerous.

1. The first of these results is found in 1 Cor. 6:19, where we read: "Know ye not that your body is a temple of the Holy Ghost which is in you, which ye have from God?" These words were spoken to believers, to regenerated men, and they plainly tell us that when one is born again, the Holy Spirit comes to take up His permanent dwelling in the man and that the man who is born again thus becomes a temple of the Holy Spirit. It is true that we may not always be conscious of this indwelling of the Holy Spirit, nevertheless He dwells in us.

2. The second result of the New Birth is found in Rom. 8:2-4, where we read: "For the law of the Spirit of life in Christ Jesus made me free from the law of sin and of death. For what the law could not do, in that it was weak through the flesh, God, sending his own Son in the likeness of sinful flesh and as an offering for sin, condemned sin in the flesh: that the ordinance of the law might be fulfilled in us, who walk not after the flesh, but after the Spirit." In the 7th chapter of Romans, we have a picture of the man who is awakened by the law of God which he approves after the inward man, which he sees "is holy and just and good," which he tries to keep in his own strength, but utterly fails to keep, until at last he comes to an end of himself and is filled with despair of ever being able to keep the law of God outside of him, because of the law of sin and death inside him, which law of sin and death says, "the good which you would do you cannot do, and the evil which you hate and would not do, you must keep on doing." When a man is thus brought to a consciousness of his own utter helplessness and turns to God and

accepts Jesus Christ, the Holy Spirit, whom Jesus Christ gives to him who dwells in him, sets him free from this law of sin and death so that by the power of the indwelling Spirit he is enabled to obey the law of God and to get the victory over the evil things that he would not do and to do the things which he would do. Whereas in a man merely awakened by the law of God, "the law of sin and death" gets a perpetual victory, in a regenerate man, the "law of the Spirit of life in Christ Jesus" gets the perpetual victory. Doubtless many of you here to-day are still struggling to keep the law of God and utterly failing in your attempt to do so. What you need is to be born again, and thus have the Holy Spirit come to dwell in you, and then to walk by the Spirit, and by the power of this indwelling Spirit to get victory every day and hour over the law of sin and death that wars in your members against the law of God.

3. The third result of the New Birth is found in Rom. 12:2, where we read, "And be not fashioned according to this world: but be ye transformed by the renewing of your mind." From this it appears that the third result of the New Birth is in outward transformation of our lives by the inward renewing of our minds so that we no longer are fashioned according to this world. Of course the regenerated man does not at once manifest perfectly that of which he has the germ in himself. He begins the new life just as we begin our natural lives, as a babe, and he must grow. As Peter puts it in 1 Pet. 2:2, we must "As new born babes, desire the sincere milk of the word, that we may grow thereby." This new life must be fed and developed. It is irrational, and unwarranted by the Word of God, to expect one who has just been born again, and who is consequently a babe in Christ, to be as perfect in character as one who was born years ago and who has grown to maturity. But the moment we are born again we receive in germ all the moral perfection that is to be ours when this germ is fully developed within us and comes to its perfect manifestation.

4. The fourth result of the New Birth we find in 1 John 5:1, "Whosoever believeth that Jesus is the Christ is begotten of God." The fourth result of being born again is that the regenerated man believes that Jesus is the Christ. Of course this faith that comes from the New Birth is a real faith. The faith that John here speaks of is not a faith that is a mere opinion, but that real faith that Jesus is the

anointed of God that leads us to enthrone Jesus as King in our lives. If you are not making Jesus King in your heart and life you have not been born again. But if you are making Jesus King in your heart and life and absolute ruler of your thoughts and conduct, then you are born again, for "Whosoever believeth that Jesus is Christ is begotten of God."

5. The fifth result of being born again we find three verses further down in this same chapter, 1 John 5:4: "For whatsoever is begotten of God overcometh the world." The fifth result of being born of God is that the one thus born again overcomes the world. The world is at variance with God, "The whole world lieth in the Evil One" (1 John 5:19). It is under the dominion of the Evil One, ruled by his ambitions and ideas. The world is at variance with God in its commercial life, social life, domestic life, and all the phases of intellectual life and educational life, and is constantly exercising a power over each of us to draw us into disobedience to God (see 1 John 5:3); but the one born of God by the power of the faith that comes through being born again, gets the victory over the world. He gets the victory over the world's ideas, purposes, plans, ambitions. He gets the victory over the world in his personal life, domestic life, commercial life, political life, intellectual life every day.

6. The sixth result of being born of God is found in 1 John 3:9, R. V., "Whosoever is begotten of God doeth no sin; because his (i.e., God's) seed abideth in him: and he cannot sin (rather, cannot be sinning), because he is begotten of God." The sixth result, then, of being born of God is that in the one born of God the seed of God remains; and, therefore, the one born of God is not making a practice of sin. Some one will ask, just what does this mean? It means exactly what it says, if we look carefully at the exact force of the words used and give due emphasis to the tense of the verbs used. First of all, let us look at the exact force of the word translated "Sin." What does sin mean? John himself has been careful to define it in the verse itself and in the context in which our verse is found. The first thing that is evident from 1 John 3:9 is that sin is a something done, not merely a something left undone, and not merely sinful thoughts and desires. What kind of a something done it is defined five verses back in verse 4. "Everyone that doeth sin doeth also lawlessness;

and sin is lawlessness." Sin here by John's own definition (and we have no right to bring the definition of any one else into the verse we are studying) is "lawlessness," i.e., such acts as reveal conscious disregard for the will of God as revealed in His word. So we see that sin, as used here, means, a conscious intentional violation of the law of God. The regenerate man will not be doing that which he knows to be contrary to the will of God. He may do that which is contrary to God's will, but which he does not know to be contrary to God's will. It is not therefore "lawlessness." Perhaps he ought to have known that it was contrary to God's will and when he is led to see that it is, he will confess his guilt to God. Furthermore, we should note the tense of the verb used in this verse. It is the present tense which denotes progressive or continuous action. A literal translation of the passage would be, "Everyone begotten out of God, sin is not doing, because His (God's) seed in him is remaining; and he cannot be sinning, because out of God he is begotten." It is not taught here that one born of God never sins in a single act, but it is taught that he is not going on sinning, not making a practice of sin. Of what he is making a practice appears in 1 John 2:29, "If ye know that he is righteous, ye know that everyone also that doeth righteousness is begotten of him." The result, then, of being born again is that the one begotten again does not go on consciously day after day doing that which he knows to be contrary to the will of God, but he does make a practice of "doing righteousness," i.e., doing that which is conformed to the will of God as revealed in His Word. The new nature imparted in regeneration renders the continuous practice of sin impossible and renders the practice of righteousness inevitable.

7. The seventh result of the New Birth is found in 1 John 3:14, R. V., "We know that we have passed out of death into life, because we love the brethren. He that loveth not abideth in death." The seventh result of being born again is that we love the brethren. We should note carefully what the thought of "love" is as brought out in the context. It is not love as a mere sentiment. It is love in that higher and deeper sense of a desire for and delight in the welfare of others, the sort of love that leads us to make sacrifices for those we love, or as we read further down in this same chapter, verses 16-18, "Hereby know we the love of God, because he laid down his life for us and

we ought to lay down our lives for the brethren. But whoso hath this world's goods, and behold his brother in need, and shutteth up his compassion from him, how doth the love of God abide in him? My little children, let us not love in word neither with the tongue; but in deed and truth." This makes it very evident that what the Holy Spirit here means by love is not a mere affection or fondness for others, not a mere delight in their society; it means that deep and genuine interest in their welfare that leads us to go down into our pockets when they are in need and supply their need; it leads us to sacrifice our own interest for the sake of their interests even to the point of laying down our lives for them. The objects of this love are "the brethren," i.e., all those who are begotten of God, as we read in 1 John 5:1, "Whosoever believeth that Jesus is the Christ is begotten of God: and whosoever loveth him that begat loveth him also that is begotten of him." Any man who is born again will love every other man who is begotten of God. The other one who is begotten of God may be an American or a German, or an Englishman, or a negro, or a Chinaman, or an Indian. He may be educated or uneducated; but he is a child of God and a brother, and as such if you are born of God, he will be the object of your love. This is a searching test of whether or not one is born of God.

8. The final result of being born of God that we will consider this morning is found in 2 Cor. 5:17, R. V., "Wherefore if any man is in Christ, he is a new creature (creation): the old things are passed away, behold, they are become new." The ninth result of being born again, including all the other results that we have been considering, is that in the regenerate man, old things are passed away, they are become new. In the place of the old ideas, old affection, old purposes, old choices, are new ideas, new affections, new purposes, new choices.

III. THE NECESSITY OF THE NEW BIRTH

For just a few moments let us look at the necessity of the New Birth. This is set forth in one of our texts and in the verses following, 1 John 3:5, 6: "Verily, Verily, I say unto you, except a man be born of water and the Spirit, he cannot enter into the kingdom of God. That which is born of the flesh is flesh; and that which is born of the Spirit is Spirit." We see here that the New Birth is a universal necessity, and we see why it is a necessity. The words translated, "Except a man be born," etc. more literally translated would be, "If any man be not born out of water and Spirit, he cannot enter into the kingdom of God." And why he cannot enter into the Kingdom of God the following verse says, and that is because all that one gets by natural generation is "Flesh" and the Kingdom of God is spiritual, and, therefore, to enter it one must be born of the Spirit. No matter how refined and intelligent our ancestry, no matter how godly our fathers and mothers may have been, we do not get the Holy Spirit from them. All we get is "flesh." It may be refined flesh, moral flesh, upright and very attractive flesh, but it is flesh; and "they that are in the flesh cannot please God," nor "inherit the kingdom of God." The flesh is incapable of improvement. No more "can the Ethiopian change his skin, or the leopard his spots" than can a man who is unregenerate attain to a life pleasing to God. (See Jer. 13:23.) He must be born again. The necessity is also absolute and imperative, so absolute and imperative that Jesus said to Nicodemus, though he was a man of most exemplary morality, a man of high moral and spiritual education, a teacher of Israel, a leader in the religious life of Israel, "You must be born again." (John 3:7.) Nothing else will take the place of the New Birth. Men are trying to substitute education, morality, religion, orthodoxy, baptism, outward reform, "new thought," "theosophy" or the knowledge of God, and other such things, for the New Birth; but none of these, or all of them together, are sufficient, you must be born again. There is absolutely no exception to this rule. As Jesus says in John 3:3, "Verily, verily, I say unto thee, except any man be born from above, he cannot see the kingdom of God."

IV. HOW CAN ONE BE BORN AGAIN?

The question, therefore, confronts each one of you, Have you been born again? There is no more important question that you could possibly face. Face it in these pages and don't dodge it. And that brings us to the immediately practical question, How are men born again, or what must any one here to-day, who is not born again, do in order to be born again right here this morning? This question also is plainly answered in the Word of God; and I can give you the answer in a very few minutes and give it so that any one here can understand it. There are three parts to the answer.

1. The first part of the answer you will find in Titus 3:4, "Not by works done in righteousness, which we did ourselves, but according to his mercy, he (i.e., God) saved us through the washing of regeneration and renewing of the Holy Ghost." These words tell us very plainly that it is God who regenerates and that He does it through the power of His Holy Spirit. The same thought is found in our text, John 3:5, 6: "Jesus answered, Verily, verily, I say unto thee, except a man be born of water and the Spirit he cannot enter into the kingdom of God. That which is born of the flesh is flesh; and that which is born of the Spirit is Spirit." Regeneration is God's work; wrought by Him by the power of His Holy Spirit working in the mind, feelings and will of the one born again, in your heart and mine.

2. Some one might infer from the fact that regeneration is God's work, which He works in our hearts by His Holy Spirit, that all we have to do is to wait until God sees fit to work; but we see plainly from other passages in the Word that this is not true. We are taught the second thing about how regeneration is wrought in James 1:18, "Of His own will he brought us forth by the word of truth, that we should be a kind of first fruits of His creatures." Here we are taught that the Word of Truth, the Word of God, is the instrument that God uses in regeneration. The same thought is found in 1 Pet. 1:23, "Having been begotten again, not of corruptible seed, but of incorruptible, through the word of God, which liveth and abideth." And Paul gives voice to the same great thought in 1 Cor. 4:15, where he says: "For though ye should have ten thousand tutors in Christ, yet have ye not many fathers: for in Christ Jesus I begat you through the gospel." From these passages it is evident that the New Birth is wrought by God through the instrumentality of His Word. It is God who works it through the power of His Holy Spirit, but the Holy Spirit works through the Word, and thus God begets men anew by "The Word of Truth," or the "Word of God," i.e., the Word which is preached by "the Gospel." So then, if you or I wish to be born again we should get in contact with the Word of God by studying the Bible

and asking God that the Holy Spirit may make that Word which we are studying a living thing in our own hearts. We should get in contact especially with that part of God's Word which is found in the Gospel of John, for John tells us in John 20:31 that "These (i.e., these things in the Gospel of John) are written, that ye may believe that Jesus is the Christ the Son of God; and that believing ye may have life in his name." If we wish to see others born again we should bring the Word of God to bear upon their minds and hearts either by preaching the Word, or by teaching it, or in personal work; and we should look to the Holy Spirit to quicken that Word in the hearts of men as we sow it in their hearts, and in this way the New Birth will result.

3. The third and last and decisive truth as to how we are born again is found in Gal. 3:26 and John 1:12, 13. In Gal. 3:26 we read, "For ye are all sons of God, through faith, in Christ Jesus." This tells us plainly that we become born again through putting our faith in Christ Jesus. This is even more explicitly stated in John 1:12, 13: "But as many as received him (i.e. the Lord Jesus), to them gave He the right to become children of God, even to them that believe on His name: which were born not of blood, nor of the will of the flesh, nor of the will of man, but of God." Here we are told that the decisive thing in our becoming children of God is that we believe in, or receive, Jesus Christ. Any one who receives Jesus Christ as his personal Saviour and trusts God to forgive him because Jesus Christ died in his place and receives him as his Lord and King, and surrenders his thoughts to His absolute control as his Lord and his life to His absolute control as his King and confesses Jesus Christ as Lord before the world, such a one immediately becomes a child of God, is immediately born again, is immediately made a partaker of the Divine nature. The same thought is illustrated by Jesus Himself in John 3:14, 15, where our Lord Jesus is recorded as saying, "And as Moses lifted up the serpent in the wilderness, even so must the Son of man be lifted up; that whosoever believeth in Him may have eternal life." The reference is to the story of the Israelites in the Old Testament when they were bitten by fiery serpents. As the dying Israelite with the poison of the fiery serpent coursing through his veins, was saved by simply looking at the brazen serpent on the

pole, a serpent made in the likeness of the one that had bitten him, and had new life coursing through his veins as soon as he looked, so we dying men, with the poison of sin coursing through our veins, are saved by looking at Jesus Christ "Made in the likeness of sinful flesh," lifted up on the cross, and have new life coursing through our veins the moment we look. All we have to do with our regeneration is to receive Christ as He is presented to us in the Word, by which we are born again. Therefore, "If any man be in Christ he is a new creature (creation). The old things are passed away, behold all things are become new."

In the New Birth the Word of God is the seed; the human heart is the soil; the preacher of the Word is the sower, and drops the seed of the Word of God into the soil of the human heart; God by His Spirit opens the heart to receive the seed (Acts 16:14); the hearer believes; the Spirit quickens the seed into life in the receptive heart; the heart closes around the seed by faith; the new nature, the Divine Nature springs up out of the Divine Word; the believer is "born again," "created anew," "made alive," "passed out of death into life."

Conclusion.

Have you been born again? I put this question to every man and woman here. I do not ask you whether you are a church member. I do not ask if you have been baptised. I do not ask, have you gone regularly to the communion. I do not ask, have you turned over a new leaf. I do not ask, are you an amiable, cultured, intelligent, moral, socially delightful gentleman or lady. I ask you, have you been born again? If not, you are outside of the Kingdom of God and you are bound for an everlasting hell unless you are born again. But if you are not already born again you may be born again to-day, you may be born again before you leave this building, you may be born again right now; for the Word of God says, "As many as received him, to them gave he the right to become children of God, even to them that believe on his name: which were born, not of blood, nor of flesh, nor of the will of man, but of God." And it says again in Rom. 10:9, 10, "If thou shalt confess with thy mouth Jesus as Lord and shalt believe in thy heart that God raised him from the dead, thou shalt be saved: for with the heart man believeth unto righteousness; and with the mouth confession is made unto salvation." These verses make it plain as day just what you must do right here and now to become a child of God. It is up to you to say whether or not you will do it.

Sanctification

"And the God of peace himself sanctify you wholly; and may your spirit and soul and body be preserved entire, without blame at the coming of our Lord Jesus Christ."—1 Thess. 5:23.

Our subject now before us is Sanctification. The subject is one of great importance. Not only is there much ignorance and error and misconception about the subject, but there is, strange to say, most bitter controversy over the subject. So bitter is the controversy over the subject that some years ago there were two rival "holiness conventions" held at the same time in Chicago at different hours of the day, in the same church, and the animosity between these two companies of "holiness brethren" was so intense that on one occasion they came near to having blows at the altar of the church. The subject of Sanctification has given rise to such bitterness and such extravagances in some quarters that many even dread the use of the word "Sanctification." But the word is not only a Bible word, but a deeply significant word, a word full of precious meaning; and it would not be the part of wisdom on our part to give up this good Bible word simply because the word is so often abused. On one occasion a man said to me in the Bible Institute of Chicago, "Are you not afraid of holiness?" Of course what the man meant was, was I not afraid of certain phases of "holiness doctrine" so-called. I replied that I was not nearly as much afraid of holiness as I was of unholiness. The teaching of the Bible on the subject is very plain and very precious. What we have to say this morning will come under three headings. First, What Sanctification Is: 2. How to be Sanctified; 3. When Sanctification Takes Place.

I. WHAT SANCTIFICATION IS

First, then, let us consider what Sanctification is.

1. In the first place let me make it clear that, Sanctification is not the "Baptism with the Holy Spirit." The two are constantly confused. There is an intimate relation between the two, but they are not at all one and the same thing; and only confusion and misconception can arise from confounding two experiences which God keeps separate. That Sanctification is not the baptism with the Holy Spirit and that the baptism with the Holy Spirit is not Sanctification, will become clear as we proceed and find out from a study of the Bible just what Sanctification is.

2. In the second place, let me say that Sanctification is not the eradication of the carnal nature. We will see this when we come to examine God's definition of Sanctification; for God has very clearly defined what Sanctification is and when it takes place. Those who teach "the eradication of the carnal nature" are grasping after a great and precious truth, but they have expressed that truth in a very inaccurate, unfortunate, and unscriptural way, and this way of stating it leads to grave misapprehensions and errors and abuses. The whole controversy about "the eradication of the carnal nature" arises from a misapprehension and from using terms for which there is no warrant in the Bible. The Bible nowhere speaks about "the carnal nature," and so certainly not about "the eradication of the carnal nature." There is such a thing as a carnal nature, but it is not a material thing, not a substance, not a something that can be eradicated as you pull a tooth or remove the vermiform appendix. "A carnal nature" is a nature controlled by the flesh. Certainly it is a believer's privilege not to have his nature governed by the flesh. Our nature should be and may be under the control of the Holy Spirit, and then it is not a carnal nature; but one nature has not been eradicated and another nature put in its place, but our nature is taken out from under the control of the flesh and put under the control of the Holy Spirit. Furthermore, while it is our privilege to have our nature under the control of the Holy Spirit and delivered from

the control of the flesh, we still have "the flesh," and shall have the flesh as long as we are in this body. But if we "walk by the Spirit" we do not "fulfil the lusts of the flesh" (Gal. 5:16). The 8th chapter of Romans describes the life of victory, just as the 7th chapter, 9-24 verse describes the life of defeat, when men are "carnal, sold under sin," but it is in the 8th chapter where life "in the Spirit" is described (Rom. 8:9) that we are told that we still have the flesh, but that it is our privilege not to "live after the flesh," but "by the Spirit," to "put to death the deeds of the body." So we see that the body is there, but in the power of the Spirit we do, day by day and (if we live up to our privilege) every day and every hour and every minute, continuously "put to death the deeds of the body."

3. So much as to what Sanctification is not. We will see exactly what it is if we look at God's definition of Sanctification. We shall find that the word Sanctification is used in the Bible in a two-fold sense.

(1) The first meaning of Sanctification we will find in Lev. 8:10-12, "And Moses took the anointing oil, and anointed the tabernacle and all that was therein, and sanctified them. And he sprinkled thereof upon the altar seven times, and anointed the altar and all its vessels, and the laver and its base, to sanctify them. And he poured of the anointing oil upon Aaron's head and anointed him to sanctify him." Now it is perfectly clear in this passage that to sanctify means to separate or set apart for God, and that Sanctification is the process of setting apart or state of being set apart for God. The word Sanctify is used in this sense over and over again. Another illustration is Lev. 27:14, 17. "And when a man shall sanctify his house to be holy unto God, then the priest shall estimate it, whether it be good or bad: as the priest shall estimate it, so shall it stand . . . and if a man shall sanctify unto Jehovah part of a field of his possession, then the estimation shall be according to the sowing thereof." Here again it is plain that to sanctify means to separate or set apart for God, and that Sanctification is the process of setting apart or state of being set apart for God. Still another illustration of this same use of the word sanctify is found in Num. 8:17, "For all the firstborn among the children of Israel are mine, both man and beast: on the day that I smote all the firstborn in the land of Egypt I sanctified them for

myself." This, of course, does not mean that God, at the time that He smote the firstborn in Egypt, eradicated the carnal nature from the first-born of Israel. It does mean that He set apart all the first-born to be peculiarly His own. Another very suggestive illustration of the same usage of the word is found in the case of Jeremiah as stated by himself in Jer. 1:4, 5, "Now the word of Jehovah came unto me saying, before I formed thee in the belly I knew thee; and before thou camest forth out of the womb I sanctified thee: I have appointed thee a prophet unto the nations." This plainly means that before his birth God set Jeremiah apart for Himself. There would still be much imperfection and infirmity in him, but he was set apart for God. Another suggestive illustration of the same use of the word Sanctify is found in Matt. 23:27, in the words of our Lord Jesus Himself: "Ye fools and blind; for which is greater, the gold, or the temple that hath sanctified the gold?" But perhaps the most striking illustration of all is in what our Lord says about His own sanctification in John 17:19, "And for their sakes I sanctify myself, that they themselves also may be sanctified in truth." Here the plain meaning is that our Lord Jesus set Himself apart for this work for God and He did it in order that believers might be set apart for God "in truth," or "in the truth." This is the most frequent use of the word sanctify. There are numerous illustrations of it in the Bible. So to sanctify means to separate or set apart for God; and Sanctification is the process of setting apart or the state of being set apart for God. This is the primary meaning of the words.

(2) But the word as used in the Bible has also a secondary signification closely related to this primary meaning. An illustration of this secondary meaning will be found in II Chron. 29:5, "Hear me, ye Levites; now sanctify yourselves, and sanctify the house of Jehovah, the God of your fathers, and carry forth the filthiness out of the holy place." Bearing in mind the "parallelism" which is the chief characteristic of Hebrew poetry, it is plain that to sanctify here is synonymous with the "Carry forth the filthiness out of the holy places" found in the last part of the verse. So to sanctify here means to separate from ceremonial or moral defilement, to cleanse; and Sanctification is the process of separating, or state of being separated from ceremonial or moral defilement. The same use of the

word is found in Lev. 11:44, "For I am Jehovah thy God: sanctify yourselves therefore, and be ye holy; for I am holy: neither shall ye defile yourselves with any manner of creeping thing that moveth upon the earth." Here again it is clear that "sanctify yourselves" is synonymous with "be ye holy" and is contrasted with "defile yourselves" and means to separate from ceremonial or moral defilement, to cleanse; and Sanctification is the process of separating or state of being separated from ceremonial or moral defilement. The same meaning of sanctification is found in the New Testament in I Thess. 5:23, "And the God of Peace, Himself sanctify you wholly and may your Spirit and soul and body be preserved entire, without blame at the coming of our Lord Jesus Christ." Here we see the close relation between entire sanctification and preserving wholly, without blame, and to sanctify here clearly means to separate from moral defilement, and sanctification here again is the process of separating or state of being separated from moral defilement. The same thing is evident from the 4th chapter of this same epistle in the 7th verse (I Thess. 4:7), "For God called us not for uncleanness, but in sanctification." Our "Sanctification" is here set in direct contrast with "uncleanness," and hence it is evident that sanctification here means the state of being separated from all moral defilement. The same thing is evident from the 3rd verse of this same chapter, "For this is the will of God, even your sanctification, that ye abstain from fornication." Here again it is evident that Sanctification means separation from impurity or moral defilement. The two meanings, then, of Sanctification are: the process of separating or setting apart, or state of being separated or set apart, for God; and the process of separating or state of being separated from ceremonial or moral defilement. These two meanings of the word are closely allied—one cannot be truly separated to God without being separated from sin.

II. HOW MEN ARE SANCTIFIED

We come now to the second question, How are men sanctified? There are several parts to the complete answer of this question.

1. The first part of the answer is found in our text of this chapter, I Thess. 5:23, "And the God of Peace himself sanctify you wholly and may your Spirit and soul and body be preserved entire, without

blame at the coming of our Lord Jesus Christ." It appears from this verse that God sanctifies men, and Sanctification is God's work. Both the separation of men from sin and their separation unto God, is God's work. As it was God who in the old dispensation set apart the first-born of Israel unto Himself, so it is God who in the new dispensation sets apart the believer unto Himself and separates him from sin. Sanctification is primarily not our work but God's.

2. The second part of the answer is found in Eph. 5:25, 26, "Husbands love your wives, even as Christ also loved the church, and gave himself up for it; that he might sanctify it, having cleansed it by the washing of water by the word." Here we are taught that Christ sanctifies the church and that Sanctification is Christ's work. The question, of course, arises, in what sense does Christ sanctify the church. The answer is found in Heb. 10:10, "By which will we have been sanctified through the offering of the body of Jesus Christ once for all." Here it appears that Jesus Christ sanctifies the church by giving Himself up a sacrifice for it. By thus giving Himself up for it as a sacrifice Christ sets the Church apart for God. Just as the blood of the Passover Lamb in the 11th and 12th chapters of Exodus set a difference between Israel and the Egyptians, so our Lord Jesus by the offering of His own body has forever put a difference between the believer in Himself and the world, and has forever set every believer apart for God. The Cross of Christ stands between the believer and the world. The shed blood of Christ separates the believer from the world, purchases him to God and thus makes him to belong to God.

3. The third part of the answer to the question, how men are sanctified, is found in 2 Thess. 2:13 and in other passages, "But we are bound to give thanks always to God for you, brethren beloved of the Lord, for that God chose you from the beginning unto salvation through sanctification of the Spirit and belief of the truth." It appears from this passage, as from other passages in the Bible, that it is the Holy Spirit who sanctifies the believer, and that Sanctification is the Holy Spirit's work. Here the question arises, In what sense does the Holy Spirit sanctify the believer? In this sense, just as in the Old Testament type, tabernacle, altar and priest were set apart for God by the anointing oil (Lev. 8:10-12), so in the New Testament

anti-type, the believer, who is both tabernacle and priest, is set apart for God by the anointing of the Holy Spirit. Further than that, it is the Holy Spirit's work in the heart that overcomes the flesh and its defilements, and thus separates the believer from sin and clothes him with divine graces of character, and makes him fit to be God's own. As Paul puts it in Gal. 5:22, 23, "But the fruit of the Spirit is love, joy, peace, longsuffering, kindness, goodness, faith, meekness, self-control." In opposition to this work of the Holy Spirit, we read in the immediately preceding verses what "the works of the flesh" are, an awful catalogue of vileness and sin, and we are told in the 16th verse, "Walk in the Spirit and ye shall not fulfil the lust of the flesh."

4. The fourth part of the answer to the question how we are sanctified is found in Heb. 13:12, "Wherefore, Jesus also, that he might sanctify the people through his own blood suffered without the gate." It is plain from this passage that believers are sanctified through the blood of Jesus Christ. Here the question arises, In what sense does the blood of Jesus sanctify? The answer is plain: The blood of Jesus Christ cleanses us from all the guilt of sin, and thus separates us from the mass of men under the curse of the broken law, and sets us apart for God (cf. 1 John 1:7, 9). In the Old Testament dispensation the blood of the sacrifice cleansed the Israelites from the guilt of ceremonial offenses and set them apart for God; in the New Testament anti-type the blood of Christ cleanseth the believer from the guilt of moral offenses and sets him apart for God.

5. The fifth part of the answer to the question, how men are sanctified, is found in John 17:17, "Sanctify them in the truth: thy word is truth." Here our Lord Jesus in His prayer indicates that we are sanctified in the truth, and that the truth is the Word of God. In what sense does the Word of God sanctify? This question is plainly answered in different parts of the Word of God, where we are taught that the Word of God cleanses from the presence of sin, and thus separates us from it and sets us apart to God. (Ps. 119:9, 11; John 15:3.) As we bring our lives into daily contact with the Word, the sins and imperfections of our lives and hearts are disclosed and put away, and thus we are more and more separated from sin unto God. (cf. John 13:10.)

6. The sixth part of the answer to the question, how men are sanctified, is found in 1 Cor. 1:30, "But of Him are ye in Christ Jesus, who was made unto us wisdom from God, and righteousness, and sanctification, and redemption." In this passage we are taught that Jesus Christ was made unto us from God sanctification. Just what does that mean? Simply this: that separation from sin and separation to God are provided for us in Christ Jesus and by the appropriation of Jesus Christ we obtain this sanctification thus provided. The more completely we appropriate Christ the more completely are we sanctified. But perfect sanctification is provided for us in Him, just as perfect wisdom is provided in Him (Col. 2:3). We appropriate either wisdom or sanctification or anything else that is provided for us in Christ in ever-increasing measure. Through the indwelling Christ presented to us by the Spirit in the Word, we are made Christlike and bear fruit.

7. The seventh part of the answer to the question of how men are sanctified is found in Heb. 12:14, "Follow after peace with all men, and the sanctification without which no man shall see the Lord." Here we are taught that we have our own part in sanctification, and that if we are to be sanctified in the fullest sense, sanctification is something that we must pursue, or seek earnestly, if we are to obtain it. While sanctification is God's work, we have our part in it, viz., to make it the object of our earnest desire and eager pursuit.

8. The eighth part of the answer to the question of how we are sanctified is found in Rom. 6:19, 22, "As ye presented your members as servants to uncleanness and to iniquity unto iniquity, even so present your members as servants to righteousness unto sanctification. . . . But now being made free from sin, and become servants to God, ye have your fruit unto sanctification." The meaning of these words is plain, and the teaching important and practical. We are here taught that we attain unto sanctification through presenting our members as servants (bondservants, or slaves) to righteousness and becoming ourselves bondservants unto God. In other words, if we wish to attain unto sanctification we should present our whole body and every member of it to God, to be His servants, belonging wholly unto Him, and we should present ourselves to God as His servants, to be His absolute property. This is the practical method of

attaining unto sanctification, a method that is open to each one of us here to-day, no matter how weak we are in ourselves.

9. The ninth and final part of the answer to the question of how we are sanctified, is found in Acts 26:18, "To open their eyes, that they may turn from darkness to light and from the power of Satan unto God, that they may receive remission of sins and an inheritance among them that are sanctified by faith in Me." Here we are told that we are sanctified by faith in Christ. Sanctification, just as justification, regeneration, and adoption, is conditioned upon faith. Faith is the hand that appropriates to ourselves the blessing of sanctification that God has provided for us through His Son Jesus Christ by His death on the cross, and through the power of the Holy Spirit working in us. And we claim sanctification by simple faith in Him who shed His blood and by surrendering ourselves to the control of the Holy Spirit, Whom Jesus Christ gives.

III. WHEN DOES SANCTIFICATION TAKE PLACE

We now come to the question about which there has been the most discussion, the most differences of opinion, the most controversy. When does sanctification take place? If we will go to our Bibles to get the answer to the question there need be no difference of opinion. There are three parts to the answer.

1. The first part of the answer is found in I Cor. 1:2, "Unto the Church of God, which is at Corinth, even them that are sanctified in Christ Jesus, called to be saints, with all that call upon the name of our Lord Jesus Christ in every place, their Lord and ours." Here the Holy Spirit speaking through the Apostle Paul, plainly declares that all the members of the church of God are already sanctified in Christ Jesus. Sanctification in this sense is not something that we are to look for in the future, it is something that has already taken place. The moment any one becomes a member of the Church of God by simple faith in Christ Jesus, for all who have faith in Christ Jesus are members of the Church of God, that moment that person is sanctified. Every saved man and woman in this building this morning, every one who has living faith in Jesus Christ, is sanctified. Our sanctification is involved in our salvation. But in what sense are we, that is, all believers, already sanctified? The answer to this question

is found in a passage of Scripture to which we have already referred, Heb. 10:10, 14, "By which will we have been sanctified through the offering of the body of Jesus Christ once for all. . . . For by one offering He hath perfected forever them that are sanctified." The meaning is plain. By the offering of the body of Jesus Christ once for all on the Cross of Calvary as a perfect atonement for sin, every believer is cleansed forever from the guilt of sin. We are "perfected forever" as far as our standing before God is concerned, and are set apart for God. The sacrifice of Christ does not need to be repeated as were the Jewish sacrifices (V. I). The work is done once for all, sin is put away, and forever put away (Heb. 9:26; cf. Gal. 3:13), and we are set apart forever as God's peculiar and eternal possession. If any one asks you if you are sanctified; if you are a believer in Jesus Christ, i.e., if you have a living faith, in Jesus Christ, you have a right to say, "I am." Every believer in Christ is a saint, a saint not in the sense in which that word is oftentimes used in modern usage, but in the Bible sense, as being set apart for God and belonging to God and being God's peculiar property. But there is another sense in which every believer may be fully sanctified to-day. This is found in Rom. 12:1, "I beseech you therefore, brethren, by the mercies of God, to present your bodies a living sacrifice, holy, acceptable to God, which is your spiritual service." In this passage we see that it is the believer's present and blessed privilege, and important and solemn duty, to present his body to God a living sacrifice—not some part or parts of the body, but the whole body with its every member and every faculty. And when we do thus present our whole body to God a living sacrifice, then we are wholly sanctified. Such an offering is well-pleasing to God. As God in the Old Testament showed His pleasure in the offering by sending down fire to take it to Himself, so when the whole body is thus offered to God, God will send down fire again, the fire of the Holy Ghost, and take to Himself what is thus presented. The moment a believer does thus present himself a living sacrifice to God, then, so far as his will, the governing purpose of his life, the very centre of his being, is concerned, he is wholly God's, or "perfectly sanctified." He may still, and will still, daily discover, as he studies the Word of God and is illumined by the Holy Spirit, acts of his, habits of life, forms of feeling, speech and action, that are not in conformity with this central purpose of his will, and these must be confessed to God as blameworthy and put away, and this department of his being and life brought, by God's Spirit and the indwelling Christ, into conformity with God's will as revealed in His Word. The victory in this newly discovered and unclaimed territory may be instantaneous. For example, I may discover in myself an irritability of temper that is manifestly displeasing to God. I can go to God, confess it, renounce it and then instantly, not by my own strength, but by looking to Jesus and claiming His patience and gentleness, overcome it and never have another failure in that direction. And so it is with every other sin and weakness in my life that I am brought to see is displeasing to God.

    2. But this is not the whole answer to the question of when we are sanctified. The second part of the answer is found in I Thess. 3:12, "And the Lord make you to increase and abound in love one toward another, and toward all men, even as we also do towards you." And the 4th chapter of this same epistle, the 1st and 10th verses, "Finally then, brethren, we beseech you and exhort you in the Lord Jesus, that as you received of us how ye ought to walk and to please God, even as ye do walk, that ye abound more and more. . . . For indeed ye do it toward all the brethren that are in all Macedonia. But we exhort you, brethren, that ye abound more and more." And in II Pet. 3:18, "Grow in the grace and knowledge of our Lord and Saviour Jesus Christ." And II Cor. 3:18, R. V., "But we all, with unveiled face reflecting as a mirror the glory of the Lord, are transformed into the same image from glory to glory, and even as from the Lord the Spirit." And in Eph. 4:15, 16, "But speaking truth in love, may grow up in all things unto him, who is the head, even Christ; from whom all the body fitly framed and knit together through that which every joint supplieth, according to the working in due measure of each several part, maketh the increase of the body unto the building up of itself in love." From these passages we see that there is a progressive work of Sanctification, an increasing in love, an abounding more and more in a godly walk and in pleasing God, a growing in the grace and the knowledge of our Lord and Saviour Jesus Christ, a being transformed into the image of our Lord from glory unto glory, each new gaze at Him making us more like Him; a growing up into

Christ in all things, until we attain unto a full-grown man, unto the measure of the stature of the fullness of Christ. Here we see there is a progressive work of Sanctification.

3. But we have not found the whole answer to the question of When Men are Sanctified, even yet. We find the remainder of the answer to the question in our text, 1 Thess. 5:23 accurately translated as it is in the Revised Version, "And the God of peace himself sanctify you wholly; and may your spirit and soul and body be preserved entire, without blame at the coming of our Lord Jesus Christ." Here we are plainly told that the complete sanctification of believers, complete in the fullest sense, is something to be sought for in prayer and that is to be accomplished by God in the future and perfected at the coming of our Lord Jesus Christ. The same thought is found in this same book, the 3rd chapter and 12th and 13th verses, "And the Lord make you to increase and abound in love one toward another, and toward all men, even as we do toward you, to the end that he may establish your hearts unblamable in holiness before our God and Father, at the coming of our Lord Jesus with his saints." It is "at the coming of our Lord Jesus with all His saints" that He is to establish our hearts unblamable in holiness before our God and Father and that our spirit and soul and body are to be preserved entire without blame. The same thought is found in I John 3:2, "Beloved, now are we children of God, it is not yet made manifest what we shall be. We know that, if he shall be manifested, we shall be like him, for we shall see him as he is." It is not in the life that now is, and it is not at death, that we are entirely sanctified, spirit, soul, and body. It is at the coming of our Lord Jesus Christ. This is one of the many reasons why the well-instructed believer constantly cries, "Even so, come, Lord Jesus. Come quickly."

XII

The Resurrection of the Body of Jesus and of Our Bodies

"Remember that Jesus Christ of the seed of David, was raised from the dead, according to my gospel."—2 Tim. 2:8.

"For I delivered unto you first of all that which also I received, how that Christ died for our sins according to the scriptures; and that he was buried; and that he hath been raised on the third day according to the scriptures."—1 Cor. 15:3, 4.

"Now, if Christ is preached that he hath been raised from the dead, how say some among you that there is no resurrection of the dead? But if there is no resurrection of the dead, neither hath Christ been raised: and if Christ hath not been raised, then is our preaching vain, your faith also is vain. Yea, and we are found false witnesses of God, because we witnessed of God that he hath raised up Christ: whom he raised not up, if so be that he did not rise. But if the dead are not raised; neither hath Christ been raised: and if Christ hath not been raised, your faith is vain; ye are yet in your sins. Then they also that are fallen asleep in Christ are perished. If in this life only we have hope in Christ, we are of all men most pitiable."—1 Cor. 15:12-19.

We commemorate to-day the resurrection of Christ from the dead. We shall see that the resurrection of Christ was a resurrection of the body of Christ, that it was not merely the indwelling Spirit of Jesus Christ, clothed upon with a new and entirely different body, that appeared to the disciples on the first resurrection day, but that it was the body that was buried, raised again, and that this involves for us not merely the immortality of our souls, but the resurrection and eternal continuance of our bodies. Yet there are many who call themselves Christians and who say that they believe in the Bible, and who consider themselves perfectly orthodox Christians, who do not believe in the Resurrection of the Body, they merely believe in the immortality of the soul.

I. THE FACT OF THE RESURRECTION OF THE BODY OF CHRIST AND OF OUR BODIES

We shall consider first the fact of the resurrection of the body of Jesus Christ and of our bodies.

1. Turn first, please, to II Tim. 2:8, "Remember that Jesus Christ of the seed of David, was raised from the dead, according to my gospel." Here Paul explicitly declares that Jesus Christ was raised from the dead according to the gospel which he preached. Now what was raised? Certainly not His soul. That did not die. Turning to Acts 2:27-31, we find that the soul of the Lord Jesus went into Hades, the abode of the dead. These are Peter's words, spoken on the day of Pentecost, there recorded, "Because thou wilt not leave my soul unto Hades, neither wilt thou give thy holy one to see corruption (i.e., in His body). Thou madest known unto me the ways of life; thou shalt make me full of gladness with thy countenance. Brethren, I may say unto you freely of the patriarch David, that he both died and was buried, and his tomb is with us unto this day. Being therefore a prophet, and knowing that God has sworn with an oath to him that of the fruit of his loins, according to the flesh, he would raise up Christ to sit on his throne; he foreseeing this spake of the resurrection of Christ, that neither was he left unto Hades, nor did his flesh see corruption. This Jesus did God raise up, whereof we all are witnesses." Peter here declares that the soul of Jesus went to Hades and that it was "His flesh," i.e., His body, that was kept from corruption and afterwards raised. Turning now to I Cor. 15:3, 4, we read these words of Paul: "For we delivered unto you first of all that which also I received, how that Christ died for our sins according to the scriptures; and that he was buried; and that he hath been raised on the third day according to the scriptures." Paul here declares that Jesus Christ died and was buried and was raised. What was raised? Paul says, that that which "was buried" was raised. But what was buried? Not the soul of the Lord Jesus, but His body. Peter makes

this even plainer, if possible, in I Pet. 3:18-20: "Because Christ also suffered for our sins once, the righteous for the unrighteous, that he might bring us to God; being put to death in the flesh, but quickened in the spirit; in which also he went and preached to the spirits in prison; which aforetime were disobedient, when the longsuffering of God waited in the days of Noah." These words clearly mean that it was the body of Jesus that was put to death, but that the spirit still lived and went into Hades; so it was the body that was raised and to which the spirit that had not died or become unconscious came back. I Cor. 15:12-19 removes all possibility of doubt on this point on the part of any man who goes to the Bible to find out what it actually teaches and not merely to see how he can twist and distort it to fit it into his own preconceived opinions. Paul's Spirit-given words here read, "Now if Christ be preached that he hath been raised from the dead, how say some among you that there is no resurrection of the dead? (Mark, not no immortality of the soul, but no resurrection of the dead.) But if there is no resurrection of the dead neither hath Christ been raised: and if Christ hath not been raised, then is our preaching vain, your faith also is vain. Yea, and we are found false witnesses of God; because we witness of God that he raised up Christ: whom he raised not up if so be that the dead are not raised. For if the dead are not raised neither hath Christ been raised: and if Christ hath not been raised, your faith is vain, ye are yet in your sins. Then they also that have fallen asleep in Christ have perished. If in this life only we have hoped in Christ, we are of all men most pitiable." There is no honest mistaking the plain meaning of these words: by the "resurrection of the dead" Paul plainly means a resurrection of the body; and in the whole chapter, beyond an honest doubt, he is not talking about the immortality of the soul, but the resurrection of the body. The whole argument turns on that, and Paul here clearly says if the body of Jesus was not raised, then the whole Christian system is a sham and our faith vain and that we Christians of all men are most to be pitied. For if the body of Jesus was not raised, and if our bodies are not to be raised, then we Christians are making tremendous sacrifices for a lie. Paul says further that if our bodies are not to be raised, then Christ's body has not been raised and Christianity is a humbug. Christianity as taught in the New Testament stands or falls with the resurrection of the body of Jesus and the resurrection of our bodies. There is no room in this argument of Paul's for "Pastor" Russell's doctrine, that the resurrection of Jesus Christ was not a resurrection of the body that was laid in the grave, the body that was crucified, and that the body of Jesus Christ, the body that was laid in the sepulchre, was carried away and preserved somewhere, or else dissolved into gases. Paul says here, if the body that was laid in the sepulchre was not raised, "then is our preaching vain" and your "faith also is vain."

In Luke 24:5, 6, the angels at the tomb from which the body of Jesus had disappeared are recorded as saying to the women who were seeking the body of Jesus to embalm it, "Why seek ye the living among the dead? He is not here but is risen." Now what were the women seeking? The body of Jesus to embalm it, and the angels say that what they were seeking was not there but was risen, had been raised. Furthermore, in the remainder of the 6th verse and verse 7, they say: "Remember how he spake unto you when he was yet in Galilee, saying that the Son of Man must be delivered up into the hands of sinful men, and be crucified, and the third day rise again." Here they told the women plainly that what was crucified, which of course was the body of Jesus, was raised. If the actual, literal body of Jesus had not been raised, then these angels were liars. Do you believe that? These are only a few of the very many passages in which it is very clearly taught that the very body of Jesus was raised from the dead. The body of Jesus was raised from the dead and our bodies shall be raised from the dead, else Christianity is a lie from start to finish. But Christ was raised from the dead and we shall be raised. Or, as Paul puts it in the 20th verse of this same chapter, "But now hath Christ been raised from the dead, the first fruits of them that are asleep." Our resurrection, the resurrection of our bodies, will be the harvest that follows the resurrection of the body of Christ, which was "the first fruits."

II. THE CHARACTER OF OUR RESURRECTION BODIES

Having clearly settled the fact of the resurrection of the body of Jesus Christ and of our bodies, let us next consider the character of our resurrection bodies.

1. First of all, we know that the body which is raised will not be exactly the same body that it was when it was laid in the grave. This appears from I Cor. 15:35-38: "But some will say, how are the dead raised? And with what manner of body do they come? Thou foolish one, that which thou thyself sowest is not quickened, except it die: and that which thou sowest, thou sowest not in the body that shall be, but a bare grain, it may chance of wheat, or of some other kind; but God giveth it a body even as it pleased him, and to each seed a body of its own." Here we are told that our bodies when they are raised will not be exactly the same as our bodies when they are buried, any more than the wheat that springs from the kernel of wheat that is planted is the same as the kernel that was planted. But just as what grows from the seed comes from the seed and bears the most intimate relation to the seed, so our resurrection bodies come from the body that is buried and bear the most intimate relation to it. The resurrection body is the outcome of the body that is buried. It is the old body quickened and transformed; or, as Paul puts it in Phil. 3:20, 21: "Jesus Christ . . . shall fashion anew the body of our humiliation, that it may be conformed to the body of his glory, according to the working whereby he is able even to subject all things unto himself."

2. The next thing that the Bible teaches about our resurrection bodies is that they are like the glorified body of Jesus Christ. This appears from the verses just quoted, Phil. 3:20, 21: "The Lord Jesus Christ . . . shall fashion anew the body of our humiliation, that it may be conformed to the body of his glory, according to the work whereby he is able even to subject all things unto himself." Christ's resurrection body was not the same body that was laid in the sepulchre. It was the old body transformed and delivered from the limitations of the body that He had while living here among men, and new qualities imparted to it, and our bodies will also be transformed into the likeness of this glorious body of Christ and thus delivered from the limitations to which they are subjected now, and new qualities imparted to them. It will be a transformed body; the character of its transformation is indicated by the transformation that took place in the body of Jesus Christ. Some suggestion as to what that transformed body of Jesus Christ was like is found in that

anticipation of His resurrection which was seen by Peter, James and John on the mount of transfiguration. Matthew in his description of the appearance of Jesus at His transfiguration, tells us that "His face did shine as the sun, and his garments became white as the light" (Matt. 17:2). Luke tells us that "the fashion of his countenance was altered and His raiment became white and dazzling" (Luke 9:29). Mark tells us that "He was transfigured before them: and his garments became glistering, exceeding white; so as no fuller on earth can whiten them" (Mark 9:2, 3).

3. The next thing that we are told about our resurrection bodies is that they will not be flesh and blood. In I Cor. 15:50, 51 we read, "Now this I say, brethren, that flesh and blood cannot inherit the kingdom of God." Paul is here talking about our resurrection bodies. It is in the resurrection chapter he says this, and he distinctly tells us that our resurrection bodies will not be "flesh and blood."

4. But while our resurrection bodies will not be "flesh and blood," they will have "flesh and bones." This appears from what our Lord Himself says about His own resurrection body in Luke 24:39. Here we read that Jesus said: "See my hands and my feet, that it is I myself: handle me, and see; for a spirit hath not flesh and bones as ye behold me having." As our resurrection bodies are to be transformed into the likeness of His, we also must have "flesh and bones" in our resurrection bodies. Some have fancied that they saw a contradiction between what our Lord says here and what Paul says in the passage quoted above (I Cor. 15:50, 51), but there is no contradiction. "Flesh" we shall have, but not "flesh and blood," i.e., not flesh, the animating principle of which is blood. The question arises, What takes the place of the blood in our resurrection bodies? The answer seems to be that in the present life, "blood is the life" of the natural body, but in the life to come our bodies are to be, as we are told elsewhere in this same chapter, "spiritual bodies," i.e., bodies, the animating principle of which is the Spirit of God, not our own blood. Our not having "blood" in our resurrection bodies involves many great and glorious possibilities, upon which we cannot dwell now.

5. In the fifth place (and closely connected with 3 and 4), our resurrection bodies will be incorruptible. We read in I Cor. 15:42:

"So also is the resurrection of the dead. It is sown in corruption; it is raised in incorruption." The thought of this word "incorruption" is that the body is not subject to decay, it is imperishable. Our present bodies are decaying all the time. We are perishing every day and every minute. My present body is disintegrating while I talk to you. But the bodies that we shall receive in the resurrection will be absolutely free from the liability to corruption or decay. They cannot disintegrate or suffer decay or deterioration of any kind.

6. The next thing that we are taught about the resurrection body is that it is a glorious body. This comes out in the first part of the following verse, I Cor. 15:43, "It is sown in dishonour; it is raised in glory." Some idea of the glory, the glorious beauty, of that body is suggested by the representation of our glorified Lord that we have in Rev. 1:13-17: "And in the midst of the candlesticks one like unto the Son of man, clothed with a garment down to the foot and girt about the breasts with a golden girdle. And his head and his hair were white as white wool, white as snow, and his eyes were as a flame of fire and his feet like unto burnished brass, as if it had been refined in a furnace, and his voice as the voice of many waters. And he had in his right hand seven stars: and out of his mouth proceeded a sharp two-edged sword: and his countenance was as the sun shineth in his strength. And when I saw him, I fell at his feet as one dead, and he laid his right hand upon me saying, Fear not; I am the first and the last." Our resurrection bodies will be like that.

7. Furthermore, our resurrection bodies will be powerful, or as we read in the last half of this same verse (1 Cor. 15:43), "It is sown in weakness, it is raised in power." Then all our weariness and weakness will be forever at an end. In our present bodies our bodies are oftentimes a hindrance to our highest aspirations, they thwart the carrying out of our loftiest purposes, we cannot put into execution our loftiest purposes, "the spirit is willing but the flesh is weak." But in our resurrection bodies the body will be able to accomplish all that the spirit purposes. The redeemed body will be a perfect counterpart of the redeemed spirit that inhabits it. No deafness, dimsightedness nor blindness, no tired hands and feet, no maimed soldier boys coming home from the war.

8. It will be a heavenly body. This appears from the 47th to the

49th verses of this same chapter. "The first man is of (literally, out of) the earth, earthy: the second man is of (literally, out of) heaven: as is the earth, such are they also that are earthy: and as is the heavenly such are they also that are heavenly. And as we have borne the image of the earthy, we shall also bear the image of the heavenly." The thought plainly is that our present bodies are of an earthly origin and an earthly character, but that the transformed body will be of a heavenly character. Paul explains it at length in 2 Cor. 5:1-4 where he says, "For we know that if the earthly house of our tabernacle be dissolved, we have a building from God, a house not made with hands, eternal, in the heavens. For verily in this (i.e., in this present earthly house, earthy body) we groan, longing to be clothed upon with our habitation which is from heaven (i.e., our heavenly body): if so be that being clothed we shall not be found naked. For indeed we that are in this tabernacle (i.e., in the present earthy body) groan, being burdened; not for that we would be unclothed, but that we would be clothed upon (i.e., with our heavenly body), that what is mortal may be swallowed up of life."

9. Our transformed bodies will be luminous, shining, dazzling, bright like the sun. This is seen in many passages. For example, Matt. 13:43, "Then shall the righteous shine forth as the sun in the kingdom of their Father." This is to be taken literally for it is in the interpretation of the parable and not in the parable. This suggests what we have already seen about the transfigured body of Jesus in Matt. 17:2, where we are told that "His face did shine as the sun, and his garments became white as the light." We have the same thought also in the Old Testament in Dan. 12:3, where we are told, "And they that are wise shall shine as the brightness of the firmament; and they that turn many to righteousness as the stars forever and ever." They shall shine literally as well as figuratively. Some suggestion of what the luminous glory of our faces and forms in our resurrection bodies will be is seen in the light that Paul tells us that he saw beaming from the person of Jesus when the glorified Jesus met him on the Damascus road. In Paul's description of what he saw on that occasion, as given in Acts 26:12, 13, we read, "Whereupon as I journeyed to Damascus with the authority and commission of the chief priests, at midday, O king, I saw on the way a light from heaven, above the brightness of

the sun, shining around about me and them that journeyed with me." The light that Saul saw, as is evident from the whole account, was the light that shone from the person of our glorified Lord, and in our resurrection bodies we shall be like Him.

10. Three interesting facts regarding our resurrection bodies are stated in Matt. 22:30 and Luke 20:35, 36. In Matt. 22:30 we read: "For in the resurrection they neither marry, nor are given in marriage, but are as angels in heaven." In Luke 20:35, 36 we read: "But they that are counted worthy to attain to that world, and the resurrection of the dead, neither marry, nor are given in marriage: for neither can they die any more: for they are equal unto the angels; and are sons of God, being sons of the resurrection." Taking these two passages together, we learn that our resurrection bodies are like the angels, that we do not marry in our resurrection bodies and that these bodies cannot die any more.

11. Though all these resurrection bodies are glorious, they differ from one another, each one having its own peculiar glory. This appears from 1 Cor. 15:41, 42: "There is one glory of the sun, and another glory of the moon, and another glory of the stars; for one star differeth from another star in glory. So also is the resurrection from the dead." Glorious as all our bodies shall be, there will be no tiresome uniformity even of glory in the world of resurrection bodies. Each body will have its own peculiar glory.

12. Let us say finally in regard to the character of our resurrection body, that the resurrection of our body will be the consummation of our adoption, i.e., of our placing as sons, our manifestations as sons of God. In Rom. 8:23 we read: "We, which have the first fruits of the Spirit, even we ourselves groan within ourselves, waiting for our adoption (i.e., our placing as sons), to wit, the redemption of our body." The resurrection body will be the consummation of our placing as sons, i.e., in the resurrection body it will be outwardly manifested that we are sons of God. Before His incarnation Christ was "in the form of God." (Phil. 2:6), i.e., in the visible appearance of God. So shall we also be in the resurrection, for our bodies shall be like His. This throws light upon what Paul meant when he said in Col. 3:4: "When Christ, who is our life, shall be manifested, then shall we also with him be manifested in glory." And also it throws

light on what John meant when he says in I John 3:2, R. V.: "Beloved, now are we the children of God, and it is not yet made manifest what we shall be. We know that, if he shall be manifested, we shall be like him; for we shall see him as he is."

III. WHEN WILL THE RESURRECTION OF THE BODY TAKE PLACE?

There remains but one question to be considered and we can deal with that very briefly. That question is, when will the resurrection of the body take place? This question is plainly answered time and again in the Bible. For example, it is answered in Phil. 3:20, 21: "For our citizenship is in heaven; from whence also we wait for a Saviour, the Lord Jesus Christ: Who shall fashion anew the body of our humiliation, that it may be conformed to the body of his glory, according to the working whereby he is able even to subject all things unto himself." Here it is plainly declared that the transformation of our bodies into the likeness of the glorious body of Christ will take place when the Lord Jesus whom we are awaiting shall appear from heaven. The same thought is given in I Thess. 4:16, 17: "For the Lord Himself shall descend from heaven, with a shout, with the voice of the archangel, and with the trump of God: and the dead in Christ shall rise first; then we which are alive, that are left, shall together with them be caught up in the clouds, to meet the Lord in the air: and so shall we ever be with the Lord." The question will arise in some of our minds, what about us in the meantime if we chance to die before the coming of the Lord? This question also is plainly answered in II Cor. 5:1-8: "For we know that if the earthly house of our tabernacle (our present bodies) be dissolved (die and decay) we have a building from God, a house not made with hands (our resurrection body that we are to get at the coming of the Lord), eternal, in the heavens. For verily in this (i.e., while living in this present body) we groan, longing to be clothed upon with our habitation which is from heaven (our resurrection body) if so be that being clothed we shall not be found naked. For indeed we that are in this tabernacle (this present earthy body) do groan, being burdened; not for that we would be unclothed (i.e., not that we would merely get rid of our present bodies), but that we would be clothed upon (i.e., that we would receive our resurrection bodies) that what is mortal may be swallowed up of life. Now he that wrought us for this very thing is God, who gave unto us the earnest of the Spirit (i.e., the Holy Ghost, whom we have received as the earnest of the full redemption in our resurrection bodies which are to be obtained at the coming of the Lord). Being therefore always of good courage and knowing that, whilst we are at home in the body (i.e., while we are still in our earthly life in this present earthly body) we are absent from the Lord (for we walk by faith not by sight); we are of good courage, I say, and are willing rather to be absent from the body (i.e., to have our present earthly body die even before we get our resurrection bodies, which we shall not get until the return of the Lord), and to be at home with the Lord." The teaching of this plainly is that if we die before the return of the Lord and therefore before we obtain our resurrection body, our spirits are unclothed, i.e., they are unclothed from this present body and not yet clothed upon with the resurrection body, but that we are "at home with the Lord" in conscious blessedness, in a condition that is far better than that that we are in in this present life (see Phil. 1:23, R. V.), but not so perfect as that condition which shall be when our redeemed spirits are clothed upon with our resurrection bodies. It will be at the return of the Lord Jesus that we get our full redemption. That is one reason why "we wait" (literally, assiduously wait) for Him (Phil. 3:20, 21, see Greek). That is one reason why we long for the return of the Lord. There are many reasons why we long for the return of our Lord. All the great problems that are confronting us at this present time in national and international life, in social, commercial and political life, will be solved when He comes, and will never be solved until He comes; and for these reasons we long for Him. But we long for Him also because while this present body serves many a useful purpose for the redeemed spirit that inhabits it, it is often a hindrance. It is often subject to aches and pains, to frailties, and it is a constant temptation to folly. But when our Lord Jesus comes again He will transform this present body of our humiliation into the likeness of His own glorious body and at that time we shall know what "full salvation" means, when we shall shine forth as the sun in the kingdom of our Father.

XIII
THE DEVIL

"The Devil. . . .is."—John 8:44.
"The Devil Sinneth."—1 John 3:8.

INTRODUCTION

Our subject in this chapter is The Devil. I have two texts—John 8:44: "The Devil. . . .is."

The second text is 1 John 3:8: "The Devil Sinneth." The Bible doctrine concerning the Devil, his Existence, Nature, Character, Work and Destiny is a fundamental doctrine of the Christian faith, and is of vital importance. The teaching of the Bible on this subject is not a mere matter of theory or dogma. It is a matter of most practical every day importance. Experience shows that if men are in error in regard to this subject, they are pretty sure to be in error on other questions that are fundamental. When men and women begin to question the existence of a personal Devil it is pretty sure that before long they will be questioning a good many other things regarding which a true child of God should have no questions. Doubt of the existence of a personal Devil is widespread to-day. Many preachers in supposedly orthodox pulpits do not hesitate to say, "I do not believe in the existence of a personal Devil." Denial of the existence of a personal Devil is one of the main points in the system which is so widespread to-day, and which is doing so much evil, that with considerable reason it has been called "The Devil's Masterpiece"—Christian Science. A well-known and popular pastor in this city some months ago proclaimed to his people that he was going to preach to them a gospel "without an atonement of blood, without an infallible

Bible, without hell, and without a personal Devil." If he does preach to them a system of doctrine without any of these he will preach some other system of doctrine than that which is contained in the book, which our Lord Jesus Christ has endorsed as the Word of God, i.e., the Bible.

I. THERE IS A DEVIL

The first point to make clear is that there is a Devil. This is plain from our first text, John 8:44: "The Devil....is." The whole verse reads: "Ye are of your father, the devil, and the lusts of your father it is your will to do: He was a murderer from the beginning, and abode not in the truth, because there is no truth in him. When he speaketh a lie, he speaketh of his own: for he is a liar, and the father thereof." These are the words of Jesus Christ. With any one who has any right to call himself a Christian, the words of Jesus Christ have infinitely more weight than the words of Mrs. Mary Baker Eddy or any one else, or all others together, and Jesus here says, "The Devil....is." But this is not the only passage by any means in which our Lord Jesus asserts in the most emphatic and most unmistakable terms the existence of the Devil. Turn to Matt. 13:19, and you will read these words: "When any one heareth the word of God, and understandeth it not, then cometh the evil one and snatcheth away that which has been sown in his heart." These words are found in the interpretation of a parable—the Parable of the Sower. It is impossible to say that these words are figurative. In parables we have figures, in the explanation of the parables we have the literal facts that the figures symbolise, and these words are not taken from the parable, but from our Lord's own explanation of the parable, and here we are distinctly told that there is a person, who is here called "The Evil One," whose business it is to snatch away the Word of God when it has been sown in hearts that do not understand and heed it. If evil is only impersonal and our Lord had only referred to impersonal influences, or human influences, as taking away the Word out of the hearts where it had been sown, these words of His would be utterly without meaning. That Jesus Christ believed that there was a person of whom He here speaks as "The Evil One" and of whom He elsewhere speaks, as we shall see directly, as "The Devil," admits of no doubt if we grant that the Lord Jesus was an honest man. We must, therefore, if we believe in the Lord Jesus, believe that there is a Devil. We can deny his existence only by questioning either the honesty or the intelligence of our Lord. He certainly taught that there was a Devil. It would be easy to show from the teachings of Peter (1 Pet. 5:8, 9; Acts 5:3) and from the teachings of John (John 13:2) and from the teachings of Paul (Eph. 6:10-12) also that there is a Devil; but that is unnecessary for any one who has any right to call himself a Christian, for if the Lord says so, that settles it, and the Lord Jesus does say "The devil. . . .is." If there is no Devil, then our Lord Jesus was either a fool or a fraud. The question of believing in the personality of the Devil involves the honour of our Lord Jesus. If His teaching is not to be trusted on this point, it is not to be trusted on any other point, and the denial of a personal Devil involves the trustworthiness of the Lord Jesus as a Teacher and a Saviour at every point. So we see that the question of the existence of the Devil is fundamental and of vital importance.

II. THE NATURE OF THE DEVIL

Having settled it that there is a Devil, we now face the question as to the nature of the Devil.

1. First of all, the Bible teaches us that the Devil is a person. This comes out in our second text, 1 John 3:8: "The devil sinneth." Only a person can sin. When we say that the Devil is a person we do not mean that necessarily he has a body, certainly not such a body as he is pictured as having in various paintings and engravings that are supposed to represent the Devil. A person is any being who knows and feels and wills. When we say that the Devil is a person we mean that he is a being who has intelligence, feeling and will, that he is not a mere principle of evil. The personality of the Devil is taught over and over again in the Bible. Just a few illustrations in addition to our texts. Turn again to Matt. 13:19: "When any one heareth the word of God, and understandeth it not, then cometh the evil one, and snatcheth away that which hath been sown in his heart." The representation of this passage is the representation of a person. He is called "The Evil One," not merely "evil," but "The Evil One," which of course is the representation of a person. If evil is only

impersonal, or if it only works through human beings, these words of our Lord Jesus would be without meaning. The personality of the Devil comes out again very clearly and very forcibly in Eph. 6:10-12: "Finally, brethren, be strong in the Lord and the strength of his might. (11) Put on the whole armour of God, that ye may be able to stand against the wiles of the devil. (12) For our wrestling is not against flesh and blood, but against the principalities, against the powers, against the world rulers of this darkness, against the spiritual hosts of wickedness in the heavenly places." Here Paul distinctly tells us that the great reason why we need to be strong in the Lord and in the strength of His might and why we need to put on the whole armour of God, is because there is a being of great cunning, subtlety and power, a person named "The Devil," and that this being has under him a multitude of other personalities of such dignity and power as to be called by the titles: "principalities," "powers," "world rulers," "spiritual hosts of wickedness." Beyond a question our Lord Jesus, and the Apostle Peter and the Apostle John and the Apostle Paul believed in and taught the existence of a personal Devil. If there is not a personal Devil we may as well give up our Bible, for in that case it is a book that is full of folly and of fraud. If there is not a personal Devil we must give up our belief in the inspired authority of the Apostle Paul, the Apostle Peter, the Apostle John, and we must give up our faith in the Lord Jesus Christ. No intelligent student of the Bible can retain his faith in the inspiration and authority of that Book, or his faith in the Lord Jesus Christ, if he gives up belief in the existence of a personal Devil. As intelligent men and women, we must take our choice between believing in the existence of a personal Devil or giving up our faith in Jesus Christ and Christianity. Any system of doctrine that denies the existence of a personal Devil is radically unchristian whatever name it may arrogate to itself.

2. The second thing that the Bible teaches as to the nature of the Devil, is that, the Devil is a being of very great power and authority. This comes out in the verses we have just read, Eph. 6:10, 11: "Finally be strong in the Lord, and in the power of his might. (11) Put on the whole armour of God, that ye may be able to stand against the wiles of the devil." These words make it clear that the Devil is

so mighty that the people of God cannot resist his cunning wiles without having on the whole armour of God, and it is also evident from the 10th verse that we cannot resist his power unless we are strengthened with the strength of God. And this is not all: in the 12th verse we read: (12) "For our wrestling is not against flesh and blood, but against the principalities, against the powers, against the world rulers of this darkness, against the spiritual hosts of wickedness in the heavenly places." These are tremendous words. If they mean anything, they certainly mean that there are beings of great authority and dignity who are under the leadership of the one supreme being of evil, the Devil. The conflict that we have on hand as believers in Christ is terrific. The conflict that the Allies have on hand with the mighty military forces of the Kaiser is nothing to the battle we have on hand with the Devil and his hosts. We are fools if we underestimate the battle. On the other hand, we must not over-estimate it. While our conflict is with the Devil, and while our wrestling is against "the principalities," against "the powers," against "the world-rulers," against "the spiritual hosts of wickedness," nevertheless He that is for us is far mightier than they. The Devil is mighty but our Saviour is almighty. It is quite possible for one to become morbid over this subject of the Devil, and to become utterly discouraged and even deranged. That is entirely unnecessary and unwarranted. While our conflict is with the Devil and his mighty hosts, God has provided for us a strength and an armour whereby we may "be able to quench all the fiery darts of the Evil One" and to "withstand in the evil day, and having done all to stand" (v. 13).

3. The third thing that the Bible teaches us as to the Nature of the Devil is that, the Devil is a being of great majesty and dignity of position. Turn to Jude 8, 9: "Yet in like manner these also in their dreamings defile the flesh, and set at nought dominion, and rail at dignities (the literal translation of the Greek word rendered dignities is "glories"). (9) But Michael the Archangel, when contending with the devil he disputed about the body of Moses, durst not bring against him a railing judgment, but said, The Lord rebuke thee." From these words it is evident that the position of the Devil was so exalted that even Michael the archangel did not dare to bring a railing judgment against him. The context seems to imply that the position of the

Devil was more exalted than that of Michael the archangel himself. The Devil of the Bible is not at all the Devil of common thought. He is not a being hideous in appearance, with hoofs and horns and tail. He is not even the being pictured by Milton or Bunyan. He is a being of very great original majesty and dignity, a being of great wisdom and power. When people talk lightly and contemptuously about the Devil they display gross ignorance of what the Bible teaches about him. It is true that he is evil in character and therefore called "The Evil One" (John 5:19, R. V.). It is true he is a liar and a murderer (John 8:44), it is true that he is full of malignity (II Cor. 4:4): but he is a being of great dignity and majesty, so that even Michael the archangel durst not bring against him a railing accusation.

4. The Bible teaches furthermore that the Devil is "the prince of this world." Our Lord Jesus Himself taught this. He says in John 12:31: "Now is the judgment of this world; now shall the prince of this world be cast out." The Greek word translated "world" in this passage is kosmos, and the thought is of the present world order, and our Lord's teaching is that the Devil is the prince of this present world order. We have the same teaching of our Lord in John 14:30, where we read: "I will no more speak much with you, for the prince of the world cometh: and he hath nothing in me." These words of our Lord are found in what many regard as the most precious chapter in the Bible, the 14th chapter of John, and if we give up this teaching of our Lord regarding Satan we must give up, not merely the Bible as a whole, but this most precious chapter in the Bible. We find the Lord teaching the same thing again on that same night, the night before His crucifixion, in John 16:11 where he says: "The prince of this world is judged"—the evident reference being to Satan.

How the Devil came to be Prince of this world it may be impossible for us to say, but that he is so admits of no question, if we are to accept the teaching of Jesus Christ, and any one who will study the ruling principles of commercial life, of political life, of social life, and above all of international relations, to such an one it will become perfectly evident that the Devil is the one who is master of the present order of things. If we ever doubted before that there was a Devil, and just such a Devil as the Bible pictures, we can scarcely doubt it now, when we consider the action of the rulers of the earth in this present mad world war. How could beings so intelligent in matters of science and philosophy and economics as the present rulers of Germany are, ever be guilty of plunging the nations of the earth into this mad war? There is but one reasonable answer: because there is a Devil who rules the present Kosmos, or world order, and he controls the Kaisers and the Reichstags of the world and will until the true Prince comes, the Prince of Peace, our Lord Jesus Christ.

III. THE CHARACTER OF THE DEVIL

1. As to the character of the Devil, the Bible teaches us that he is a being absolutely wicked. In Matt. 13:19 he is called, "The Wicked One." That is to say, he is one who is the personal embodiment of absolute wickedness. In I John 5:19 R. V. also he is called "The Wicked One." God is "The Holy One," that is to say the One who is the personal embodiment of perfect holiness. The Devil is just His opposite, the personal embodiment of consummate wickedness.

2. The Devil is to evil what God is to good. In I John 3:8, we read: "He that doeth sin is of the devil; for the devil sinneth from the beginning. To this end was the son of God manifested, that he might destroy the works of the devil." This does not mean that the Devil sinned from the very origin of all things and that he was created sinful, for we learn from Ezek. 28:15 that the Devil was created upright. The verse does mean, however, that Satan is the original sinner. The expression "from the beginning" is characteristic of the epistle from which these words are taken and does not necessarily mean from the origin of things (see for example verse 11). In a similar way we are told in one of our texts—John 8:44—that the Devil was a murderer from the beginning and that he is "A liar and the father of it." There is absolutely "no truth in him." So much for the nature and character of the Devil.

IV. THE WORK OF THE DEVIL

We come now to the question of the Work of the Devil, or How the Devil Manifests Himself, and What He Does.

1. In the first place we are taught that the Devil tempts men to sin. We have a most striking illustration of this in his temptation of

our Lord. We have in the Bible three accounts of this temptation. We will look at Matthew's account. Matt. 4:1-9: "Then was Jesus led up of the Spirit into the wilderness to be tempted of the devil. (2) And when he had fasted forty days and forty nights, he afterward hungered. (3) And the tempter came and said unto him, If thou art the son of God, command that these stones become bread. (4) But he answered and said, It is written, man shall not live by bread alone, but by every word that proceedeth out of the mouth of God. (5) Then the devil taketh him into the Holy City; and he set him on the pinnacle of the temple. (6) And saith unto Him, If thou art the Son of God, cast thyself down: for it is written, he shall give his angels charge concerning thee: and, on their hands they shall bear thee up, lest haply thou dash thy foot against a stone. (7) Jesus said unto him, Again it is written, thou shalt not make trial of the Lord thy God. (8) Again, the devil taketh him unto an exceeding high mountain, and showeth him all the kingdoms of the world, and the glory of them; (9) And He said unto him, All these things will I give thee, if thou wilt fall down and worship me." Of course we have not time this morning to go into the whole question of our Lord's temptation, but this much is certainly plain, that the Devil is represented as the tempter, tempting our Lord. If there is no personal Devil, as so many would have us believe, or if he is not the tempter, there would be absolutely no reason for bringing him into this account. As the Devil tempted our Lord, so he tempts us to-day. And it is to be noticed that he does not tempt us merely to gross animal lusts and vile sins, but with subtle spiritual temptations, and above all he tempts us to doubt God's Word. It was with this form of temptation that he first assaulted our Lord. God had just said to the Lord Jesus at His baptism, "Thou art my beloved Son; in thee I am well pleased" (Luke 3:22), and Satan came insinuating doubt of God's Word by beginning his temptation with these words: "If thou art the Son of God," and again further down in the temptation, he repeats the doubt, saying to the Lord Jesus again: "If thou art the Son of God." In just the same way Satan began his assault upon Eve in the Garden of Eden, by insinuating a doubt of God's Word and of God's goodness. He began by saying: "Yea, hath God said. ...?" (Gen. 3:2), and further on when Eve stated exactly what God had said, the Devil flatly contradicted and said: "Ye shall not surely die" (literally, Dying, thou shalt not die) when God had said: "Thou shalt surely die" (Dying, thou shalt die). This is Satan's favourite method of attack to-day. He gets us to doubt God's Word. Satan's most effective mode of work is by leading men into doubt and into error on fundamental points. The saloons and the gambling hells and the brothels are not the chief spheres of Satan's activities, but the schools and colleges and theological seminaries where he is inducing men and women, and callow youths and maidens, to doubt the truth of God's Word, and to reject the fundamental truths of God's word and accept Satan's errors in their place. Satan knows well; that, if he can get men to doubting God's Word, it is easy to lead them into the vilest sins. False doctrine has been a more prolific source of the vilest sins than even the saloons.

2. But Satan not merely tempts men to sin by insinuating doubts of God's Word, he also has his synagogues and ministers among men to do his work. Turn to Rev. 3:9: "Behold, I give of the synagogue of Satan, of them that say they are Jews, and are not, but do lie; behold, I will make them to come and worship before thy feet, and to know that I have loved thee." What I wish you to notice here are the words, "The synagogue of Satan." In this case it was a Jewish synagogue, but now-a-days, it is often a so-called Christian church. In II Cor. 11:14, 15 we have an even more remarkable passage: "For even Satan fashioneth himself into an angel of light. (15) It is no great thing therefore if his ministers also fashion themselves as ministers of righteousness; whose end shall be according to their works." Here we are told that Satan has his ministers. They do not advertise themselves as ministers of Satan, oftentimes they are not even conscious that they are; but they put themselves forward as "ministers of righteousness." They advocate "ethical culture," a system of salvation without atoning blood. They are frequently men of very attractive personality and great intellectual brilliance and ability, but they are doing the Devil's work. Satan is never so dangerous as when he "Fashioneth himself into an angel of light," and no other ministers of his are so dangerous as the men and women of attractive personality and brilliant intellectual gifts who are undermining the faith of God's children, or who are teaching

various forms of seductive and alluring error, "Christian Science," "New Thought," "Theosophy," "Occultism" (Spiritualism), and all that species of cults.

3. We have not time to speak here of Satan's work as the author of sickness (Acts 10:38; Luke 13:16), and as the one who has the power of death (Heb. 2:14).

4. But we must also speak of another work of the Devil. It is set forth in II Cor. 4:3, 4, R. V.: "And even if our gospel is veiled, it is veiled in them that perish: (4) In whom the god of this world hath blinded the minds of the unbelieving, that the light of the gospel of the glory of Christ, who is the image of God should not dawn upon them." We read here that it is the work of Satan to blind the minds of unbelievers in order "That the light of the gospel of the glory of Christ, who is the image of God, should not dawn upon them." It is evident then that the Devil is the author of false views, especially false views of the person of Christ. He is the author of Unitarianism, and the denial of the Deity of our Lord in all its forms. He so blinds the minds of men who submit to his blinding that the Divine "Glory of Christ," "who is the very image of God," is hidden from them. This explains why it is that Unitarianism in all its various forms persists even after its folly has been so often exposed. Satan's work along this line is to culminate at the appearing of the Anti-Christ, "Even he, whose coming is according to the working of Satan with all power, and signs and lying wonders, and with all deceit of unrighteousness for them that perish; because they received not the love of the truth, that they might be saved." (II Thess. 2:9, 10, R. V.)

V. THE DEVIL'S DESTINY

We come now to the fifth general division of our subject—The Devil's Destiny.

1. Turn in the first place to Rev. 20:1-3: "And I saw an angel coming down out of heaven, having the keys of the abyss and a great chain in his hand. And he laid hold of the dragon, the old serpent, which is the devil and Satan, and bound him for a thousand years, and cast him into the abyss, and shut it, and sealed it over him, that he should deceive the nations no more, until the thousand years

should be finished: After this he must be loosed for a little time." We are here taught that at the Second Coming of our Lord Jesus Christ Satan shall be bound with a great chain and cast into the abyss for a thousand years. The abyss, or as it is translated in the Authorised Version, "bottomless pit," does not mean hell. Satan, as we shall see further on, shall be cast into hell later.

2. Turn now to Rev. 20:7, 8: "And when the thousand years are finished, Satan shall be loosed out of his prison, and shall come forth to deceive the nations which are in the four corners of the earth, Gog and Magog, to gather them together to the war: The number of whom is as the sand of the sea." We are here taught that at the end of the Millennium, the thousand years, Satan shall be loosed for a little season from the abyss into which he has been cast chained, and that he shall come forth to deceive the nations. But the time of his power then will be very brief.

3. In Rev. 20:10 we find the ultimate destiny of the Devil: "And the devil that deceived them was cast into the lake of fire and brimstone, where are also the beast and the false prophet; and they shall be tormented day and night for ever and ever." Here is one of the points at which the theories of the "Reconciliation" people and "Universalists" generally break down. The argument of the Reconciliationists and Universalists, by which they attempt to prove that all men must ultimately be saved, carried to its logical issue, if it proved anything, would prove the salvation of Satan also, and this many of them do teach. They say plainly that the Devil will ultimately be brought to repentance and saved. Indeed that is what I believed and taught in my early ministry. But this passage which we have just read shows the impossibility of this being true. "The lake of fire" was "prepared for the Devil and his angels." Our Lord Himself says in Matt. 25:41 that when He comes back to judge this world He will say to those on His left hand: "Depart from me, ye cursed into the eternal fire, which is prepared for the devil and his angels." Hell was not prepared for men, but for the Devil and his angels. If any man goes there it will be because he has chosen to cast in his lot with the Devil rather than with God. Therefore they go where the Devil goes. Every one who rejects Jesus Christ is throwing in his lot with

the Devil.

VI. HOW TO GET VICTORY OVER THE DEVIL

Now just for a few moments let me show you from the Word of God, how, in practical every day life, to get the victory over the Devil. There are four things to be borne in mind.

1. Read first, James 4:7, "Be subject therefore unto God: but resist the devil, and he will flee from you." This teaches us that, we are first of all to surrender to God and then to resist the Devil and that, if we do resist him, for all his cunning and power, he will flee from us. Although the Devil is strong, it is ours in God's strength to withstand him and overcome him.

2. Now turn to I John 2:14: "I have written unto you, fathers, because ye know him which is from the beginning. I have written unto you young men, because ye are strong, and the word of God abideth in you, and ye have overcome the evil one." This passage teaches us that, it is when we feed upon the Word of God and store the Word of God in our hearts, thus having it abiding in us, that we shall be able to overcome the Devil. If we neglect the study of the Bible for a single day, we leave an open door for the Devil to enter. I have been a Christian for forty-three years, but I would not dare to neglect the study of God's word for one single day. Why not? Because there is a Devil; and, if I neglect the study of the Word of God for a single day, I leave a window open for him to enter and leave myself too weak to cope with him and conquer him. But if we will feed upon the Word of God daily, and trust in God, we can resist the devil at every point. Though the Devil is cunning and strong, God is stronger, and God imparts His strength to us through His written word.

3. Turn now to Eph. 6:11: "Put on the whole armour of God, that ye may be able to stand against the wiles of the devil." Here we are taught that, in order "to stand against the wiles of the Devil" we must "Put on the whole armour of God." What that armour is, is found in the verses that immediately follow. This armour, this whole armour, this "panoply of God," is at our disposal. The fact that there is a Devil, that he is a being of such majesty, dignity, cunning, and power, that he is so incessantly plotting our ruin and to undermine our faith, is no reason for fear or discouragement. By taking "the

shield of faith" we shall be "able to quench all the fiery darts of the evil one," by taking "the helmet of salvation," and the "sword of the Spirit which is the Word of God," and by "praying always with all prayer and supplication in the Spirit," it is our privilege to have victory over the Devil every day of our lives, every hour of the day, and every minute of the hour.

4. The final step in the way to get victory over Satan is found in Eph. 6:10: "Finally, be strong in the Lord, and in the strength of his might." The way to get victory over Satan is to give up all confidence in our own strength and believe in the almighty strength of Jesus Christ and claim that strength for ourselves. It is in the strength of Jesus Christ's might that we shall get the victory over "the evil one." In the strength of His might, as we have already said, it is our privilege to have victory over the Devil every day of our lives, every hour of the day and every minute in the hour. Hallelujah!

XIV
Is There a Literal Hell?

"In danger of the hell of fire."—Matt. 5:22.

My subject is "Is There a Literal Hell?" I wish that the things that I am going to preach to you were not true. God wishes so, too, "The Lord is longsuffering to usward, not wishing that any should perish, but that all should come to repentance" (2 Peter 3:9). But God has made us in His own image, with a moral nature, with a capacity for self-determination, with a power of choice; and men can if they will choose darkness instead of light. They can choose to trample God's saving love under foot. They can choose to reject the One who was wounded for their transgressions and bruised for their iniquities, and upon whom the chastisement of their peace was laid; and some will so choose. I am sorry that they will. I would be willing to die to save them. The Lord Jesus did die to save them. But they spurn Him. So these things that I am to speak to-night are true and I am going to preach them in order that you may know them, and in order that you may be sure of them. I am going to preach about hell to keep as many of you as possible from going there.

Is There a Literal Hell? Almost all intelligent people who believe that there is a future life at all, believe that men and women who sin in the present life and who die impenitent and unsaved will be punished to some extent at least in the life that is to come. They believe that whoever sins must suffer, and that the suffering which sin causes will not be limited to this present life. But, while almost all intelligent people who believe in a future life at all believe that there is some kind of future punishment, there are many that do not believe in a literal hell, that is, in a place of awful and unutterable torment. Is there a hell? Is there a place to which impenitent men and women will go some time after death and suffer agonies far beyond those that any one suffers here on earth? Some say, "yes," there is a hell. Many, even including not a few supposedly orthodox preachers, say, "No, the only hell is the inward hell in a man's heart." How are we to settle this question? How are we to determine who is right? We cannot settle it as some are trying to settle it by "counting noses." Majorities are not always right. Especially is it true that majorities are not always right in science and in philosophy and in theology. What the majority of scientists firmly believed a century ago the majority of scientists laugh at to-day. What the majority of philosophers once believed, the majority of philosophers to-day regard as ridiculous. So majorities cannot always be right. And, therefore, we cannot settle this question by asking what the majority believe.

We cannot settle the question by reasoning as to what such a being as God must do, for how can finite and foolish man judge what an infinitely holy and infinitely wise God would do? Man never appears more foolish than when he tries to reason out what an infinite God must do. All these arguments about hell by reasoning as to what God must, or must not, do are stupid. A child of seven cannot reason infallibly as to what a wise and good man of fifty will do, much less can puny creatures of the dust (such as you and I are, such as the most learned philosophers and theologians are) reason infallibly as to what an infinitely wise and infinitely holy God must do. It is, however, far easier to believe in a literal hell, and an everlasting hell, from the standpoint of pure reasoning to-day than it was three years and a half ago. Nevertheless, we cannot settle the question as to whether there is a literal hell by reasoning even to-day as to what such a being as God must do.

There is only one way to settle this question right, that is by going to the Bible and finding out what it says, and taking our stand firmly and unhesitatingly upon that. We have seen the last three Sunday nights that the Bible is beyond an honest question God's word, so whatever the Bible says on this subject, or any other subject, is true and is sure. Especially is it true that we must go to the Bible and find what it says in the matter of future punishment and future blessedness. All we know about the future is what the Bible tells us. All reasoning about the future outside of what the Bible tells us is pure guessing, it is a waste of time. We know nothing about heaven but what the Bible tells us, and we know nothing about hell but what the Bible tells us. On a subject like this one ounce of God's revelation is worth a thousand tons of man's speculation. The whole question is what does the Bible say about Hell? But while we are dependent entirely upon the Bible, the Bible clearly reveals all that we need to know. The Bible tells us a great deal about heaven, and it tells us still more about hell, and it is an interesting fact that the Lord Jesus Himself, whose authority many are ready to accept who do not accept the authority of the rest of the Bible, is the One Who tells us the most about hell, and the most clearly about hell. Indeed, all that I am going to show you is what the Lord Jesus Himself says on this subject.

I. HELL AND HADES ARE NOT THE SAME

First of all, in order to clear the way for the study of what Jesus says on this subject, let me call your attention to the fact that Hell and Hades are not the same. There are numerous places in the Authorised Version where we find the word "Hell" but where that word does not occur in the Revised Version, and where the word "Hades" is substituted for the word "Hell." The Revised Version is right at that point, as every Greek scholar knows. Hades is not Hell. "Hades" is the Greek equivalent of the Old Testament Hebrew word "Sheol." This Hebrew word "Sheol" is frequently translated in the Authorised Version of the Old Testament by the English word "Grave." It ought never to be so translated, as it never means "Grave." I have taken the pains to look up every passage where this Hebrew word is used and in not a single instance does it mean "Grave." There is an entirely different Hebrew word which can properly be translated in that way. "Sheol," or New Testament "Hades," means the place of departed spirits. Sheol (or Hades) before the coming, life, death, resurrection, and ascension of our Lord, was the place where all the spirits of the dead, good and bad, went. Before the ascension of Christ, in Hades was Paradise, the place of the blessed dead, and Tartaros, the place of the wicked dead. At His ascension Christ emptied the Paradise of Hades, and took it up to Heaven with Him, as we read in Eph. 4:8, "When he ascended on high, he led captivity captive, and gave gifts unto men." Before Christ ascended Paradise was down, now it is up. Christ said to the repentant thief on the cross, "Verily I say unto thee, to-day shalt thou be with me in Paradise," and Jesus Himself taught us He went down into "the heart of the earth" (Luke 12:40) and the dying thief went down with Him into this subterranean Paradise. I think Jesus Himself went also into that part of Hades where the lost spirits were (1 Peter 3:18-20), but that is another story that we will consider later. All that is important now is that the repentant, dying thief went down into Paradise, but after the ascension of the Lord, when Paul went to Paradise, he was "caught up even to the third heaven into Paradise" (II Cor. 12:2-4). No blessed dead are now left in Hades, and ultimately "death" and "Hades," i.e., all that are dead who have not yet been raised, or caught up into the Celestial Paradise, all who are still in Hades, shall be "cast into the lake of fire" (Rev. 20:14). This "lake of fire" into which death and Hades are to be cast, is the true and ultimate Hell.

II. THERE IS TO BE A LITERAL HELL

Having cleared the way by removing the misapprehension so common in the minds of people to-day, that Hades and Hell are the same, now let us say next that there is to be a Hell. The Bible says so, Jesus says in Matt. 5:22, "but I say unto you, that every one who is angry with his brother, shall be in danger of the judgment; and whosoever shall say to his brother, Raca, shall be in danger of the council; and whosoever shall say, Thou fool, shall be in danger of the hell of fire." In the 29th verse of the same chapter the Lord Jesus says: "And if thy right eye causeth thee to stumble pluck it out, and cast it from thee; for it is profitable for thee that one of thy members should perish, and not that thy whole body should be cast into hell." And in the 30th verse He says: "And if thy right hand causeth thee to stumble, cut it off, and cast it from thee; for it is profitable for thee that one of thy members should perish, and not that thy whole body should be cast into hell." We read again what our Lord Jesus said in Mark 9:45-48, "and if thy foot causeth thee to stumble, cut it off; it is good for thee to enter into life halt, rather than having thy two feet to be cast into hell. And if thine eye causeth thee to stumble, cast it out; it is good for thee to enter into the kingdom of God with one eye, rather than having two eyes to be cast into hell; where their worm dieth not, and the fire is not quenched." Some one may say that these words of our Lord are figurative. There is not the slightest suggestion that they are figurative. The whole context is against their being taken figuratively. It is indeed wrong to interpret figurative language as if it were literal, but it is just as unwarranted and just as wrong to interpret literal language as if it were figurative. Of course, the word "Gehenna," which is translated "Hell" is derived from the valley of Hinnom, where in ancient times human sacrifices were offered, but the use of the word is literal throughout the New Testament, though its derivation is figurative. Many words that are figurative in their derivation are literal in their use, and the meaning of words is never determined by derivation, but by usage. For example, our word "eclipse" is a figure of speech. According to the figure it is a leaving or failing or fainting of the moon or sun, whichever it may be that is eclipsed. But though it is figurative in its derivation, the ordinary usage of it is literal. The universal use in the New Testament of "Gehenna" or "Hell" is literal. The word here translated "Hell" is found twelve times in the New Testament, eleven of these twelve times it is used by our Lord Jesus Himself, and He uniformly uses it, as in the passages which I have just read, of a literal hell. If there is no literal hell, then our Lord Jesus was either a fool or a fraud. He certainly meant to convey the impression that there was a literal hell. There can be no doubt of that, if we go to His words to find out what is the natural meaning of them. If there is no literal hell then either Jesus thought there was one when there was not, in which case He was a fool; or else He knew that there was not, but tried to make men think that there was, in which case He was a fraud. There is no other alternative but either to believe that there is a literal hell or else to believe that Jesus of Nazareth, our

Lord and Saviour, was a fool or a fraud. I know that Jesus was not a fool. I know that He was the only begotten Son of God, that in Him dwelt all the fullness of the Godhead bodily, that He and the Father are one, that all men should honour the Son even as they honour the Father. I know that He spoke the very words of God, therefore I know that there is a literal hell, for He said so. It is worthy of note, furthermore, that most of these words about hell that I have read you to-night are taken from the Sermon on the Mount, the one part of the Bible that pretty much all men claim to believe. There are many who say they do not know about the Bible as a whole, but they do accept the Sermon on the Mount. Well, these passages are for the most part from the Sermon on the Mount. Either accept this part of the Sermon on the Mount or else throw the whole thing overboard as the utterance of a fool or a fraud. There is no other ground possible for any man who is willing to think things through.

III. IS THE FIRE OF HELL LITERAL FIRE?

The next question that confronts us is, Is the fire of hell mentioned in some of the passages we have read, literal fire? This is not so vital a question as the question, is there a literal hell, but nevertheless it is an important question, and I believe the question is plainly answered in the Bible, and plainly answered by Jesus Christ Himself. To turn again to the passage already referred to, Matt. 5:22, we read: "But I say unto you, that every one who is angry with his brother shall be in danger of the judgment; and whosoever shall say to his brother, Raca, shall be in danger of the council; and whosoever shall say, Thou fool, shall be in danger of the hell of fire." These are Christ's own words. He not only speaks of hell, but a "hell of fire," and this too is from the Sermon on the Mount. In Matt. 18:9 the Lord Jesus says again, "And if thine eye cause thee to stumble, pluck it out, and cast it from thee; it is good for thee to enter into life with one eye, rather than having two eyes to be cast into the hell of fire." And again in Mark 9:43-49, the passage read a few moments ago, we read, "And if thy hand cause thee to stumble, cut it off; it is good for thee to enter into life maimed, rather than having thy two hands to go into hell, into the unquenchable fire. And if thy foot cause thee to stumble, cut it off; it is good for thee to enter into life halt, rather than having thy two feet to be cast into hell. And if thine eye cause thee to stumble, cast it out; it is good for thee to enter into the kingdom of God with one eye, rather than having two eyes to be cast into hell, where the worm dieth not, and the fire is not quenched." Here again some may say the fire is figurative. Turn to Matt. 13:30, 41, 42, we read these words: "Let both grow together until the harvest; and in the time of harvest I will say to the reapers, gather up first the tares, and bind them in bundles to barn them; but gather the wheat into my barn." Now here is a parable and we have figures and there would be warrant, if this were all that we had, for saying that the fire was figurative, as other things in the verse are figurative; but in the 41st and 42nd verses of the same chapter we read, "The Son of man shall send forth his angels, and they shall gather out of His kingdom all things that cause stumbling, and they that do iniquity, and shall cast them into the furnace of fire; there shall be the weeping and gnashing of teeth." Here we have the interpretation of the parable. Now in parables, as already said, we have figures, but in the interpretation of parables we have the literal facts which the figures represent, but we see clearly that here in the interpretation as well as in the parable, we have fire. Everything else in the parable is explained, every item in the parable except the fire, but that remains fire in the interpretation of the parable as well as in the parable itself. We find the same thing in another parable in verses 47 to 50, the parable of the net cast into the sea. Here, also, in the interpretation of the parable as well as in the parable itself we have fire. Every other figure of the parable is explained by the literal fact that it represents, but in the interpretation of the parable we have "fire." In the light of these facts we cannot deny the literal fire of hell without doing violence to every reasonable law of interpretation. Furthermore still, we read in Rev. 20:15 that at the judgment of the great white throne, "and if any was not found written in the Book of Life, he was cast into the lake of fire." There is nothing in the whole context that suggests a figure. And in the 21st chapter and the 8th verse we read: "But for the fearful, and unbelieving, and abominable, and murderers, and fornicators, and sorcerers, and idolators, and all liars, their part shall be in the lake that burneth with fire and brimstone; which is the second death."

Remember furthermore that the wicked in the eternal world are not mere disembodied spirits. This is plain both from the Old Testament and the New. We read in Dan. 12:2: "And many of them that sleep in the dust of the earth shall awake, some to everlasting life, and some to shame and everlasting contempt." Now this says "them that sleep in the dust of the earth." The soul departs into Hades. It is the body that crumbles into dust, and it is the body that is to be raised. In the New Testament, in John 5:28, 29, our Lord is recorded as saying: "Marvel not at this; for the hour cometh, in which all that are in the tombs shall hear His voice, and shall come forth; they that have done good, unto the resurrection of life; and they that have done evil, unto the resurrection of judgment." Now it is not the souls of men that are in the tombs, it is the bodies of men, and this passage teaches the resurrection of the bodies, both of the good and of the wicked. In I Cor. 15:22 we read, "For as in Adam all die, so also in Christ shall all be made alive." What Paul is talking about in this entire chapter is the resurrection of the body, not merely the immortality of the soul, and we are here distinctly told that every child of Adam gets resurrection of his body in Christ.

Furthermore, in Matt. 5:30 Jesus says: "If thy right hand causeth thee to stumble, cut it off, and cast it from thee; for it is profitable for thee that one of thy members should perish, and not thy whole body go into hell." Here in the plainest possible terms the body is spoken of as going into hell, and in a similar way in Matt. 10:28, the Lord Jesus says: "Be not afraid of them that kill the body, but are not able to kill the soul; but rather fear him who is able to destroy both soul and body in hell." From these plain and definite words of our Lord it is plain as day that in the future life we are to have bodies, and that the bodies of the lost are to have a place in a literal physical hell of fire. While the bodily torments of hell fire are not the most appalling feature of hell, while the mental agony, the agony of remorse, the agony of shame, and the agony of despair, is worse, immeasurably worse; nevertheless, physical suffering, a physical suffering to which no pain on earth is anything in comparison, is a feature of hell.

IV. IS THE LAKE OF FIRE A PLACE OF CONSCIOUS TORMENT, OR IS IT A PLACE OF ANNIHILATION, I.E., A PLACE OF NON-EXISTENCE OR IS IT A PLACE OF NON-CONSCIOUS EXISTENCE?

There is one other question that remains to be answered, and that is, is the lake of fire a place of conscious torment, or is it a place of annihilation, i.e., a place of non-existence, or is it a place of non-conscious existence? There are those who believe in a literal hell, but they do not believe that those who are consigned to it will consciously suffer there for any great length of time. They hold either that those who are sent to hell are annihilated, or else that they exist there in a non-conscious state. Of course, this would be an everlasting hell, and everlasting punishment, but is it the hell that is taught in the Bible? Is the lake of fire a place of continued conscious torment, or is it a place of non-conscious existence? In answer to this question let me call your attention to the fact that the punishment of the wicked is spoken of in the Bible most frequently as "Death" and "Destruction." What do these words mean in biblical usage?

1. Let us look first at the biblical usage of the word "Death." Many tell us, time and time again, that death means non-existence, or at least non-conscious existence, and therefore that is what it must mean in the passages where it is spoken of as the future punishment of the impenitent. But does "death" as used in the Bible mean either non-conscious existence, or annihilation? Look first at 1 Tim. 5:6; here we read, "She that liveth in pleasure is dead while she liveth." Death here certainly does not mean either non-existence, or non-conscious existence. The woman that lives in pleasure still exists, and she certainly exists consciously, but she is "dead." Death means wrong existence rather than non-existence. It is just the opposite of life, and life in the New Testament usage does not mean mere existence, it means right existence. God-like existence, holy existence. It means the ennoblement and glorification and deification of existence; and death means just the opposite, it means wrong existence, debased existence, the ruin, the shame, and the ignominy and the despair of existence. In a similar way we are told in Eph. 2:1, that men until they are quickened, or made alive, by the power of God are "Dead in trespasses and sins." It is perfectly

clear then that death does not mean either non-existence, or non-conscious existence. But even more decisive than this is the fact that God Himself has defined death very accurately and very fully in Rev. 21:8: "But the fearful and unbelieving, and the abominable, and murderers, and whoremongers, and sorcerers, and idolators, and all liars, shall have their part in the lake which burneth with fire and brimstone; which is the second death." Here we are told in so many words that the "death" which is the final outcome of persistent sin and unbelief is a portion in the place of torment, the lake of fire. That this lake of fire is a place of conscious suffering is made clear in the preceding chapter, Rev. 20:10, where we are told that "the devil that deceived them was cast into the lake of fire and brimstone, where the beast and the false prophet are, and shall be tormented day and night for ever and ever." The beast and false prophet had already been there a thousand years when the devil was cast into the lake of fire, and they were tormented consciously, without rest.

2. Now let us look at what "Destruction" means in the New Testament. We are told by a certain school of religious thought that "destruction" means destruction. Yes, "destruction" means destruction, but what does destruction mean? They say it means annihilation, or ceasing to be, but the Greek word so translated never means that in the Bible, nor even out of the Bible. In the best Greek-English lexicon of the New Testament extant, Thayer's translation of Grimm's great work, we are told that when a thing is said to "perish" (and the verb from which the noun commonly translated "destruction" and "perdition" is derived, is the one translated "to perish") it is not meant that it ceases to be, but that it is "so ruined that it no longer subserves the use for which it was designed." Furthermore, here again God has been careful to define His terms. He Himself has given us in the [300]Bible a definition of "destruction." We read in Rev. 17:8, 11: "The beast that thou sawest was, and is not; and shall ascend out of the bottomless pit, and go into perdition; and they that dwell on the earth shall wonder . . . and the beast that was, and is not, even he is the eighth, and is of the seven, and goeth into perdition." Here we are told that the beast goes into "perdition." The word here translated "perdition" is precisely the same word that is elsewhere translated "destruction" and should be so translated here; or else

in the other instances it should be translated, as here, "perdition." Now if we can find what the beast goes into, then we shall know exactly what "destruction" means, for we are told that he goeth "into destruction." In the 19th chapter of Revelation, the 20th verse, we are told exactly where the beast goes: "And the beast was taken, and with him the false prophet that wrought miracles before him, with which he deceived them that had received the mark of the beast, and them that worshipped his image. These both were cast alive into a lake of fire burning with brimstone." Now looking forward to the next chapter, the 10th verse, which I have already quoted, we read: "And the devil that deceived them was cast into the lake of fire and brimstone, where are also the beast and the false prophet, and they shall be tormented day and night for ever and ever." Putting these passages together we see that the beast goeth into "destruction," and the destruction into [301]which he goes is a place in the lake which burneth with fire and brimstone, where for a thousand years he is in conscious torment, and where after the thousand years are over he is still there and is still tormented. So then "destruction" is clearly defined in the New Testament in the same way in which "death" is defined, as the condition of beings in a place of conscious torment.

Again in Rev. 14:10, 11, we read regarding those who worship the beast and his image and receive his mark in their foreheads or in their hands: "The same shall drink of the wine of the wrath of God, which is poured out without mixture into the cup of his indignation; and he shall be tormented with fire and brimstone in the presence of the holy angels, and in the presence of the Lamb; and the smoke of their torment ascendeth for ever and ever; and they have no rest day nor night, who worship the beast and his image, and whosoever receiveth the mark of his name." The Bible makes it clear as language can make it that the lake of fire to which "whoever is not written in the Lamb's book of life" is consigned, is a place of continued, conscious torment. There is no escaping the clear teaching of the Word of God unless we throw our Bibles away and discredit the teaching of the Apostles and the teaching of Jesus Christ Himself.

Next Sunday night we will take up the question, Is the Punishment of the Wicked Everlasting, but we must stop at this point to-night. Sherman said, [302]"War is hell." Of course, in the way in which

Sherman meant it, this is true. It is far more true of war to-day than it was in the worst and most inexcusable phases of our Civil War—Libby and Andersonville, for example, on the part of the South, and the march through Georgia on the part of the North. But even war to-day as carried on by Germany in all its appalling frightfulness, is not hell. Hell is incomparably more awful than the war now raging in Europe, and this awful hell of which we have been studying to-night is the destiny of some of you here in this room, unless you soon repent and accept the Lord Jesus Christ. Other appalling facts about hell we will take up next Sunday night, but we have already seen enough to make any true Christian determine to work with all his might to save others from this awful hell. And we have seen enough to make every honest and sensible person here to-night determine to escape this awful hell at any cost.

Is Future Punishment Everlasting?

Jesus Christ plainly taught that there was to be a literal hell and that this hell would be a place of conscious suffering, suffering far beyond that experienced by any one here in this present life, but we are faced by another question of great importance, Is this future, conscious suffering of the impenitent to be endless? There are many who believe in future punishment of a very severe and awful character, and who indeed believe in a literal hell of awful, conscious suffering, but they deny, or at least doubt, that this future hell will be a place of endless, conscious suffering. Many of them admit and teach that the suffering may go on for a long time, and perhaps for thousands of years, but they hold that it will end at last and that all men will ultimately come to repentance, accept Jesus Christ, and be saved. What is the exact truth about the matter? We cannot decide this by asking what the majority of supposedly reliable theologians believe, for majorities are often wrong and minorities are often right. Neither can we decide it by reasoning as to what such a being as God is must [304]do. It is impossible for finite and foolish men such as we are, and such as the wisest philosophers and theologians are, to judge what an Infinitely wise and Infinitely holy God must do. All reasonings by finite men as to what an Infinitely wise God must do are utterly futile and an utter waste of time. All we know about the future is what God has been pleased to tell us in His Word. The Bible, as we have seen, is beyond a question the Word of God, and therefore what it has to say on this subject, or any other subject, is true and absolutely sure, and in a question of this character one ounce of God's revelation is worth more than a thousand tons of man's speculation. The whole question then is, what does the Bible teach in regard to this matter?

I. WHAT THE BIBLE TEACHES REGARDING THE ENDLESSNESS OF FUTURE PUNISHMENT

1. To find out exactly what the Bible teaches as to the endlessness of future punishment let us turn first of all to the words of our Lord Jesus Himself in Matt. 25:46 (R. V.), "And these shall go away into eternal punishment: but the righteous into eternal life." The first question that confronts us in studying this passage is what the word aionios (aionion) which is here translated "eternal" means. The best Greek-English dictionary of the New Testament is Thayer's. In this dictionary Thayer after a careful study of the [305] word, its derivation and its usage, gives these three definitions of the word, and these three only: (1) "Without beginning or end, that which always has been and always will be." (2) "Without beginning." (3) "Without end, never to cease, everlasting." It is frequently said that the word aionios according to its derivation means age-lasting, and therefore may refer to a limited period. Even admitting this to be true, we should bear in mind that the meaning of words is not determined by their derivation but by their usage, and the most important question is not what the derivation of this word may be, but as to how it is used in the New Testament. It is used 72 times in the New Testament. Forty-four of these 72 times it is used in the phrase "eternal life," or as it is sometimes rendered, "everlasting life." No one questions that everlasting life is endless and that in connection with the word "life" "age lasting" (if that be its proper derivation of the word) means lasting through all ages, never ending. Once it is used in connection with the word "habitations," referring to the habitations which the blessed are to have in the world to come, and, of course, these also are never-ending. Once it is used of the "weight of glory" that in the world to come awaits the believer in Jesus Christ who endures affliction for Christ in the life that now is. In this case again, of course, by universal consent it means endless. Once it is used of the "house not made with hands" that believers in Christ are [306]

to receive at the coming of the Lord Jesus (II Cor. 5:1-8). Of course, this "house not made with hands" is everlasting. In fact the very point that is being brought forward in this passage is the contrast between our present bodies which are but for a brief time and our resurrection bodies which are to exist throughout all eternity. Once it is used of the future unseen things that never end, contrasted with the present seen things that are for a season (II Cor. 4:18). Of course, these are never-ending. That is the very point that is being brought out in the contrast. Once it is used of the everlasting "comfort" (R. V.) or "consolation" (A. V.) that "our Lord Jesus Christ Himself, and God our Father" give us, and that is certainly never ending. Twice it is used of the "glory" that those in Christ obtain (II Tim. 2:10). That, of course, by universal consent is endless. Once it is used of the "salvation" Christ brings, which is beyond question never ending. Once (Heb. 9:12) it is used of the "redemption" that Jesus Christ secures for us by His blood. This redemption is never ending. In fact, the chief point of contrast in the context in this case is between the temporary redemption secured by the constantly repeated sacrifices of the Mosaic ritual and the never ending redemption secured by the perfect sacrifice of Christ made once for all. Once it is used of the "inheritance" that those who are in Christ receive (Heb. 9:15). Here again beyond a question it is never ending. Once it is used of [307]the "everlasting covenant" through Christ's blood contrasted with the temporary covenant, based on the blood of bulls and goats, given through Moses. Here again it necessarily and emphatically means never ending. That is the very point at issue. Once it is used of the "everlasting kingdom" of our Lord and Saviour Jesus Christ (II Peter 1:11), and we are told in Luke 1:33, "of His kingdom there shall be no end." Once it is used of "everlasting gospel" (or good news) and that, of course, also never ends. Once it is used of the "everlasting God" (Rom. 16:26) and He certainly endures not merely through long ages, but without end. Once it is used of the Holy Spirit who is called "the eternal (or everlasting) Spirit," and He certainly endures, not merely through long ages, but throughout an absolutely endless eternity. This covers fifty-nine of the seventy-two times it is used, and in these fifty-nine instances the thought of endlessness is absolutely necessary to the sense, and in not a single one of the thirteen remaining times where it is used is it used of anything that is known to end. If usage can determine the meaning of any word then certainly the New Testament use of this word determines it to mean never ending, or, as Thayer defines it, "without end, never to cease, everlasting."

Nor is this all, God Himself determines it to mean never ending: He defines it to mean never-ending by specifically using it in contrast with that [308]which does end. For example, in 2 Cor. 4:18 we read, "While we look not on the things which are seen, but the things which are unseen: for the things which are seen are temporal (literally, for a season); but the things which are not seen are eternal." Here the whole point is that the unseen things in distinction from the seen which are for a season are for a never ending duration.

But even allowing that the word according to its usage could be used of that which, though it last throughout an age, or ages, has an end; even if that were true (which it is not), then the meaning of the word in any given instance would have to be determined by the context in which it is found. Now what is the context in the passage which we are studying? Let us read it again, "And these shall go away into eternal punishment: but the righteous into eternal life." The same Greek adjective is used in connection with "punishment" and with "life." (In the Authorised Version it is differently rendered, but in the Greek and in the Revised Version it is exactly the same.) Certainly this qualifying adjective must mean the same in the one half of the sentence that it means in the other half of the sentence. We must at least admit that Jesus Christ was an honest man, and He certainly was too honest to juggle with words: He would not use a word to mean one thing in one half of a sentence and something utterly different in the other half. He evidently sought to convey the impression that the punishment [309]of the unsaved was of the same duration as the life of the saved. No one questions that the life is endless. It would be the destruction of all our hopes if it were not endless. Therefore, if we are to deal honestly with our Lord's words, He taught that the punishment of the unsaved was to be endless. We have exactly the same reason in God's Word for believing in endless punishment that we have for believing in endless life. If you give up the one you must give up the other, or else deal dishonestly with the words of Jesus Christ.

2. We might rest the case here and call it proven, but let us turn to another passage, Rev. 14:9-11, "And another angel, a third, followed them, saying with a great voice, If any man worshipeth the beast and his image and receiveth a mark on his forehead, or upon his hand, he also shall drink of the wine of the wrath of God, which is prepared unmixed in the cup of His anger; and he shall be tormented with fire and brimstone in the presence of the holy angels, and in the presence of the Lamb: and the smoke of their torment goeth up for ever and ever; and they have no rest day and night, they that worship the beast and his image, and whoso receiveth the mark of his name." Here we have another expression for the duration of the punishment and suffering of the impenitent, the expression rendered for ever and ever. There are in the Greek two slightly differing forms of expression that are so translated. [310] The one form of expression literally rendered is "unto the ages of the ages," the other form is "unto ages of ages." What thought do these expressions convey. It has been said by those who seek to escape the force of these words as referring to absolute endlessness, that the expression "is a Hebraism for the supreme one of its class," and as an illustration of the same alleged Hebraism the expressions, "Lord of Lords" and "Holy of Holies" are cited. But this is not so. In the first place, the form of neither of the two expressions is the same; and, in the second place, that is not the meaning of the expression "The Lord of Lords" or the meaning of the expression "The Holy of Holies." The expression "Lord of Lords" does not mean merely the supreme Lord, but one who is Himself Lord of all other Lords, and this expression "unto the ages of the ages" never means merely the ages which are the supreme ages in distinction from other ages (nor as another puts it, the ages which come out of the other ages, i.e., the closing ages before eternity). The expression according to its form means ages which are themselves composed of ages. It represents not years tumbling upon years, nor centuries tumbling upon centuries, but ages tumbling upon ages in endless procession. It is the strongest

possible form of expression for absolute endlessness. Furthermore, the way to determine conclusively what the expression means is by considering its usage. Usage is always the [311]decisive thing in determining the meaning of words and phrases. What is the usage of these expressions in the book from which we have taken our passage? These expressions are used twelve times in this book. In eight of the twelve times they refer to the duration of the existence, or reign, or glory of God and His Son, Jesus Christ our Lord. Of course, in these instances it must stand not merely for the supreme ages, or any individual ages, it must refer to absolute eternity and endlessness. Once it is used of the duration of the blessed reign of the righteous, and, of course, here again it refers to an endless eternity: and in the three remaining instances it is used of the duration of the torment of the Devil, the Beast, the False Prophet, and the finally impenitent. It is urged by those who would deny that the expression means an absolutely endless eternity, that it is used in Rev. 11:15, where we are told that "the kingdom of the world is become the kingdom of our Lord, and of His Christ: and He shall reign for ever and ever (unto the ages of the ages)," and that we are told in 1 Cor. 15:24 that Christ "shall deliver up the kingdom to God, even the Father"; and that therefore His kingdom must come to an end, and consequently "for ever and ever" in this passage cannot mean without end. There are two answers to this objection, either of which is sufficient. The first is that the "he" in "he shall reign for ever and ever" in Rev. 11:15, does not necessarily refer to the Christ, but [312]rather to the Lord Jehovah, in which case the argument falls to the ground. The second answer is that while we are taught in I Cor. 15:24, etc., that Jesus Christ will deliver up His mediatorial kingdom to the Father, nevertheless we are distinctly taught that He shall rule with the Father, and we are told in so many words in Luke 1:33 that "of His kingdom there shall be no end," so that even if the "he" in Rev. 11:15 referred to the Christ and not to the Lord Jehovah, still the statement would be exactly correct that He, the Christ, was to reign for ever and ever, i.e., without end. There is not a single passage in the whole book in which this expression is used of anything but that which is absolutely endless. So the question is answered again and answered decisively that the conscious suffering of the persistently impenitent is absolutely endless.

3. Now let us look at another passage, II Thess. 1:7-9: "The Lord Jesus shall be revealed from heaven with His mighty angels, in flaming fire taking vengeance on them that know not God, and that obey not the gospel of our Lord Jesus Christ: who shall be punished with everlasting destruction from the presence of the Lord, and from the glory of His power." Here we are told that the punishment of those that know not God and obey not the gospel is "everlasting destruction."

What does "everlasting destruction" mean? In Rev. 17:8, 11 we are told that the beast goeth into [313]"destruction," so if we can find out where the beast goes, or into what he goes, we shall know what "destruction" means in the Bible usage. In Rev. 19:20 we are told that "the beast was taken, and with him the false prophet that wrought the signs in his sight, wherewith he deceived them that had received the mark of the beast and them that worshipped his image: they two were cast alive into the lake of fire that burneth with brimstone," so we see that "destruction" is a portion in the lake of fire. And in the next chapter, Rev. 20:10, we are told that "The devil that deceived them was cast into the lake of fire and brimstone, where are also the beast and the false prophet (after having already been there for one thousand years, see context); and they shall be tormented day and night for ever and ever." So we see that destruction means a portion in the lake of fire where its inhabitants are consciously suffering without cessation for ever and ever. It is clear then, from a comparison of II Thess. 1:7-9 with these passages, that those who know not God and obey not the gospel of our Lord Jesus Christ shall be punished with never-ending, conscious suffering.

4. Let us look at one more passage, Matt. 25:41 (these again are the words of the Lord Jesus Himself): "Then shall he say also unto them on the left hand, Depart from me, ye cursed, into the eternal fire which is prepared for the devil and his angels." What I wish you to [314]notice here is that the punishment into which the impenitent are sent is the "eternal fire" which is "prepared for the devil and his angels." We have an exact description of just what the eternal

fire prepared for the devil and his angels is in the passage read a few moments ago, Rev. 20:10: "And the devil that deceived them was cast into the lake of fire and brimstone where are also the beast and the false prophet; and they shall be tormented day and night for ever and ever." By a comparison of these two statements we have another explicit declaration of our Lord that the punishment of the impenitent is to be a conscious agony, where they are punished without rest day and night for ever and ever.

From any one of these passages and especially from all taken together, it is clear that the Scriptures make it as plain as language can make it that THE FUTURE PUNISHMENT OF THE PERSISTENTLY IMPENITENT IS ABSOLUTELY ENDLESS.

II. OBJECTIONS

There are several passages of Scripture which those who believe that all men will ultimately repent and be brought to accept Christ and thus saved, urge against what seems to be the plain teaching of the passages we have been studying.

1. The first of these is 1 Peter 3:18-20: "Because Christ also suffered for sins once, the righteous for the unrighteous, that he might bring us [315]to God; being put to death in the flesh, but made alive in the spirit; in which also he went and preached unto the spirits in prison, that aforetime were disobedient, when the longsuffering of God waited in the days of Noah, while the ark was a preparing, wherein few, that is, eight souls, were saved through water." It is urged that as Christ went and preached to the spirits in prison there will be another chance after men have died. But this the passage in question does not assert or imply in any way.

(1) First of all there is no proof that "the spirits in prison" refers to the departed spirits of men who once lived here on earth. In the Bible departed spirits of men are not spoken of in this way. These words are used of other spirits, but not of human spirits disembodied, and there is every reason for supposing that these "spirits in prison" were not the sinful men that were on earth when the ark was preparing, but the angels who sinned at that time, just as we are told in Gen. 6:1, 2 that they did sin (cf. Jude 6, 7).

(2) Furthermore, even if "the spirits in prison" here spoken of were the spirits of men who were disobedient in the time of Noah, there is not a hint in the passage that they were saved through the preaching of Christ to them, or that they had another chance. There are two words commonly used in the New Testament for preaching, one is kerusso and the other is euaggelizo. The first of these means to herald, as to herald a king, or to herald the kingdom. It may, however, be used of preaching a message, the gospel message or some other message. The second word euaggelizo, means to preach the gospel. In the passage that we are studying it is the first word that is used, and there is not a hint that Christ preached the gospel to these spirits in prison. He simply heralded the triumph of the kingdom. It was not a saving message. So there is nothing in this passage to put up even inferentially against the plain, direct statements regarding the destiny of the wicked found in the passages we have been studying.

2. The second passage that is appealed to by those who deny the endlessness of future punishment is Phil. 2:9-11: "Wherefore also God highly exalted Him, and gave unto Him the name which is above every name; that in the name of Jesus every knee should bow, of things in heaven and things on earth and things under the earth, and that every tongue should confess that Jesus Christ is Lord, to the glory of God the Father." Here it is said, we are told, that all those "under the earth" as well as in heaven and on earth should bow the knee in the name of Jesus and confess that Jesus Christ is Lord, and that this implies that they are saved. But it does not imply that they are saved. Every knee of lost men and of the devil and his angels too will be forced some day to bow in the name of Jesus and every tongue forced to confess that He is Lord. If any one does that in the present life of his own free choice, he will be saved, but otherwise he will do it by compulsion in the age to come and every one has his choice between doing it now willingly and gladly and being saved, or doing it by compulsion hereafter and being lost. There is absolutely nothing in this passage to teach universal salvation or to militate even inferentially against the plain statements we have been studying.

3. The third passage that is appealed to is Acts 3:19-21: "Repent ye therefore, and turn again, that your sins may be blotted out, that so there may come seasons of refreshing from the presence of the Lord; and that He may send the Christ who hath been appointed for you, even Jesus: Whom the heaven must receive until the times of restoration of all things whereof God spake by the mouth of His holy prophets that have been from of old." Here we are told of a coming "restoration of all things" and those who contend for the doctrine of universal salvation hold that this means the restoration to righteousness of all persons. But that is not what it says, and that is not what it refers to. We are taught in Old Testament prophecy and also in the book of Romans, that in connection with the return of our Lord Jesus there is to be a restoration of all nature, of the whole physical universe, from its fallen state. For example, in Rom. 8:19-21 we read: "For the earnest expectation of the creation waiteth for the revealing of the sons of God. For the creation was subjected to vanity, not of its own will, but by reason of him who subjected it, in hope that the creation itself also shall be delivered from the bondage of corruption into the liberty of the glory of the children of God." And in Isa. 55:13 we read: "Instead of the thorn shall come up the fir-tree; and instead of the brier shall come up the myrtle-tree: and it shall be to Jehovah for a name, for an everlasting sign that shall not be cut off." And in Isa. 65:25 we are told: "The wolf and the lamb shall feed together, and the lion shall eat straw like the ox; and dust shall be the serpent's food. They shall not hurt nor destroy in all my holy mountain, saith Jehovah," and in Isa. 32:15, we are told that "until the Spirit be poured upon us from on high, and the wilderness become a fruitful field, and the fruitful field be esteemed as a forest." It is to this restoration of the physical universe, here plainly predicted in Rom. 8:19-21 and these Old Testament prophecies, that the "restoration of all things" spoken of in Acts 3:21 refers. There is not a hint, not the slightest suggestion, of a restoration of impenitent sinners.

4. Still another passage that is urged is Eph. 1:9, 10, where we read: "Having made known unto us the mystery of His will according to His good pleasure which He purposed in Him unto

a dispensation of the fulness of the times, to sum up all things in Christ, the things in the heavens, and the things upon the earth." Here it is urged that [319]things in heaven and things in earth are to be summed up in Christ. This is true, but it should be noticed that the Holy Spirit has specifically omitted here the phrase that is found in Phil. 2:10, the "things under the earth," that is the abode of the lost, so this passage, so far from suggesting that the lost ones in hell will be restored, suggests exactly the opposite thing. There is then certainly nothing in this passage to militate even inferentially against the plain statements we have been studying.

5. One more passage that is urged against the doctrine we have been studying remains to be considered, that is 1 Cor. 15:22. Here we read, "For as in Adam all died, so also in Christ shall all be made alive." It is urged in connection with this passage that we are distinctly told here that all who die in Adam, that is every human being, shall be made alive in Christ, and that "made alive" means "obtain eternal life," or "be saved." For years I thought that this was the true interpretation of this passage, and for that reason in part, I held and preached at that time that all men ultimately, some time, somewhere, somehow, would be brought to accept Jesus Christ and be saved; but when I came to study the passage more carefully I saw that this was a misinterpretation of the passage. Every passage in the Bible, or in any other book, must be interpreted in its context. The whole subject that Paul is [320]talking about in this chapter is not eternal life, not the immortality of the soul, but the resurrection of the body, and all this passage declares is that as all lose physical life in Adam, so also all will obtain a resurrection of the body in Christ. Whether that resurrection of the body is a resurrection to everlasting life or a resurrection to shame and everlasting contempt (Dan. 12:2) depends entirely upon what men do with the Christ in whom they get it. There is absolutely nothing here to teach universal salvation. It only teaches a universal resurrection, resurrection of the wicked as well as of the righteous.

To sum up the teaching of all these passages that are so often urged to prove universal salvation, there is nothing in any one of the passages, nor in all of them together, to teach that all men will ultimately be saved, and there is nothing in them to in any way conflict with what we have seen to be the honest meaning of the passages studied above, namely, that the future punishment of sin is absolutely endless. There is not a passage to be found in the Bible that teaches universal salvation, or that all men will ultimately come to repentance and be saved. I wish that there were, but there is not. I have been searching diligently for such a passage for nearly forty years and I have not found it, and it cannot be found.

III. WHERE ARE THE ISSUES OF ETERNITY SETTLED?

There remains one other important question; and that is, where are the issues of eternity settled. There are those who believe that the punishment of the persistently impenitent is everlasting, that it has no end, but they also believe that the issues of eternity are not settled in the life that now is, but that with many they are settled after death and that when men die impenitent they will have another chance. Believing in endless punishment does not necessarily involve believing that there is no chance after death. There are many who believe that there will be a chance after death, and that many will accept it, who also believe that some will not accept it and will therefore be punished for ever and ever. Now what is the teaching of the Word of God on this point? Let me call your attention to four passages, any one of which settles the question, and taken together they leave no possible room for doubt for any candid man who is willing to take the Bible as meaning what it says, any man who is really trying to find out what the Bible teaches and not merely trying to support a theory.

1. The first passage in 2 Cor. 5:10: "For we must all be made manifest before the judgment seat of Christ; that each one may receive the things done in the body, according to what he hath done, whether it be good or bad." In this passage we [322]are plainly told that the basis of judgment in the world to come is "the things done in the body," i.e., the things done this side the grave, the things done before we shuffle off this mortal coil, the things done before the spirit leaves the body. Of course, this particular passage has to do primarily with the judgment of the believer, but it shows what the

basis of future judgment is, viz., the things done this side of the grave.

2. The second passage is Heb. 9:27: "It is appointed unto men once to die, and after this cometh judgment." Here we are distinctly told that "after death" there is to be, not an opportunity to prepare for judgment, but "judgment," and that, therefore, our destiny is settled at death, and that there is no chance of salvation "after death."

3. The third passage is John 5:28, 29: "Marvel not at this: for the hour cometh, in which all that are in the tombs shall hear His voice, and shall come forth; they that have done good, unto the resurrection of life; and they that have done evil, unto the resurrection of judgment." Here also it is clearly implied that the resurrection of good and bad is for the purpose of judgment regarding the things done before their bodies were laid in their graves.

4. A fourth passage, if possible more decisive than any of these, gives our Lord's words, John 8:21: "He said therefore again unto them; I go away, and ye shall seek me, and shall die in your [323]sin, whither I go, ye cannot come." Here our Lord distinctly declares that the question whether men shall come to be with Him or not depends upon what they do before they die, that if they die impenitent, if they "die in their sins," that whither He goes they cannot come. To sum up the teaching of all these passages, the issues of eternity, the issues of eternal life or eternal destruction, the issues of eternal blessedness and glory, or eternal agony and shame, are settled in the life that now is.

IV. CONCLUSION

The future state of those who reject in the life that now is the redemption offered to them in Christ Jesus is plainly declared in the Word of God to be a state of conscious, unutterable, endless torment and anguish. This conception is an appalling one, but it is the Scriptural conception. It is the unmistakable, inescapable teaching of God's own word.

I wish that all men would repent and accept Christ. If any one could show me one single passage in the Bible that clearly taught that all men would ultimately repent, accept Christ and be saved, it would be the happiest day of my life, but it cannot be found. I once thought it could, and I so believed and taught. These ideas so widely noised about to-day as something new, these theories of "Pastor" Russell, formerly of Pittsburg, [324]Mr. Gelesnoff of this city, and Dr. Mabie of Long Beach, and Mr. Pridgeon of Pittsburg, and many others, are not at all new to me. I held and taught substantially the same views regarding ultimate universal salvation years before these men were heard of, indeed nearly forty years ago. I was familiar with the arguments that they now urge, and other arguments which they do not seem to know, but which were to me more decisive than those that they urge. But the time came, as I studied the Bible more carefully, when I could not reconcile my teaching with what I found to be the unmistakable teaching of God's Word. I had to do one of three things: I had to either give up my belief that the Bible was the Word of God, or else I must twist the words of Jesus (and others in the New Testament) to mean something else than what they clearly appeared to teach, or else I must give up my doctrine of ultimate universal restoration and salvation. I could not give up my faith that the Bible was the Word of God, for I had found absolutely overwhelming proof that it was God's Word. I could not twist the words of Jesus and of others to mean something else than what was clearly their intended meaning, for I was an honest man. There was only one thing left to do and that was to give up my doctrine of universal restoration and salvation. I gave it up with great reluctance, but I was compelled to give it up or be untrue to my own reason and conscience. It is the inescapable teaching of the [325]Word of God that all who go out of this world without having accepted Jesus Christ, will spend eternity in hell, in a hell of unutterable, conscious anguish.

This Bible conception is also a reasonable one when we come to see the appalling nature of sin, and especially the appalling nature of the sin of trampling under foot God's mercy toward sinners, and rejecting God's glorious Son, Whom in His love He has provided as a Saviour.

Shallow views of sin and of God's holiness and of the glory of Jesus Christ lie at the bottom of weak theories of the doom of the impenitent. When we see Sin in all its hideousness and enormity, the Holiness of God in all its perfection, and the Glory of Jesus Christ in all its infinity, nothing but a doctrine that those who persist in the choice of sin, who love darkness rather than light, and who persist in the rejection of the Son of God, shall endure everlasting anguish, will satisfy the demands of our own moral intuitions. Nothing but the fact that we dread suffering more than we loathe sin, and more than we love the glory of Jesus Christ, makes us repudiate the thought that beings who eternally choose sin should eternally suffer, or that men who despise God's mercy and spurn His Son should be given over to endless anguish.

If, after men have sinned and God still offers them mercy, and makes the tremendous sacrifice of His Son to save them—if they still despise that [326]mercy and trample God's Son under foot, if then they are consigned to everlasting torment, I cannot but say, "Amen! Hallelujah! True and righteous are thy judgments, O Lord!"

At all events the doctrine of conscious, eternal torment for impenitent men is clearly revealed in the Word of God, and whether we can defend it on philosophical grounds or not, it is our business to believe it; and leave it to the clearer light of eternity to explain what we cannot now understand, realising that God may have many infinitely wise reasons for doing things for which we in our ignorance can see no sufficient reason at all. It is the most ludicrous conceit for beings so limited and foolish as the wisest of men are, to attempt to dogmatise how a God of infinite wisdom must act. All we know as to how God is to act is what God has seen fit to tell us.

In conclusion, two things are certain. First, the more closely men walk with God and the more devoted they become in His service, the more likely they are to believe this doctrine. Many there are who tell us they love their fellow men too much to believe this doctrine; but the men who show their love in more practical ways than by sentimental protestations about it, the men who show their love for their fellow men as Jesus Christ showed His, by laying down their lives for them, they believe this doctrine, even as Jesus Christ Himself believed it.

As Christians become worldly and easy-going [327]they grow loose in their doctrine concerning the doom of the impenitent. The fact that loose doctrines are spreading so rapidly and widely in our day is nothing for them, but against them, for worldliness is also spreading in the church (1 Tim. 4:1; 2 Tim. 3:1; 4:2, 3). Increasing laxity of life and increasing laxity of doctrine go arm in arm.

Second, men who accept a loose doctrine regarding the ultimate penalty of sin, be it Universalism, Restorationism, or Annihilationism, or that fantastic combination, or conglomeration, of them all, Millennial Dawnism, lose their power for God. I have seen this proven over and over again. These men may be and are very clever at argument, and very zealous in proselyting, but they are seldom found beseeching men to be reconciled to God. They are far more likely to be found trying to upset the faith of those already won by the efforts of those who do believe in everlasting punishment than trying to win men who have no faith at all. If you really believe the doctrine of the endless torment of the impenitent, if the doctrine really gets hold of you, you will work as you never worked before for the salvation of the lost. If you in any wise abate the doctrine, it will abate your zeal. Time and time again I have come up to this awful doctrine and tried to find some way of escape from it, but when I have failed, as I always have failed at last, when I have determined to be honest with the Bible and myself, I have [328]returned to my work with an increased burden for souls and an intensified determination to spend and be spent for their salvation.

Eternal, conscious suffering, suffering without the least ray of hope of relief, awaits every one of you here to-night who goes on persistently rejecting Jesus Christ, as you are rejecting Him to-night, and who shall pass out of this world having rejected Him. In that world of never ending gloom there will be no possibility of repentance. As you look out into the future there will not be one single ray of hope. "Forever and ever" will be the unceasing wail of that restless sea of fire. After you have been there ten million years and look out toward the future you will see eternity still stretching on and on and on and on, with no hope. Oh, men and women out of Christ, why will you risk such a doom for a single year, or a month, or a week, or a day? Hell is too awful to risk for five minutes the chance of going there. There is but one rational thing for you to do, that is to accept Christ and accept Him right now as your Saviour, surrender to Him as your Lord and Master, confess Him as such before the world, and strive from this time on to please Him in everything day by day. Any other course is utter madness.

R. A. TORREY

Published By Parables

OUR MISSION

The primary mission of Published By Parables, a Christian publisher, is to publish Contemporary and Classic Christian books from an evangelical perspective that honors Christ and promotes the values and virtues of His Kingdom.

Are You An Aspiring Christian Author?

We fulfill our mission best by providing Christian authors and writers publishing options that are uniquely Christian, quick, affordable and easy to understand -- in an effort to please Christ who has called us to a writing ministry. We know the challenges of getting published, especially if you're a first-time author. God, who called you to write your book, will provide the grace sufficient to the task of getting it published.

We understand the value of a dollar; know the importance of producing a quality product; and publish what we publish for the glory of God.

Surf and Explore our site --
then use our easy-to-use "Tell Us" button
to tell us about yourself and about your book.

We're a one-stop, full-service Christian publisher.
We know our limits. We know our capabilities.
You won't be disappointed.
We Publish Christian Books -- FREE

www.PublishedByParables.com

R. A. TORREY

The Fundamental Doctrines of the Christian Faith

R. A. TORREY

www.ingramcontent.com/pod-product-compliance
Lightning Source LLC
Chambersburg PA
CBHW071732080526
44588CB00013B/1991